Charles Jennings was born in London and was educated there and at Oxford University. He is married with two children, and lives in London where he works as a writer and journalist. His previous books, *Up North*, *People Like Us*, *Father's Race* and *Greenwich*, are also published by Abacus.

Praise for Charles Jennings

'Very funny indeed . . . in the way that Bill Bryson was funny in *The Lost Continent*' *Sunday Times*

'Jennings is blessed with a tremendous sense of humour and a gift for piercingly evocative prose' *Sunday Telegraph*

'Jennings is a spry reporter and an effervescent writer' *Financial Times*

'One of the canniest social commentators in Britain today' *Daily Telegraph*

'Like Orwell, Jennings has an unerring eye for tat and bright-eyed failure . . . very funny, appalled and unbelieving' *New Statesman*

'Wickedly hilarious . . . a mirror-image of George Orwell' *Independent on Sunday*

FAINTHEART

An Englishman Ventures
North of the Border

Charles Jennings

An *Abacus* Book

First published in Great Britain by Abacus in 2001
This edition published in 2002
Reprinted in 2002

A CIP catalogue record for this book
is available from the British Library.

ISBN: 0 349 11440 4

Typeset in Berkeley by M Rules
Printed and bound in Great Britain
by Clays Ltd, St Ives plc

Abacus
An imprint of
Time Warner Books UK
Brettenham House
Lancaster Place
London WC2E 7EN

www.TimeWarnerBooks.co.uk

FAINTHEART

PREFACE

This could have been Scotland, if only the Darien Scheme had worked: temperatures up around ninety degrees Fahrenheit, 140 inches of rain a year with attendant raging humidity, tropical rainforests and swamp woods abundant. Scotland would have been a place filled with mangroves and a kind of eighty-foot tree called a cativo. Jaguars, tapirs and crocodiles would have patrolled the vegetation. There would have been spider monkeys and numerous quetzals – the sacred bird of the ancient Mayas and Aztecs, a large and brilliantly plumaged creature somewhere between a parrot and a bottle brush.

Scotland would not, in fact, have consisted of just the dour granitic wedge atop the British Isles that it currently does. It would also have been a place somewhere on the Gulf of Darien on the eastern edge of Panama, now home to the Panama Canal and one of the world's great international trading centres. A good chunk of Scotland would have been malarial, sweaty and brightly coloured. This Scotland would have been more or less the inverse of the actual Scotland – it would have been transformed, represented a colonial presence in the world, been hotter than New York in July. That it didn't and isn't was because of a predictably Scottish mixture of pride, obsessiveness, poor resources and a loathing of the English.

Where did the idea for the Darien Scheme spring from? The answer lies back in the 1600s, a period when the Scots were becoming increasingly irritated by the fact that, while other countries were getting rich by trading with their colonies across the globe, the Scots had no colonies to trade with and hence little chance of real international enrichment. Anglo-Scottish hostility and bad faith saw to it that they had no chance of sharing in the wealth generated by England's colonial holdings either. So the Scots decided to cut out the middle-man, grab a piece of the world for themselves and establish the first proper offshore Scottish colony, thereby – in theory – laying the foundations of a new trading empire.

The piece of land they picked was Darien, the marshy isthmus joining Central with South America. It looked good on paper. It was where the Pacific and the Atlantic met; it was at the crossroads of the world; and it was apparently unoccupied by any other major European power. This was unquestionably the one to go for. With the encouragement of the Scottish Parliament, 'The Company of Scotland Trading to Africa and the Indies' came into being in 1693. It started to amass funds for the great Darien expedition, drawing freely on money from Scots investors, English backers (those, principally, who'd been frozen out of the East India Company) and eager Dutch entrepreneurs. Before long, the Company of Scotland was well capitalised and ready to colonise.

It was at this point that the English Parliament saw the danger. Small numbers of Scotsmen would begin to colonise large parts of the world, it was feared, cutting off trading opportunities from the English and threatening that nation's vital stability and economic interests. William III was obliged to pass a law compelling English investors to withdraw from the scheme. Once the English pulled out, the Dutch backers promptly followed and the Company of Scotland was left staring into a future as hollow as a bell.

Except for the fact that the Scots, mad and full of desperation and wounded pride as they were, refused to let the matter lie. Faced with a catastrophic financial shortfall in the Darien Scheme's finances, the nation rose up and paid in every spare penny it had to keep the dream afloat. Estimates vary as to whether this amounted to a quarter of the country's entire wealth, or half: but whoever could buy a share in the Scheme did so. Those who couldn't afford a share in their own right would club together with friends and neighbours and buy one jointly. This startling – and, retrospectively, insane – endorsement of the project meant that it not only came back from the brink, but amassed some £400,000. By July of 1698, it had five ships ready to set sail from the port of Leith, near Edinburgh.

The adventurers were led by William Paterson, a Dumfriesshire-born financier who had been a key player in the founding of the Bank of England. For their trip to the steaming, mosquito-infested tropical swamps of Central America, the expeditionary party had packed serge, wigs, linen, socks, bonnets, canvas, slippers, blankets, heavy shoes and homespun cloth. They had an awful lot of oatmeal for porridge, plus a good stock of Presbyterian Bibles and twenty-nine barrels of clay pipes. Clearly, they were not really equipped for one of the hottest, vilest places in the world – an area which even today is thinly populated and resistant to the onward march of civilisation. As late as 1994, the only unfinished part of the Pan-American Highway from Alaska to Chile was at Darien.

Even more significant, perhaps, was the expedition's Protestant indifference to the presence of the highly Catholic Spanish in the rest of Panama. The Scots had concluded that, given the lack of recorded activity on the map, Darien had simply been overlooked by the colonising nations. The truth was that the Spanish had taken it in 1501 and regarded it as wholly their own, but considered it too disgusting a spot to be worth bothering with much.

So the Scottish optimists set sail. Many died on the voyage; once in Darien, more succumbed to malaria and the predations of the native Indians. They did manage, however, to set up a base called Fort St Andrew, to which they clung tenaciously while the Spanish mobilised their forces to drive them out. Reinforcements arrived in 1699 from Leith; and again in that year from Rothesay, but not enough to make any difference. The Spanish closed in on the small, disease-ravaged Protestant community, which begged the English governors of Jamaica and Nova Scotia (the irony!) for help. No chance, of course, as these were under strict orders from London to offer no assistance. In 1700, the little garrison surrendered to the Spaniards, who, impressed by their bravery, allowed the wrecked survivors to march out with their honour intact.

Two thousand Scottish lives were lost in the adventure. William Paterson lost both his wife and his son. Scotland's dreams of becoming a colonial power were ruined – and the Scottish Exchequer was bankrupted.

The upshot? When the English pressed the Scots to surrender to the authority of the English Parliament early in the eighteenth century, Scotland hadn't got a financial leg to stand on. The Scots caved in, in 1707, and it was the Act of Union which put an end to four hundred years of Scottish independence. Thus ended the dream of a sub-tropical Scotland, in which the Equator would have been a scant eight degrees away, the Pacific on one side, the Caribbean on the other.

Colombia, with its *mestizos*, its *cordilleras*, its *Bogotáños*, would have been just across the border. The sea would have been a milky opal colour and a good proportion of colonial Scots would have had walnut tans and black hair, just the occasional ginger shock appearing suddenly on crowded streets or in airport lounges. Instead, 'Great Britain', the term officially used first under James I of England, VI of Scotland – Britannia Prima and North Britain under one sway – became a matter of fact.

ONE

God it was cold and wet. I'd walked – *walked*, mark you – all the way from Edinburgh's Picardy Place, down the Leith Walk to where the River Leith itself exits into the Firth of Forth, and I was so cold my face wouldn't move. It was as stiff as a block of wood. Here's an irony: despite its loathsome reputation, Scotland's weather is, on paper, not the killer most people would have you believe. Average temperatures in winter are actually about the same as those of England. It's the summer which can be an easy fifteen degrees less.

But while the average annual rainfall in the Thames Valley is a mere 20-plus inches, Scotland is home to the wettest place in the UK: Wester Ross, with an irrational 200 inches per annum. It's this deluge which sets the tone for the rest of Scotland, plus the wind – horizontal rain, blown at 70 m.p.h., most of the time, everywhere. Wester Ross, Renfrew Street in Glasgow, Constitution Street in Leith, wherever, it rains and the wind blows. It's not *that* cold behind the slats of the meteorologist's data-collection box, but add in the wind-chill and it turns into a slow death. Cue Irvine Welsh, the D. H. Lawrence of the schemes: '*Supposed tae be August, but ah'm fuckin freezing ma baws oaf here.*' Of course it wasn't August when I was there. So it was even colder than *that*.

You can sort of kid yourself while you're in the centre of Edinburgh that it's not as cold as it actually feels. Cities are warmer places anyway, and the movement of the crowds, the labouring buses, the neon shop fronts, all bespeak life and heat. That and the dignity of all those fantastic Edinburgh buildings – this is civilisation, all right, and you don't die of hypothermia in the heart of civilised Europe unless you're a vagrant. But as I scraped a left at Waterloo Place (under the shadow of Calton Hill, Nelson's Monument, the City Observatory, the failed memorial of the Napoleonic Wars, all that lumber stuck on a tump, like the leftovers of a house clearance) I found that the bracing vitality of Princes Street and George Street was draining away, bit by bit. There weren't so many people down this end of town, once I cleared Picardy Place. The ones who were there had that scrunched, chewed-slipper look on their faces: a mixture of too many long-term bevvies and being wind-dried on street corners for a couple of decades. Scraps of garbage had exploded from a bin bag and were capering along the pavements. Away went your tasty Edinburgh shopping opportunities – Jenners, The Tartan Gift Shop, James Thin the booksellers, a pant-wetter called Thistle Do Nicely. Up instead, past Pilrig Street, came the stop'n'shop snout-and-booze outlets, along with a few dockers' tattoo parlours and the usual (for Scotland) free hand of bakeries selling cardiac pastries and death-dealing cakes.

Down the side-streets off Leith Walk and Constitution Street stood rows of council houses. From somewhere near here, the doomed Darien expedition had set sail three hundred years earlier. This was where Mary, Queen of Scots landed in 1561 to claim her throne. Adding to my unease at the slow disappearance of the known world was the fact that I couldn't properly read the signals of the world that was replacing it. There weren't any trees, for instance. And there was a terrific amount of roughcast housing. Down in the south, bald treelessness is a function of urban deprivation; 'roughcast' a token of tastelessness or the council's desire to stick poor, beaten-up people in cheap, unburstable houses. Up here, it was hard to tell how much was brutally frank social housing and how much was simply a response to the weather.

There are urban trees in Scotland, quite a lot of them. But they seem exceptional, praiseworthy in a way that wouldn't be the case in, say, Kensington. They're more like daring foreign tourists, in groups, herded together.

The further north-east I got, the keener the wind and the bleaker the landscape. Finally, right down at the moribund Leith docks themselves, I was not only the only person for half a mile in any direction, I could *see* that I was the only person, on account of the barren flatness of the old dockland environment. A guy rumbled past me in a knackered Morris Marina, looking at me as if I was out of my mind. Which I was, in a very real sense. I was lost, dislocated, completely adrift from the real world, two miles back up the road. '*We look to Scotland for all our ideas of civilisation,*' Voltaire once said, but did he ever hang around the lorry park in Leith in mid-winter?

But then, why was I there at all? Why wasn't I back in the centre of town with all the other tourists? How jaded do you have to be to make it to Leith? My guidebook reckoned it took a day to do the Royal Mile, another day for the New Town, a third for the big galleries. At that point you either go to another place altogether, or, totally parched for stimulation, make your way down to the old docks.

Which is what I'd done. I'd done the Royal Mile and the bare sublimity of Arthur's Seat (which you can drive most of the way up with all the other layabouts). I'd done the Scott Monument (*Saturn V* in stone Gothic, Sir Walter lost inside like a man in a conservatory rather bigger than what he had really had in mind). I'd done the eighteenth-century super-refinement of the beautiful New Town. I'd done the bent, twisting medieval steps of the Old Town, glistening in the rain and street lamps like obsidian. I'd done Princes Street, the thoroughfare that is Edinburgh's Oxford Street – same dimwit chainstores running along the north side, same guy out on the pavement telling you to go to a golfing equipment sale, but, unlike Oxford Street, with a king-sized cleft in the earth and an immense castle on the south side. I'd been up Nelson's Monument, I'd blundered around the Castle and felt the pervy warlike thrill of standing in the Esplanade where they hold the Military Tattoo.

I'd inspected the doom-laden St Giles' Cathedral and tried to stifle any unseemly bodily noises in the little wardrobe that is the Chapel of the Thistle (designed in 1911, crammed with carvings of heraldic gear, knights' helmets, Disneyland beasts). I'd watched while parties of very old, puzzled ladies quizzed a Cathedral attendant about the Presbyterians' horror of the English, Roman Catholics and indeed ethical loose-nesses of all kinds. I'd been to the National Gallery of Scotland, so warm, stuffy and clarety that I felt like moving my bed in there so that I could sleep while The Reverend Robert Walker Skated on Duddingston Loch and Alexander III of Scotland was Rescued from a Stag.

I'd even battled round the stunning new Museum of Scotland, begun in 1991 and clad in lovely Morayshire sand-stone like a great misshapen golden drum of industrial chemicals. This is a wonderful structure, but entirely baffling to visit. Every floor is divided up into sub-sections which can only be reached by unnamed staircases and truncated flights of steps such as you get in ship engine-rooms or power stations. No section is linked to any other except by sheer chance.

Once I'd got past the single biggest exhibit in the Renaissance section – which turned out to be 'The Maiden', a primitive fifteenth-century version of the guillotine – I ended up trapped with a couple of oldsters who, like me, had got lost in the 3-D logical puzzle that was the museum's interior. 'Is this downstairs the same level as the level we're on?' one of them asked me.

They followed me round like a couple of private detectives. I never made it as far as the top floor and 'Scotland in the New Millennium', which allegedly had a picture of Kirsty Wark in a Saab.

And yes, I reached for the most muscular thesaurus when faced with all this, because like all great cities, Edinburgh turns you into a pure tourist, turns your thoughts into guidebook *précis*. This is one of the defining characteristics of a real city: its capacity to make you feel like an awed spectator, an out-of-towner forever clock-watching in case there aren't enough moments in the day to do everything that has to be done. Meanwhile, the city's real inhabitants work to a different, unknowable beat, to emphasise their singularity. *Edinburgh is a cross between Bath and St Malo*, I noted in my jotter, adding, with equal acuity, *but nicer than either*.

In fact, Edinburgh is more civilised than almost all English cities, which is why I'd started there, was still there after several days, and why I was so unhealthily reluctant to leave it. Every time I thought about pushing on, either to some other town (terrifying Glasgow; dreary Dundee) or to somewhere which wasn't a town at all (terrifying Highlands; dreary Lowlands) I lost my nerve and couldn't move. Edinburgh, I tried to persuade myself for quite a long time, *is* Scotland. See one and you've seen the other. It's a kind of metonymy for

Scottishness. It was a one-stop event. Which was why I found myself in the privileged position of being able to walk down to Leith in the first place, in the freezing cold and the persistent gale. I just couldn't get away from the place.

By noon I'd made it to Leith's Commercial Street and had exhausted a couple of normally reliable manoeuvres to bring some life back. First I ate a Snickers bar. When that failed, I crept into a boozer, demolished a packet of crisps, downed a whisky and debated whether or not to take up smoking again so that I could warm myself internally with some hot cigarette fumes.

The place was deserted apart from me and a sorrowing barmaid with her hair cut *en brosse*. After she'd pushed my drink across the counter to me and admitted that, yes, it was cold today, she got on the phone and began a long morose conversation about a financial crisis she was facing.

A gas fire on the far wall hissed, and dew started to form on the lino. Brown was the colour of the day, apart from the burgundy Naugahyde on the banquettes. You could hear the clock ticking, broken by the occasional clattering of my teeth.

Things only looked up when a Scottish chancer dressed like Les Dennis in *Family Fortunes* rushed in with a suitcase.

'Do you want to buy any duvets?' he asked me. 'Any bedding for your house?'

I mimed *no thanks* and he went over to the bar. Turned out the barmaid didn't want any bedding either, but wouldn't say no to a nice watch.

'Hold on,' the chancer said, and ran out. He came back thirty seconds later with a briefcase full of watches, and he and the barmaid spent the next ten minutes choosing a gold item with expanding metal bracelet and date window.

To pacify me, she switched the pub telly on. This was showing the news in Gaelic. Scottish Gaelic is like Dutch,

Danish and Norwegian passed through a blender and then served up as a kind of vegetable health language that you know you ought to enjoy but never will. After all, there are a mere sixty thousand (and falling) Gaelic-speakers left in Scotland. The greatest number of these is found in the Western Isles. Somewhat alarmingly, the next biggest number is in the Strathclyde region (although we must view this proportionally, noting that over half the Western Islanders are Gaelic-speakers with less than 1 per cent of those living in Strathclyde bothering to speak the language). Edinburgh, in the Lothians, barely registers. Nevertheless, BBC Scotland were taking no chances, and out it all came into this Leith pub.

It pointed up the truth that Scottish Gaelic is really less a language and more a token of resistance. The Welsh are happy to persist in speaking Welsh in many parts of Wales, in order to preserve a culture which has just about no other forms of expression. Durable plastic arts and architecture aren't a Welsh thing: speaking is. But the Scots have always had bigger fish to fry than the Welsh, more tangible and permanent things to participate in (such as the British Empire). The fact that the number of Gaelic-speakers dropped from ninety thousand in the 1980s to sixty thousand in the 1990s suggests that speaking Gaelic is only useful if you really are eking out a living in the Outer Hebrides, or as a defiant urban pastime for fans of Sorley MacLean and Iain Crichton Smith. Or for, say, a prog-Celtic musician like Paul Mounsey, who in 1994 produced a tune called 'Passing Away'. This lamented in a contemporary groove style the disappearance of spoken Gaelic, even though Mounsey was sensibly living at the time in São Paulo, Brazil.

These are doomed linguistic recusants. It's impossible to believe that the inhabitants of Cessnock or Motherwell are crying out to learn *tha e òg agus gòrach* (he is young and stupid) or *tha an t-iasg làn chnàmhan* (the fish is full of bones) or even *briosgaidean* (biscuits). So the news was gibberish, but delivered with such cow-eyed significance and sincerity that I felt bad at being unable to make out anything more than the words 'Mel Gibson' and 'airport'. I also wanted to say aloud that this TV news Gaelic was nothing but a gestural language, a symbol. But that would have meant dropping my normal English liberal guard and setting out to affront every proud Scotsman. An unsayable sentence, in other words.

I ate my crisps and realised that I was getting colder rather than warmer.

'Fiver,' the chancer said, allowing the gold watch to sprawl in the palm of his hand.

'It's for a present,' said the barmaid.

'He'll like that one.'

It was the coldest part of the year, I was on the outskirts of Edinburgh, and after another eight minutes' freezing, I worked out that unless I was genuinely ready to drop dead, I was going to have to keep moving.

This was, indeed, a theme: the constant rhythmic swing from street to shelter to street to shelter again, the half-crazed hunt for warmth, the frustrated bewilderment that whatever I tried, I never really reached an acceptable operating temperature. It made me wonder in a nasty, supremacist sort of way about the ideal operating temperature for civilised urban life. In the end I worked out that this was to be found only between the thirtieth and fiftieth parallels. Which would, of course, have ruled out Stockholm, Delhi, half of Cairo and the whole of Sydney.

Inevitably there's no mileage in wanting to transport every-where to Provence or Tuscany. But I might point out that the eighteen months I spent putting this book together were sus-piciously punctuated by colds, flu, bronchitis and the general miasma of the valetudinarian. Would this have been the case if Edinburgh were nearer, say, Lyon? I doubt it.

So I crawled out of the bar and into the showrooms of kiltmakers Kinloch Anderson on the corner of Dock Street. The great thing about Kinloch Anderson is that they are kiltmakers by appointment to HM The Queen, HRH The Duke of Edinburgh and HRH Prince Charles. This makes it a kind of spiritual home of the tartan, and tartan is one of those terrible obsessional cultural problems for the English. The problem can be stated thus: we love it but we're not meant to wear it. Kinloch Anderson and its Tartan Problem was one of the reasons – the principal reason – I'd trudged down the Leith Walk in the first place. The other three reasons were: to look at the ex-Royal Yacht *Britannia*, which was moored at Leith docks; to inspect the new *dolce vita* food and retail developments near the Dock Offices (Isle of Dogs/Covent Garden, they said, with a John Duns Scotus twist); and to see if the Leith police really existed and if so to stand and titter at their premises, muttering 'The Leith police dismisseth us' under my breath.

Kinloch Anderson live in a big corrugated shed near the waterfront, done up inside in Retail Park Baronial style and with a no-expense-spared central heating system. Once in there, I started to turn my normal greyish shrimp-pink again. I'd been in the icy rain, of course, in the short dash from boozer to kiltmaker. So as well as resembling a fresh corpse I smelled of crisps, Snickers, alcohol and now wet tramp's trousers as I prepared to waste the time of the charming lady in charge.

As I stood there dripping, I drank in the fact that all around me were blazing pieces of tartan, done up as men's kilts, women's kilts, kilties for children or dwarves. There were, too, all the barbarous accessories of sporrans, golfer-effect socks, *skean-dhus* or 'Black Knives' – these concealed down the sock for the stabbing of the loathed English. Not much in the way of pure Caledonia in the actual showroom itself, mark you. It was pretty much like one of those con-the-passenger retail outlets you get in airport terminals, all pre-fab veneers and armies of chrome clothing racks cooking slowly under the spotlights. But then what else could I expect from the interior of a brand-new lightweight commercial shed? What else could I expect such a long way away from the Royal Mile, with its gussied-up shoplets full of Celtic Twilight Scotch and fudge that costs the same per pound as fillet steak?

Anyway, there I was, looking queasily at all these garments, knowing that on the one hand this is a blatant Scottish heritage come-on, but that on the other hand your tartan kilt is bestially appealing, like the skirl of the pipes, something that goes beyond reason. I was painfully conflicted. Half of me quite properly wanted to dismiss this as stuff for the tourists and a handful of Texan cranks who insist on doing Burns Night the right way down in Houston and Abilene. The other half, unfortunately, gets horribly worked up by the sheer drama of the tartan sett and the wild virility of a skirt a man can wear.

On top of which, a kilt is not (of course!) just a banal tube of cloth wound round the buttocks, even though that's precisely what it looks like. It is much more fascinating than that. Your kilt turns out to be a masterpiece of complexity, with reinforcements and detailed stitching and over eight yards of cloth in a man's kilt, exactingly folded and pressed into permanent pleats by super-heavy medieval irons. Hence, a full dress evening outfit will set you back in the region of £1,000 if you want Kinloch Anderson's levels of craftsmanship. It turned me on terribly, and the turn-on was made more perversely irresistible by the fact that, as an almost completely Scots-free Englishman, I can't really wear tartan.

Despite my unease about its heritage and my heritage, I felt a sudden urgent hypocritical need to try one on.

Well, now, I wondered, clearing my throat, if I wanted to shell out £1,000 for a full dress evening outfit with coatee and vest, would that not be an unwise investment, given the minimal amount of wear I was likely to get out of it?

'Oh no,' the showroom chatelaine said, twinkling. 'You'd find all sorts of reasons for wearing it if you had one.'

She was about four foots' worth of pure genteel, silvery-haired Scottish lady. She wore a bomb-proof tweedy suit and unostentatious jewellery, like a school headmistress, and spoke with one of those china-plate Morningside accents that makes your head resonate in a particular way. She also had a don't-fuck-with-me look in her eye which made me careful of my language and my gestures.

Then what about the delightful tartan trews, as favoured by many regimental wearers? When would I affect that?

'As the fancy takes you. But the trews are cut higher at the waist than the normal trousers and have to be worn with braces so that a gap doesn't open up between the jacket and the trousers and show your shirt.'

Because the jacket's the shorty one, much like the abbreviated jacket worn with the kilt?

'Because, of course, it's the short jacket that you wear with it.'

Through a window I could see a platoon of ladies sewing the tartan in the workshops next door. A man stood and shoved an iron the size of a small car up and down ranks of pleats. There was even a little museum of tartan beyond an archway, with designs for Bertie Wooster-style gentlemen's plaid outfits from the 1930s and books of historic tartan. Not only did this roomlet provide a brief *tour d'horizon* of tartan, it also contained a Scottish regiment's paralysingly scary table ornament from the nineteenth century. This latter was a complete (and real) ram's head, stuffed, with a cigar dispenser and a snuff holder built into its skull, the tips of its horns adorned with silver. The whole thing was mounted on little castors so that it could be rolled down the regimental table in the direction of anyone who wanted to partake of tobacco. I wondered how it would strike someone in the grip of, say, paranoid schizophrenia or an acid trip to see this freak rumbling towards them.

I couldn't help myself. I yearned to get it on with one of those big, hairy sporrans. The Scottish lady eyed me.

'Well, yes, you could wear the Royal or Stuart Tartan if you were up here.'

But Royal Tartan is the boring one. It's the quintessential shortbread-biscuit-tin tartan, the only one any low Englishman can wear. It is the one you are shamefully loaded into if you want to go Highland reeling, but have no clan pedigree to speak of. If I dug deep enough into my past and rousted out some spurious Highland ancestry, was there no way I could use it to get into something a little more exciting?

She tilted her head and allowed her lips to turn down in apology.

'Not really,' she said.

I thought that, very distantly, I might have some Campbell blood in me.

'That would just make it worse,' she smiled, alluding no doubt to the contemptible treachery shown by the Campbells to the MacDonalds at the Glencoe Massacre.

'You reckon?'

'Ah, well,' she said.

End of discussion.

So after a bit of hemming and hawing and fiddling with the materials on display, I gave up and stumped fiercely and conflictedly out of Kinloch Anderson and back on to the wet pavement. Smoothing my dripping hair with a free hand, I then turned down to Commercial Street and on to Portland

Place, near the huge Stalinist offices of the Scottish Executive (overlooking the old Victoria Dock, cold and blank as the North Sea itself).

Here stands what used to be the Queen's private ocean-going boat, the yacht *Britannia*. Now a tourist attraction owned by a trust, this most desirable of vessels – built in 1953, the eighty-third Royal Yacht – costs an arm and a leg to get into, but, as attractions go, is pretty good (voted *Which? Tourist* Attraction Award Winner, 2000). Not only does it enable you to get a peek into the private world of the Queen, it also gives you the chance to fondle some pointedly superior fixtures and fittings; while at the visitors' centre, designed by non-Scottish Sir Terence Conran, you get the latest in plate-glass windows and anodised steel tubing, as well as hypertalkative handsets to guide you round. *And* the staff are all tricked out like airline stewards and spend a lot of time making sure you don't wander back into the multimedia film show after you've only just seen it. It is a class production.

I went round, partly to get over not being able to wear a kilt or speak Gaelic, partly because I was pruriently and masochistically interested in behind-the-scenes glimpses of the House of Windsor. So the moment I stepped aboard, the inevitable unresolved internal argument went off like a home-made bomb in my head. Thus, at the same time as I excoriated the Royal Family for living high on my taxes and clouds of impotent republican rage issued from my ears, I had to admit that *Britannia* would do nicely as my own recreational transport. This would be on condition that I could keep it in the manner of Her Majesty: when *Britannia* was in its pomp, the old grasper, as well as having her normal retinue of ladies-in-waiting and personal adjutants, enjoyed the services of not fifty, not a hundred, but over *two hundred* stupefyingly fastidious crewmen to get her around the world.

Among other things, these hand-picked obsessives used to clean the brightwork to a pitch of perfection never seen on any other boat; they dealt with, on average, five tons of royal luggage on any given trip; and they laid the dinner services on the mahogany dining tables using tape measures in order to get the positioning exactly right. The antique engine rooms were so beautifully kept that when General Norman Schwarzkopf was shown them, he said, 'Okay, I've seen the museum exhibits. Now where are the real engines?' Like any healthy adult faced with these intelligences, I wanted to confront the anality of *Britannia* by defiling the super-comfy doll-sized royal beds and crapping in the royal toilets, but they were sealed off by Plexiglas.

To my surprise, as I lurched through the dining salon, I found a guy in whites laying the Queen's own mahogany table without a tape measure. What, was She coming back on board?

'Oh, it's for a function tonight. We do about three or four a week.' A Sikh chef rushed out of what used to be the Royal Galley, clutching a plastic flagon of double cream. Function? Can anyone hire *Britannia*?

'Oh, yes,' the guy in whites said, jinking round the table's edge. 'We do a lot of corporate stuff.'

True: one of its first clients was the drug company Pfizer, who used it as a launch venue for Viagra. The Ford Motor Company have also borrowed it, as have Capital Bank, Jaguar and the Royal Bank of Scotland. Altogether, this grosser commercial appropriation of the Queen's former property made me feel a lot better. This, plus the smart onshore museum presentation, plus the presence of a magnificent motor launch, which was once the Royal Barge. The ex-barge, built by the Gosport firm of Camper & Nicholson in 1964, is kept in conditions of unparalleled luxury in a tank of *perpetually rippling* water, near the ticket desk. Titillation and disapproval: the

British way. I was so outraged and entranced by the whole experience that I ended up spending £29 on tea-towels in the gift shop.

. After which, my only problem was the logical one of Leith itself, the irrational yoking of Leith's historic destitution with a Royal Yacht. Some sort of pan-Scottish genuflection? After all, *Britannia* was built by John Brown & Co. on the Clyde; why then was it not on the Clyde? Was it there just because Leith has extensive water frontage going begging, like any superannuated docklands? Was it none other than chronic English guilt, penitently gifting a leftover to the Scottish tourist industry? What did *Britannia* really have to do with Edinburgh, Leith, Scotland, anyway?

I left, clutching my tea-towels, and started back towards Edinburgh city centre. And I got lost straight away in a Leith council estate, light years removed from the measured opulence of HM's secret world. After a few minutes' walking into the standard gale, I was among bare bricks, pre-fab medium-rise social housing, rusting padlocks. A steel column rose up in a central courtyard, bearing closed-circuit TV cameras and halogen security lights like a magic tree.

I knew that there were four-square, dourly handsome family homes, my kind of world, somewhere round the corner in Leith central: I'd seen them on the way in. I'd also seen the sophisticates' corner opposite the Custom House and spied on executive types forking in mouthfuls of mussels and rocket in the handful of big-city eateries that had started up among the ruined fortresses of old Leith. I'd even seen Leith Police Station. But now I was trapped in a rough end of town. *The further ye go doon the Walk at this time ay night, the mair likely ye are tae git a burst mooth . . .*

It looked like Irvine Welsh territory all right. I started framing questions in my head to ask the drug-crazed maniacs whom I was sure were about to jump out from behind stairwells and start kicking me around. 'So you're the famous Leith smackheads, then? I'm writing a book.' That kind of thing. Here I am, coupla minutes off the Fit ay the Walk, waiting for all the wee radges. So where are they? Where's the schemies?

After all, tartan and drug abuse are Scotland's claims to fame at the turn of the century. The statistics fall out of the sky like rain. At one stage, 25 per cent of all babies born in the special maternity unit of the Aberdeen Royal Infirmary were found to be already drug dependent. A recent survey found that in Scotland, 19 per cent of boys and 16 per cent of girls aged 11–15 had experimented with drugs – half as many again as for the same age group in England. The cost of distributing free syringes in Aberdeen recently reached £120,000. In the Grampian area between 1985 and 1995, the number of registered heroin addicts rose by a factor of sixteen . . . *Johnny ran oot ay veins and started shooting intae his arteries. It only took a few ay they shots tae gie um gangrine. Then the leg hud tae go.*

But there was no one to attack me, no one to ask. I was lost in the estate for a good ten minutes, creeping around blind walls like Inspector Clouseau and hurrying cravenly past doorways, in which time I did not see another soul. I didn't even see any graffiti, although every wall, every barricaded door cried out for some. Plainly, it is just too cold to spray. It freezes before it gets out of the can. So where do they go when it's too cold to go anywhere? Just hide away with the junk?

This is the thing about visiting Scotland if you're English. It's not like visiting somewhere you don't, frankly, know – Thailand, Morocco, Mexico. Instead, you're visiting somewhere with which you share a long, complicated, awkward history, even if you've never physically been there before.

Admittedly, you could say as much about France – but then at least France is separated by water and language from England. It's foreign enough to keep the distinctions clear. With Scotland it's a bit like paying a call on some tricky, bonkers relative your family once did something terrible to (an event or events which *you* can't remember much about, but which *they* can, in pinpoint detail) and having to watch your every move for fear of provoking a fight. You're not just going to another country; you're getting embroiled in someone else's argument. There's all this baggage lying around.

Consider this tangle of relationships. At the very moment that I was buying myself a Collins Edinburgh Easyfold Map in the Waverley shopping mall a few days earlier, the Monarch and her Consort were gearing up to be shepherded around the new offices of The Scotsman Publications, just down the road. Which meant that even as I was blundering around my Leith council estate, wondering *what* the Irvine Welsh inhabitants (I knew they were there somewhere: I saw their laundry hung out on jaded balconies) were making of *Britannia*, the embodiment of English rule, stuck at their back door, so the Queen and the Duke of Edinburgh had just finished visiting the printing works of the *Scotsman* and the *Edinburgh Evening News* up at Holyrood. 'HAPPY AND GLORIOUS' sobbed the *Evening News*, as if it were really the *Daily Telegraph*. 'Royal's pressing engagement,' it went on, pictures in a special pull-out supplement of Her, holding a bunch of posies, looking clueless, wearing a hat like a roll of electrical flex. 'The royal seal of approval . . . It was a tremendous honour for the *Evening News* to have her visit . . . The Queen spent almost *half an hour* [my italics] touring the *Evening News* . . .'

Why were they even bothering with those balsaheads from the House of Windsor? Why didn't they get someone Scottish and very slightly famous, like hysteria-inducing Carol Smillie or Ian McCaskill? Increasingly few people in England care about the Royal Family, and even fewer in Scotland. So why all this Windsor love? How can the Scots be so supine as to welcome the old Hanoverian inheritrix to Edinburgh *and* put up with her fleece-the-taxpayer Unionist boat, stuck tactlessly right outside one of the more neglected parts of the capital city? Why are Kinloch Anderson so proud of their royal associations when most of Scotland wants to leave the monarchy to die an abandoned death? Except, presumably, for the fact that the Royal Warrant always goes down big with credulous Japanese whisky'n'tartan lovers, and if we love anything it's a foreign export. And how – conversely – is all this connected with the fact that an Englishman can never wear a tartan kilt with an easy conscience?

Once you start posing these buttonholing you-yes-you-sir questions, you can't stop. At least, *I* can't stop: one of Kinloch Anderson's trophies is their licence to keep the Balmoral Tartan for the Royal Family, for example, but the Balmoral Tartan was designed by Prince Albert in 1857, and Prince Albert was no more Scottish than Mao Tse-tung. So how come he gets top billing? A man called David Hilton played rugby for Scotland at international level forty-one times without actually *being* Scottish and only had to stop when someone formally objected. So what kind of Scot is *he*? A London pub called Boisdale's, round the back of Victoria Station, is allegedly a Scottish theme pub, on account of its tartan carpets and pictures of beeves on the walls: the crudest of branding, American in its reductiveness, but Scottish?

Then again: how much faith do we place in tartan at all? Yes, in normal conditions, one's reaction to the tartan/kilt combo is sensibly one of revulsion and fear – Jimmy Shand, Andy Stewart, 'Donald Where's Yer Troosers?', Hogmanay specials, 'The Waggle o' the Kilt', shortbread biscuit tins. That stale breath of 1960s TV and the willed bonhomie of men in sporrans and tidy haircuts smacking one another on the back before turning to the camera and saying, *Well, we've taken you over the sea to Skye. But now I'd like to meander down to one of my very favourite places, Campbeltown Loch . . .*

On the other hand, you have to admit that a tartan kilt is all showbiz, drama, intense masculinity. 'Join a Highland regiment, me boy,' says a character in John Masters' *Bugles and a Tiger*. 'The kilt is an unrivalled garment for fornication and diarrhoea.' It's weirdly sexy. And it has a tradition of persecution to act as guarantor of its proprieties. After the Jacobite Rebellion of 1745 was crushed, the English forbad the wearing of tartan in Scotland, except by certain Scottish regiments. This drove the whole culture underground, only for it to re-emerge, blinking in the daylight, in 1822. This was when George IV paid a visit to Scotland and fell in love almost overnight with the romance of the plaid, courtesy of Sir Walter Scott's tartan-orgy Edinburgh reception. From which springs the whole royal fixation with Scotland – Victoria's *Highland Journals*, Balmoral – and also the rediscovery of the plaid's cultural centrality.

So, in the right circumstances, the romance works. The magic of tartan overwhelms any scepticism, and it becomes impossible to look at a tartan kilt without involuntarily summoning up connected images of glens, stags, waterfalls, Highland warriors, proud defiance, crags, forts, honour, varieties of ling. Given the right context, close contact with a kilt can drive away all those Andy Stewart tartan-twat images and replace them with a teary-eyed yearning to be wild and free and legitimately Caledonian.

But there is also a darker side. You don't have to try very hard to determine that tartan is a purely confected bit of romance. There is precious little evidence, pre-1800, for clan tartan regulations of any kind. You couldn't tell who was who simply by examining their tartan sett. The fierce identification of tribe and tribal colour isn't there. There are some fifteenth- and sixteenth-century texts that refer to the concept of tartan, but the earliest known depiction of Highland dress (John Michael Wright's *Highland Chieftain* in the Scottish National Portrait Gallery) shows – almost certainly – a member of the Clan Campbell wearing a tartan that has nothing to do with the Campbells, or indeed any other known clan. Wright's painting is dated 1660. The taxonomy, the semi-historical codifying, all happens later.

The people who boosted tartan most were, unsurprisingly, the people who had a vested interest in it. The Highland Societies of London (formed 1778) and Edinburgh (1780) spent decades trying to pin down clan allegiances and tartan significances and give the stuff a gloss of authenticity. It was Sir Walter Scott, the incredibly Scottish balladeer, romanticist and fiction-writer, who won the King's seal of approval for the tartan. It was William Wilson, a prominent eighteenth-century weaver of tartan, who claimed to be reproducing 'perfectly genuine patterns', based on scrupulous researches carried out by his Highland agents, and which were now freely available to interested purchasers.

Meanwhile, a kilt, looked at dispassionately as the solution to a design problem, looks like nothing, looks as if centuries ago they couldn't be arsed to work out how to make trousers out of a bolt of cloth and ended up simply winding it round their waists in the old *breacan féile*. The end which they couldn't work out what to do with went over the shoulder in a kind of virile shawl, or *plaid*. It was an Englishman called Rawlinson who had the idea – in the early eighteenth century – of separating the plaid from the skirt of the kilt, so that his workers (in a Glengarry foundry) could move around more easily. Even then, it's fair to say, a kilt was becoming a bit of an anomaly.

What, then, if this outfit isn't every Scotsman's birthright? What if it's rather more ham than we English have been led to believe? Are the kilt and plaid really no more than a piece of

Anglo-Scottish pantomime for the majority of Scotsmen, worn mainly just to feel good and excite the tourists? File it, presumably, along with other such Scottish cultural embroidery as the made-up poet Ossian and the Stone of Destiny – which is not the boring lump of rock the English gave back in 1996, but is actually an intricately carved slab, protected by hereditary guardians in a secret cave, somewhere.

Or then *again*: on the train up to Scotland, I was awash with illegitimate tartan. There was the fake tartan lining of my waterproof coat, a sort of blancmange-pink tartan lining my bag, some tartan M&S underpants and a modified Black Watch shirt I'd bought at a Gap in New York. I was sampling the stuff already. Phoney plaid, of course, deracinated plaid, not the sort to give them sleepless nights at KA, but plaid all the same.

But is this tartan? Or is it some kind of reduced-strength, export-only tartan, safe for English wankers to wear without it short-circuiting the electrics or making it dangerous to operate machinery? I can wear paisley, from near Glasgow. I can wear tweed. These are just fabrics. But real tartan, hard-core tartan, like the Gaelic language (which, come to think of it, I probably wouldn't be allowed to speak even if the chance ever arose), is hedged about by its own sacredness. Like the ceremonial dress of the Geisha, a policeman's uniform or a Shriner's Fez, it is that oddest of things, clothing with restrictions concerning who may or may not wear it. Unless, that is, you're a Massachusetts golfer in plaid trews or a French schoolgirl with a kiltette fastened by a big chrome nappy-pin – in which case, you simply steal the look without fear of reprisal, because you're not English.

I hit a lucky turn and found myself back out somewhere in the Newhaven part of Leith and just within sight of a main road. I turned my back on the estate, legged it towards a bus stop (stopping on the way for a fresh Snickers) and waited for the rain to start again.

This *is* the thing (I fretted, standing at the bus stop) about Scotland. It *is* an argument waiting to happen. You can't just come here if you're English and expect to have a good time. You're visiting an idea, a proposition, one half of a heated debate. It simply isn't like this in Portugal or Turkey – although it might be interesting to conjecture what it would be like if it was.

TWO

The Queen-loving *Scotsman* ('Scotland's National Newspaper') had a thing in the business section. It was a large black-and-white photograph of a former England international rugby player standing at Liverpool Street Station. He was wearing a T-shirt and a kilt. The expression on his face suggested that he was experiencing one of those anxiety dreams where you discover yourself to be unaccountably naked in public, on a street somewhere or (why not?) at Liverpool Street Station. On the T-shirt was printed *www.returntoscotland.com*, an Internet company dedicated to wooing people either back to Scotland or to Scotland in the first instance.

The population of Scotland is now fairly steady at a little over 5 million, but historically the country has always been haunted by the ghost of chronic emigration – quite apart from the forced expatriations of the past – in which anyone with enough zest or industry or imagination has tended to go abroad (Andrew Carnegie, Sean Connery) or at the least, south to England (too many to mention). But *returntoscotland.com* is out to reverse this historic trend. 'Do you dream of a new life,' it asks, 'where commuting to work is calmer and quicker, the air is cleaner and where you can nurture those unfulfilled ambitions? Or maybe you already live in Scotland, know how good it is, but long for a change of direction?'

Offering advice on job opportunities, relocation options, infrastructure and leisure potentialities, *returntoscotland.com* aims to redirect the flow, making it easy and attractive for people to move north rather than south. They also have a picture of a rusty red Highland longhorn beef on their website to clear up any ambiguities about where you might be moving to.

Do we take this is as a sign of weakness or strength? Is it Scotland's enterprising, independent self which is in play here? Or is it a gloomy incidental recognition of the fact that London and the south-east suck in people and money like a great oily drain, and that however happening Scotland may be, it is cold and northern and a long way from anywhere much except Esbjerg? Would things be clearer if a Scottish international rugby player stood at Waverley Station wearing a T-shirt and cargo pants ineffectually proclaiming the south-east's ruinous expense, inconvenience, hysteria, hypocritical smarminess and general all-round shittiness, while hundreds of highly qualified Scottish people leapt aboard the first train to Euston?

THREE

Back from Leith, I went to my room for a think. Kilts and the Queen. Love and hate. Is dour, wet, resentful Scotland absorbing principally because of the energy it expends in exasperating the English? 'Scotland, land of the omnipotent No,' wrote the Scottish biographer and poet, Alan Bold. 'It is never difficult to distinguish between a Scotsman with a grievance and a ray of sunshine,' wrote P. G. Wodehouse. Are we only drawn to what we find painful? Is Scotland interesting because it is so withholding?

First of all, I had to get the bedside light working. On the ceiling of my bedroom was a gilt candelabrum with three functioning bulbs. The two lamps on the bedside tables were bulbless. Easy enough in theory to get a bulb out of the ceiling light and bung it in the bedside light. But the ceiling was incredibly high, easily as high as the roof of a cathedral, so I had to balance on a chair to get up there and extract a bulb. I wedged the chair against the wardrobe, climbed up like a burglar, teetered Blondini Brothers-style on the chair's arms and worked the bulb out. Dropped to the floor again, fixed the bulb in the bedside light, turned off the main light, rubbed my hands together, ready to enjoy the effect.

The whole room was plunged into a subterranean darkness. Just a few pathetic fingers of yellow gloaming made their way out past the lampshade. This is what you get if you stay in cheap Scottish hotels. You get a lot of darkness. I suppose if I'd been up there in June I could have read all night by the interminable summer twilight. But I was not completely discouraged. After all, as Edinburgh hotel rooms went, it had good points as well as bad.

The bad points were:

– The room was breathtakingly dark.

– It had an intimidatingly high ceiling, much higher than the room was wide: effectively a vast underlit fridge with carpeting.

– The looming vertigo this induced was made worse by the doominess of the fleur-de-lys wallpaper.

– There was the suggestion of threat in a table knife which I found lying on the carpet, with marmalade or Marmite or, just possibly, shit adhering to the blade.

– There were also bloodstains or vomit stains splashed across my en suite bathroom door.

– The sheets were nylon and gave off the full solemn aura of the previous user.

– There was a folk evening in the bar downstairs one night. I meant to catch it but was too weary and cold to get off my flabby mattress. So the music drifted up the stairwell, and through my door, a pair of voices echoing. It was a real Highland dirge that they sang: 'McAul type of sheep / The whair guid time / Naff rememberrrr / Noo-oo-oo . . . / An' noo-oo-oo agin . . .' And so on. I fell into a doze, but the music penetrated my dreams and I was chased by Scottish voices across perverted landscapes.

*

On the upside, however, was the fact that it was on the edge of Edinburgh's magnificent New Town and shared with the buildings of that eighteenth-century masterpiece many of their finer architectural points. Even though the place I was in – once a private home of great style and splendour – was Victorian in origin, it had the same stately ashlared façade and dignified classical proportions and motifs as the Georgian quarter. It had the same pediments, pilasters and mouldings. It also had the same huge rectangular windows as the best of the New Town – windows through which I had been randomly staring at Edinburgh life ever since I hit the city. So far I had seen a drum kit; a number of offices with grey steel filing cabinets and dreamy-looking staff prising the lids off yoghurt pots, and shuffling envelopes; a surprising number of claret-coloured walls; and an old lady trying to get a telly to work while two teenage girls looked on, anxiously.

I had also witnessed several apparently perfectly preserved Victorian interiors, full of sombre paintwork, dado rails, old-fashioned potted plants like mother-in-law's tongue and aspidistra, paintings in gilt frames, stuffed birds mounted on little artificial outcrops of rock and covered by bell-glasses, vases and urns of fantastic size and ugliness, bookcases filled with Royal Automobile Club-style uniform bound volumes and surmounted by classical broken pediments. It was impossible to tell whether they were kept this way out of aesthetic conservatism or stinginess. Sometimes there would be an old man, seated in a leather armchair, reading a newspaper, sometimes scratching his leg.

My own gaff had a monumental hall and staircase, the sort you don't get in London any more unless you're hugely rich and can afford a full-sized period London townhouse. If my place was at all typical, then your average Edinburgh hotelier, unlike a rich Londoner faced with such space and prodigality, will leave the staircase very much in the nineteenth-century mould. The paintwork will be dark to the point of blackness. The lights will be never more than 60 watts. The woodwork will bear the same morbid varnishes of 140 years ago. There will be strange mesh trays hanging over the upper banister rails, either to put plants on or to stop people committing suicide by hurling themselves down on to the tessellated floor of the entrance hall.

The hotelier will also have a door marked Cocktail Lounge on the landing of the first floor. Every time I tried this door in my hotel, it was locked. And then, one evening, it fell open and I found inside a medium-sized room with all the lights on, and with some Formica tables dotted around. One of these tables had a half-finished game of chess on it. An anorak had been slung over the back of a neighbouring chair. There was no one there. It was like reading a book and finding a chapter from another, wholly unrelated book intercalated about halfway through, thanks to an error at the binder's.

Over time, I realised that all this was pure Edinburgh, inside and out. It was like being inside Gordon Brown: rigorous, solid, lumpily handsome, old-fashioned, forbidding, short of *élan*, humourless, stuffy, imposing, suffocating, defiant, prim. I decided that in fact the bad bits – the shortage of light, the vertigo, the unease, the strong reek of the past – were so glumly Edinburgh that they were good bits after all, and that everything was really as perfect as it was going to get.

I'd made a short, random and unscientific survey of friends and acquaintances to see what they understood by Scotland before I came up. The list went from the expected – golf, shortbread, Rangers football team, whisky, rain, Sean Connery, heroin addicts, Scottish currency you can't persuade anyone to take in London, haggis, Balmoral, Burns Night, Jimmy Shand, Hogmanay, probity/meanness – to slightly more unanticipated things – Sir Harry Lauder's bendy walking stick, Moira Stewart, heavy (as in draught beer), getting beaten up for being English, *Macbeth*, the Willow Tea Rooms in Glasgow, midge bites, 'hen' – to one or two freaks, like neds, soup, a spirtle and 'blown-over lorries'.

I was in a mood for lists. Supine on my scratcher, I lay in the subaqueous gloom and then started to catalogue exactly what had dragged me up there from the fume-filled warmth of London.

The thing that set all this off, the principal culprit, was the government's White Paper of July 1997. This enabled the referendum of 11 September 1997, which then produced clear majorities for the two propositions about the creation of a Scottish Parliament and the capacity of that Parliament to vary taxes in Scotland. January 1998 saw the Scotland Bill introduced in Westminster. This then became law as the Scotland Act 1998 the following November. And so the deed was done.

The Scottish Parliament, elected on 6 May 1999, sat for the first time on 12 May. Dr Winnie Ewing MSP announced, 'I have the opportunity to make a short speech and I want to begin with the words that I have always wanted either to say or to hear someone else say: the Scottish Parliament, which adjourned on 25 March 1707, is hereby reconvened.' The Parliament finally took up its full legislative powers on 1 July after a lot of fires had been lit in Edinburgh and Saltires had been waved in the axiomatically nippy summer air.

Then, apocalypse! Suddenly, everything was up for grabs. The arrival of Scottish devolution in 1999 was rapidly followed by an outbreak of navel-gazing in England, as the state of the Union was thrown into stark and inquisitorial relief. The southern newspapers began a long and aimless campaign of hand-wringing and rhetorical posturing (often by head-in-the-sand right-wing commentators) at the way our homeland was slipping through our fingers like the waters of life itself. Questions were asked about the future Balkanisation of the United Kingdom. With Scotland gone, and Wales and Northern Ireland on the way out, what did it mean for, say, Sheffield? Or Exeter? Visions were conjured up of a once-great nation now composed entirely of implausible diminishing city-states or principalities, run from provincial HQs by bearded men with insane provincial grievances.

Meanwhile, the Scots at once started to fan the flames of national disintegration by threatening to interfere with Clause 28 of the 1988 Local Government Act, ban fox-hunting, create discrepancies in the university tuition fee system and not provide a satisfactory answer to the West Lothian Question. There appeared a rash of books on and around the subject of Scotland, England, constitutional change, the tortured relationship between the English and the Scots and national character generally. Alan Taylor edited a collection of Scottish-born essays under the title *What a State!*. Jeremy Paxman wrote a bestseller called *The English*, yet another attempt by an English writer to see if fair play/tolerance/eccentricity were still core English values; which, it turned out, they were. Tory philosopher Roger Scruton produced *England: An Obituary*. Gavin Esler (Scottish) did a radio series called *The Brits*, in which the Home Secretary, Jack Straw, famously confirmed the fact that the English had a 'propensity to violence'. Writer and critic Darcus Howe did a TV series about the real identity of white England, calling it *The White Tribe*. Andrew Marr (Scottish) wrote a TV series-plus-book called *The Day Britain Died*. Even as I write, the BBC's Fergal Keane (Irish) has launched another piece of UK introspection called *Forgotten Britain*.

And, yep, this book is a late arrival to that queue, panting and wheezing up to the check-in desk of the devolutionary argument long after all the others have wandered off to the departure lounge of dialectic. But let me say in my own defence that, as a Londoner first and last, I nevertheless am one-eighth Scottish, on my mother's side, and this absolutely qualifies me to mouth off on the whole Scottish question, late or bang on time. Absolutely.

With the Scotland Act out of the way, my list carried on with:

– The fact that Westminster was, at the time, being run by Scotsmen. The Chancellor of the Exchequer, the Foreign Secretary, the Lord Chancellor, the Secretary of State for Scotland and the Secretary of State for Social Security were all Scottish. The Prime Minister, Tony Blair, was educated in Scotland. The former Defence Secretary and now Secretary-General of NATO, George Robertson, was Scottish. Likewise Charles Kennedy of the Liberal Democrats. And, of course, the late John Smith, former leader of the Labour Party, was crucial in rehabilitating the party in the opinion polls. Why? Because he was the miraculously perfect Scottish bank manager of all our Jungian dreams.

– Talking of which, the Royal Bank of Scotland and the Bank of Scotland (the oldest surviving clearing bank in the UK), not content with being allowed to print their own tiresome banknotes, were both trying to take over the pointedly English NatWest. A few weeks after I left Edinburgh, the Royal Bank of Scotland did just that, and now what's left of my bank account is being overseen by a load of Jocks.

– England's best-known woman barrister after Cherie Booth is the Scottish Helena Kennedy QC.

– The English – or at least Londoners – have a morbid interest in Scottish things, even if Scotland itself is just a pain in the arse. The fact that a lot of Scottish stuff (tartan, tourism, layout of Edinburgh, famous Scottish actors) is an Anglo-Scottish co-production is neither here nor there. Scotland lures the English like a bristly siren and, in return, the English make room for terrible quantities of Scots people and Scottish things down here. Hence the insistent presence of Ewan McGregor, Macallan malt whisky, Kirsty Wark, Irvine Welsh, salmon, Robbie Coltrane, all that stuff about Glasgow, Carol Smillie, Travis, James Naughtie, Gordon Ramsay (just barely Scottish) and Evelyn Glennie – but no longer, mercifully, Andrew Neil.

– The food, which is famously the most dangerous and disgusting in Europe; worse, even, than the food in England.

– Edinburgh University. According to the *Tatler* magazine for socialites and hairdressers, Edinburgh University is now more chic than Oxford. The colleges at Oxford are admittedly very pretty and they're a lot handier for London than anywhere in Edinburgh. But the town as a whole is perilously close to lapsing into a shithole, clogged with traffic, mystified tourists, cornflake-packet modern architecture and dismal chainstores. Edinburgh is a real capital city with bars that stay open all hours, magnificent vistas, tenement flats, an inviolable sense of self. And now Prince William is down for St Andrews, which is no distance.

– Glasgow – once the Second City of the Empire, once, even, the richest city in the kingdom after London – had just been named, yet again, as the unhealthiest city in the UK, this time by a team of researchers at Bristol University.

And then there was Edinburgh itself, the most potent reason for going all that horrible way north. But there's more to the city than just urban good looks, so far as I am concerned. Because me and Din Eidyn (hey!) go way back. In moments of intense, relaxed optimism, I even picture us as being more like brothers than man and city. We have a past and nothing binds you like history.

First off, there is evidence that I once went there as a child, on a family holiday. I was maybe ten. We have a family photograph, now bleached with age, of the cannons on top of

Edinburgh Castle. I can just remember standing behind the parapet, waiting for the wind to catch me and blow me off my feet and head-first down to a gory death on the Esplanade below, while my father tried to wind the film on. More to the point, I remember being so hungry by the time we got there – on account of my father's ludicrously underestimating the distance by car from Alnwick, where we were staying – that I actually ate sprouts for lunch. That was in a hotel of gigantic drabness and smelliness, light years removed from the cute bar/brasseries all over the centre of today's Edinburgh, but quite like the place I was now staying in.

Jump forward a decade and I am back, this time for the Edinburgh Festival. I am not performing: I am a hanger-on with my girlfriend, who is performing. I am a groupie, which means that I have plenty of time (while the rest are rehearsing their tough-but-tender student production which will get them all theatrical agents and TV shows) to wander the streets. I am theoretically quite cultured enough by now to respond to the splendour all around me. Amazingly, I do not. Instead I have a bad time.

I get backache from sleeping on the lino floor of a Freemasons' Hall, which is where all the student performers and their boyfriends/girlfriends are kipping down, communally, in sleeping bags. Some kinky Masonic shingle painted like the eye of Jehovah squints down at me from the end wall, which may have something to do with it. A few days pass, then someone offers me the floor of a tenement flat down the road, where I gratefully decamp. This is not bad. The flat is very cold and narrow and filthy and has a carpet filled with bogies and carpet bugs; but it is private and the bogies and bugs make the floor quite spongy. But the landlady throws me out after two nights for breaking the terms of the tenancy.

So I go back to the Freemasons' Hall in a sulk, pausing only to be mildly attacked outside a pub. This is an act which instantaneously freezes my view of Anglo-Scottish relations and leaves it in a bad way for two further decades. I am walking past this dark, miasmic boozer doorway when a hand reaches out and grabs me by the front of my shirt and starts pulling me in. I am wearing red braces at the time and a headful of poncey, floppy hair, so I am asking for it. I stare for a second at the hand and the bunched-up material of my shirt front, feeling the inexorable force pulling me in. My fight/flight adrenal mechanism dithers uselessly and then gives up altogether, leaving me about as capable of self-preservation as an aphid. I am going to get stomped. Then a voice calls out, *Ah, leave him be. He's no worth it.* The hand lets go and I run weeping and laughing back to the arms of society. My girlfriend is curiously unimpressed. I spend another few days wandering around feeling hungry, stiff, and, above all, threatened by the existence of Scotland, and then I go home.

(Now, was I grabbed because somehow the assaulting hand simply *knew* I was English? Was I talking to someone else at the time? I don't remember. I only remember the big hand. Would it have grabbed me if I'd been Norwegian or Spanish? Or even Scottish? To what extent am I projecting my paranoia on to the nation as a whole? As chance would have it, at about the same time as I was being grabbed in Edinburgh, a friend of mine who'd gone to study at St Andrews University was being beaten up by some Edinburgh medical students who took exception to his being a bouncer at a dance. 'They obviously enjoyed it that bit more because I was English,' he notes.)

But no matter, because a few more years go by and then I have to come up to appear as a makeweight performer at the Edinburgh Literary Festival. Immediately – or as soon as we make it in from the airport – I am astonished and entranced, comprehensively, southerner-style. This feeling increases as I sit in a marquee doing the graveyard slot (right after lunch) yapping on about regionalism to an audience of the other speakers' friends, other speakers waiting to do their acts later in the day and a confused old man with a ball of tissue paper in his hands.

My gig done, I then have the city at my feet, plus the chance to get drunk at one in the morning in the bar of the Traverse Theatre with some Anarchist Libertarians. I experience (along with all the other makeweight hacks) the dizzy sensation of partying in a magnificent all-night city (the bars didn't shut! They never shut!) along with a host of similarly bedazzled nanocelebrities. All my old misgivings go out of the window. When I get back to London I begin to shout the city's virtues with all the interminable stamina of a proselyte. Those who already know about Edinburgh nod and their eyes shine. The rest just scowl and change the subject. Together, the old hands and I explore our furtive passion for the burg, unable or unwilling to reveal it to a sceptical English public.

And so I ended up lying in this room like a fishtank with no water in it, inhaling the deep vapours of the bed and gearing myself up for the high point of my Edinburgh trip, the most symbolically charged thing an Englishman can do in the New Scotland: my first visit to the Scottish Parliament. The very thought of it was enough to send me into a long and tremendous sleep.

FOUR

Can I briefly lurch towards the problem of our Anglo-Scottish shared history, before I go on? There isn't a great deal of it, and what there is – is what, exactly? An inexhaustible supply of perfidy, emanating from the English and directed against the Scots. A one-way history, a pipeline of awfulness flowing from south to north.

This, at least, is the conventional Scottish line, embracing such horrors as:

– The William Wallace nightmare (see *Braveheart*).

– The killing of King James IV of Scotland, plus the flower of his nobles and kinsmen, at the battle of Flodden in 1513.

– Henry VIII attacking the south of Scotland in the 1540s in a series of vicious campaigns known as the 'Rough Wooing'.

– Elizabeth I having Mary Queen of Scots beheaded in 1587.

– Cromwell formerly subjugating Scotland by force of arms in the seventeenth century, following which the English were behind the Glen Coe Massacre of 1692, in which men,

women and children of the MacDonald clan were cruelly put
to death just outside Fort William.

– The crushed Rebellion of 1745, which in turn was followed by things which were sometimes uniquely our fault
and sometimes weren't: the Highland Clearances, then the
collapse of the kelp industry, followed by the potato famine of
1846 which caused starvation and death among what was
left of the Highland population, followed by mass emigration, followed by the Crofters' War of 1882 and, bringing this
litany temporarily to a close, the exploitation of generations
of working-class Scotsmen in the factories and slums of
Victorian industrial north Britain.

As a consequence, our capacity for being English and being
detestable has barely wavered since the eleventh century. The
Scots have expended unimaginable sums of spiritual energy
simply loathing us.

On the other hand, this morgue-like grip on the past
looks like a kind of willed insanity by the time we get to the
twenty-first century. After all, Denmark co-exists with
Germany, Portugal with Spain, Canada with the USA – yes,
with frictions, misunderstandings, irritations. But they
don't see it as an essential pre-condition of nationhood to
characterise their larger neighbours always and forever as
predatory, hypocritical, self-obsessed bastards.

In fact, it's possible to point out that the long dirge that is
Scotland's past is actually punctuated by all kinds of affirming
moments, many of them dependent on the benign intervention of the filthy English neighbour for their very success. For
instance, the defeat of the English by Robert the Bruce at
Bannockburn in 1314; the Scottish Enlightenment in the
eighteenth century (Edinburgh, Athens of the North) and
the boom of the nineteenth century (Glasgow, Second City
of the Empire); the foundation of the Scottish Labour Party in
the 1880s; and the theft of the Stone of Destiny by Scottish

Nationalists on Christmas Day, 1950, when they took it from Westminster Abbey in a rented car, dropped it and broke a bit off by mistake.

Also, that roll-call of famous Scottish men and women of destiny, including Robert Burns, Joseph Black, James Watt, The Sensational Alex Harvey Band, Alexander Graham Bell, Lord Kelvin, Lulu, Robert Louis Stevenson, Groundskeeper Willie (from *The Simpsons*, the irascible gingery school janitor), Walter Scott, Willie Carson, John Knox, Billy Connolly, Andrew Carnegie, The Bay City Rollers, the Queen Mother, Jim Clark, Robert Adam, Alastair Sim, Oor Wullie and Rod Stewart. None of whom would have been half as big without the active support and encouragement of the English.

To put it another way. Paint us an undifferentiated shade of shit if you want to, but ask yourselves, as good pious Scotsmen, how seriously do you want to be taken in this day and age? How much do you need someone else to blame?

Which leads me to the New Scottish Parliament of 1999.

FIVE

Well, all right: the Athens of the North now had its own Areopagite Council. As the writer Ian Bell put it, the day after the reconvened Parliament sat for the first time in May 1999, 'Edinburgh was the only place in the world to be.' Two consecutive days I'd earmarked for watching the new Scottish Parliament in action, to see where 'memory' was 'reclaimed, a right restated, a truth reaffirmed'. Two consecutive days to see what was, in effect, a nation reborn. A sacred trust.

After another weird night in my Bela Lugosi room, I found that the weather had got its retaliation in early and it was too freezing to get anywhere. I got so cold stumbling from base camp to the Mound – the outcrop of rock on which the temporary Parliament building was standing while they built a new one down the road – that I had to warm up in a boozer yet again, this time opposite Waverley Station. The minutes were slipping away. I had a date with destiny, but I was too busy being cold to make it.

Nursing my pint of 80/- heavy, my *eighty*, I earwigged a conversation between yet another sorrowful barmaid and a man who looked like the actor Billy Crystal when he wears a beard.

Billy marched in, took off his gloves and laid an old-fashioned brown paper parcel on the counter. Turned out the parcel contained biology textbooks.

'Oh, thanks,' the barmaid cried, holding them up as if they were wads of a currency she couldn't spend. 'That's *just* what I wanted.'

She gazed at them. She seemed both proud and suspicious at the same time. Then the phone behind the bar rang – same as the pub in Leith, same tense intervention – and the barmaid left Mr Crystal with a small lager and started on a long dialogue with someone who (I inferred) was a legal operative of some sort. There was mention of kids and money and the little one getting upset at school. Divorce was in the air. Hence the biology books, the unease, the mournfulness: life falls apart, a better career becomes a priority, things get harder as you get older.

Once she'd put the phone down and clamped a smile back on her face, she turned back to Billy Crystal and sighed, 'Oh, I hope I pass.'

'You don't *hope* you pass. You *will* pass.'

'I'm feeling my age a bit. And I'm no good at maths.'

Billy leaned forward, concerned.

'There will be people on the course who are *much* worse than you. *Believe* me.'

I think he was a little bit in love with her.

I sat and rubbed my hands together to get enough circulation going for me to clutch my glass without it sliding straight through my icy fingers and on to the floor. I wanted to join in, tell her that yes, it was the right thing to do, and yes, she *would* pass and become a pharmacist or lab technician. Two sad barmaids in a row, endemic Scottish melancholy. One trying to buy her way out of it with a watch; the other by going to adult education classes. A voice a bit like conscience prompted me to say something. The Edinburgh barmaid seemed so apprehensive of her life that I wanted to platitudinise in some way, tell her that if *I* could make it, then *she* certainly could, all it took was the will to persist, and so on.

First, though, I was reluctant to barge into someone else's conversation. Admittedly, it was a small boozer and there were only the three of us in it at the time, so I could have justified it. I could even have claimed to be a lapsed biotechnician. A barefaced lie, obviously, but why not? Human contact is the important thing. I didn't do it, though, inhibited as I was by my own modesty.

But the other reason I didn't speak was because I am English. Billy wasn't Scottish, but nor was he English. I had him down as a post-grad at the university, maybe Czech or Hungarian, a faint, appealing Central European halo around his eloquence. He sounded fine, adaptable, very go-anywhere. But I knew that if I opened my mouth, everything I said would come out as a paradigm of London snottiness, a regional nightmare. In the context of Scotland, my words would emerge helplessly like a lecture from a Tory party boss, each phrase starched with southern condescension. So you're having a spot of *bother*, are you? Well, take it from *me*, all you need is a bit of *pluck* and *there you are* . . . I was a prisoner of speech. So I sat there, the English mute, just trying to look pleasant.

After a few more clenched moments had passed, I decided that not only was I not going to speak, I wasn't going to warm up in this pub any more than I had in the one in Leith. I wandered out, up the hill towards the Parliament, to be met by a big ginger dog running down the hill towards the station. A couple of seconds later, a man appeared, running after it and shouting 'Jason!' or 'Dyson!' or 'Tyson!' It was hard to tell.

Then a middle-aged woman rushed into view.

'Oh, God,' she muttered, heading off after the first two.

Then a younger woman appeared.

'We only just bought him this morning,' she said to me as she sprinted past, hair flying. Tyson, meanwhile, was disappearing at speed through the doors of a recently opened Scottish–Italian brasserie next door to the pub I'd just left.

I headed into the Parliament buildings.

When I get there, the SNP leader, Alex Salmond, is absent. This makes me deeply unhappy. Why? I might as well come out with it now. I have been nourishing an unhealthy fixation on Alex Salmond for some years – ever since he rose to stardom with the SNP at the end of the 1980s and then became the party's National Convenor in 1990. Maybe 'fixation' is the wrong word. I just find him transfixing. There's something about the shape of his head and his crinkle-cut-chip smile that makes me wonder if he was born with one of those Victorian joke faces, one of those invertible cartoons that smiles when you hold it one way up and goes cross-eyed with indignation when you turn it the other way round. That and the waves of 1950s stolidity that come off him, the sense that even though he's about the same age as me, I know he'd talk to me patiently and patronisingly, as if explaining the world to an idiot. I can see myself, my head slowly nodding up and down like an old horse, murmuring *Oh, I see . . . now I get it* while he drones on and on, putting the detritus in my head into some kind of order.

This is not to say that, viewed in the cold light of day, he doesn't come out with a constant stream of measured political rubbish. He does. One year it is 'abundantly clear that a devolved assembly would not be safe in Westminster's hands, and that only an independent Parliament can entrench the sovereignty of the Scottish people'. The next year, 'What Scotland wants is – very simply – to be normal.' A bit later, in an interview with the *Guardian*, he says, 'Balls. Absolute balls,' like an English prep-school master pushed beyond the limit thirty years ago.

But when Salmond speaks, he always distracts you from the shallowness of whatever he's saying by keeping this perpetual half-smile on his face, gently incredulous, as if he can scarcely believe that he needs to articulate things which are so evidently true that they barely need to be spoken at all. It's a wondering smile, wondering why we the English are so blinkered we don't already hold to his point of view. He knows what's best for me and the United Kingdom, better than I know myself, and his head is shaped like a turnip: Rob Roy meets Reginald Perrin.

Back in the Parliament, Donald Dewar and Sir David Steel (the latter as red-faced and genial as Santa Claus) are, however, both in attendance. Up in the public gallery, a surprisingly large number of men in suits, plus some trenchy student types, have congregated to watch democracy in action. They twiddle their thumbs and con the daily 'Business Bulletin'. I take my seat (comfy like a cinema seat) and brood on Salmond's absence. Without him, it's like going to see a play only to find that the lead's indisposed and an understudy is on instead.

So I stare at the room around me. The temporary accommodation we are all occupying is actually the Assembly Hall of the General Assembly of the Church of Scotland. The exterior of this Victorian heap (built between 1858 and 1885, demolishing some sixteenth-century treasures in the process) is massive Late Scottish Baronial, somewhere between Hampton Court Palace and Colditz. Inside, there are exposed wooden beams, painted the colour of French mustard, quartering the room. These give the upper reaches of the debating chamber a Mead Hall feel, while the lower parts are just plain-dealing Chamber of Commerce-style tongue-and-groove panelling. A ceiling full of grimy windowpanes with laughing faces drawn in the dirt by impish service operatives keeps the atmosphere free of daylight.

A guy called Jack McConnell (Labour) is addressing the MSPs as I settle myself and my handful of rain-damp papers. McConnell is Finance Minister in the new administration, and attracts a lot of attention from the press for his take-no-prisoners style. 'You expect,' says one commentator, 'to see him tuck a Tommy gun under his arm.' It takes me a long while to work out where Labour broadly is – apart from around the corvine form of Mr Dewar – thanks to the anti-confrontational U-shaped seating plan of the debating chamber. All the MSPs sit behind desks arranged in a succession of tiered horseshoes. Every desk has a microphone to speak into, so there's no screaming; and each microphone has a red light which comes on to indicate who's talking at any given moment, so there's no confusion, no room for jostling ill-temper. There are even electronic timers on the walls to make sure that MSPs don't blab on for the rest of everyone else's lives. There is no ranting, braying opposition in the sense that we Westminster-fixated southerners understand it. The physical reality of the new Scottish Parliament is a calculated reproach to the Parliament in England, a gesture of disapproval. It is also like a seminar for middle managers who want to improve their public speaking skills.

Labour hold the middle – and largest – part of the overall horseshoe, with their power-sharing colleagues, the Lib Dems, next to them. The Tories are over to the right of the Presiding Officer. You can spot the Tories easily because of the way they lounge around in their seats, making low *nyarr nyarr* noises in the direction of Jack McConnell. The rest, including the Scottish Nationalists, are over on the other side. But they lack definition in comparison with the Tories, because there is no Alex Salmond, the Rod Stewart to their Faces.

McConnell is well into his speech, which centres on what is to be the Scottish Parliament's first piece of legislation: the Public Finance and Accountability (Scotland) Bill. 'Borrowing limits,' he says, '. . . accountability . . . water and sewage . . . companies . . . prudent use of public money . . . accountability . . .' Then his preamble comes to an end. Sir David Steel and about half the audience leave. This caesura in events is followed by a torrid set of exchanges between McConnell and various other MSPs. They all speak at about 100 m.p.h. in order to beat the clock, sprinting down the platform of language, chasing after the departing express train of compelling oratory. Some more of the audience pick up their bags and go. Soon, there are only me and a handful of other weirdos gazing down.

I can't follow what McConnell and the other interested MSPs are on about and nor, I suspect, can my co-auditors. Not even if you offered to swap my hotel room for a suite at the Caledonian could I make an exegesis of his text or the replies he elicits. But this is the first bill before Parliament, and an important symbolic moment, and it is Scotland, so words like 'prudence', 'fiscal responsibility' and 'appropriate' swirl through the air like dust clouds. They have to. No one wants to strike the wrong note. But it is kind of dull. Many of the MSPs (the men, especially) are lolling in their seats, doodling on notepads, composing letters, filling in crosswords. Of the 129 Members of the Scottish Parliament in existence I would say that about 70 of them have bothered to turn up.

On the other hand, dullness is a prerequisite of democracy. Dullness is respectable; dullness conveys an apt sense of the burden of power. Is parliamentary democracy in the UK really a sham, a skimpily concealed oligarchy with a top-dressing of *bien-pensant* suffrage? Who cares? If it looks as if it's being taken seriously, then that'll do for most of us. McConnell has that side of it down pat, despite having recently undergone the experience of 'Lobbygate' – a cash-for-questions scandal which blew up a few months earlier and then receded, leaving him untainted but mildly dog-eared by the exposure. He has a snarling eagerness in his performance which is easy to interpret as a hunger for the right decision. Satirists remark on the neatness of his personal appearance and the depth of his tan, even in winter: 'A beautifully browned piece of meat' is how one put it. But the old Michael Foot/Tony Benn paradigm no longer holds: you can yearn for social justice without having to look like a product of Care in the Community.

Then the talk is all over. Seamlessly, the debate has wound itself up. Without even realising it, I have watched history being made. I am like a casual passer-by at the signing of the American Declaration of Independence. I have even warmed up at last – the first time I can recall being warm in Scotland without actually being in bed. A Labour MSP gets churchily to his feet and testifies that, 'This is a framework which will gain worldwide recognition.' He is followed by a Lib Dem MSP who does his best to top him by proclaiming that, 'This is a model for Westminster,' and 'I don't think that Parliament will pass a more important bill this session.' Then the rest of the MSPs get up, one by one, to slap Jack McConnell on the back verbally, apart from a Tory who produces the mandatory Conservative list of nit-picking detractions. But even he allows a small approbation to the Parliament as a whole. After all, it has given him something to do in the afternoons and keeps him in with his Scottish neighbours, no matter how principled the Tories' opposition to the whole idea of a Parliament at the time of the referendum in 1997.

In fact, the only dissenting voice comes from that notorious firebrand, Dennis Canavan MSP. The too-hot-to-handle left-wing Canavan was excluded from the Labour list of candidates at the time of the Scottish parliamentary elections, so he stood as an independent in the Falkirk West seat and – Ken Livingstone-style – won the biggest majority in Scotland. He is the mischievous genie in the New Labour experiment. Earlier this year he took part in a blockade of the Faslane naval base, in protest against the nuclear weapons kept there. We do not know that soon he will force a by-election by standing down from his seat. Today he looks as if he has eaten a bag of jalapeño peppers. Canavan lays into McConnell. He turns red; he strikes the desktop with his hand. He raises his voice above the businesslike *rowl* used by the other male MSPs. There is finally a ripple of excitement among the more comatose members. It is real politics at last, rather than the sanitised millennialist variety which has gently engulfed us up to this point. Then Canavan's electronic timer runs out on him and flashes him into oblivion. He sits down with little shreds of steam still escaping from his ears and everyone goes on to the next piece of business, pleased with themselves and with the way that Canavan has torn off the procedural sanitary wrapper: a real Parliament at last!

So what do we make of this?

What was incontestable was that the proceedings embodied the traditional Scottish virtues of civility, decency and lack of side, as opposed to the traditional English vices of unruliness, snobbery and cant. Of course, with fewer than a quarter of Westminster's 650-plus seats, the Scottish Parliament ought to be able to control itself and act like a responsible gathering of adults rather than *The Battle of the Bulge*.

Nevertheless, it looked the part – like Open Day at a school, the inmates projecting self-restraint, clean shoes on, almost no fighting. It didn't take long for human nature to assert itself, of course. Pretty soon after the opening pleasantries in Parliament we had the more understandable political business of McConnell falling out then falling in again with his boss, Gordon Brown; we had Donald Dewar's competence coming under fire; we had the new Parliament buildings at Holyrood effectively doubling in cost, ballooning from around £100 million to nearly £200 million, making David Steel, the Parliament's Presiding Officer and notional overseer of the building programme, full-time butt of the national press; and we had Alex Salmond arguing so viciously with the treasurer of the SNP, Ian Blackford, about the handling of the party's finances that Blackford decided to sue Salmond for defamation. A year goes by, war breaks out. Still. It looked great to begin with.

But then, we've just elected a mayor down here in London, for the first time, and it's hard to tell whether the licence we've been granted to act in self-determination in this way is a step towards a true extension of the franchise, or just a niggardly gesture towards a city's aspirations; a piece of mere politics. No one really knows what powers the new Mayor of London has (circumscribed, malleable, one assumes) and no one really knows how much freedom the new Scottish Parliament will enjoy in the next few years. Does Scotland require a Parliament because it has always been a separate country and to deny it its own seat of democracy is an injustice? Or does Scotland need a Parliament as a starting-point, to act as a focus for its evolving nationhood and give legitimacy to its ambitions?

Either way, a Mayor of London is a pretty finite creation. It doesn't prompt any serious discussion of London's seceding from the rest of England. In Edinburgh, by way of contrast, the reopening of Parliament does little else. The Scottish Parliament is a single term in a succession of terms, part of a sequence of events which can, if you like, be seen to stretch back through the deeds of generations of Scottish freethinkers, from the signatories of the Declaration of Arbroath in 1320, to the radicals involved in the 1820 Rising, to the first Home Rule supporters, through the Scottish Nationalists of the 1930s, to the latter-day SNP. The Parliament can even be seen as a revisiting of the Liberal concept of 'Home Rule All Round' – a federalist scheme from the 1890s – given the way it naturally tends to place itself within a chain of causation. As such it implies bigger and better things: devolution, sovereign independence, Scotland taking its seat at the UN, the full Balkanisation package.

This is the agenda. At first glance, however, Parliament can look like the equivalent of the news in Gaelic: just a pacifier for Scottish resentments, something lobbed up from south of the border to shut the stroppy bastards up. But a second glance reveals that there is a process at work here, and this kind of process, once started, is hard to stop.

And Day Two?

Well, let's not go mad. The imagery is as important as the reality. The main reason I turn up for a second day of this stuff is that Day Two is the day of Question Time, in which Donald Dewar, the First Minister, can be semi-spontaneously grilled by colleagues and opponents from all parties. Fireworks are promised. Questions lined up by other MSPs include:

– What account will be taken of geographical location in the review of maternity services within the greater Glasgow area?

– What measures is the Scottish Executive taking to promote sport for people with disabilities?

– When did the First Minister last meet the Chancellor of the Exchequer and what did they discuss?

This last (put by Liberal Democrat Jamie Stone) is a standard fixture whenever Dewar is available for comment; a recurrent quibbling tease which Dewar now shrugs off with robotic disdain, on auto-pilot. But it gives a clue to the character of

Question Time and its sibling, Open Question Time. This is much more knockabout stuff, showbiz for the crowds. It also guarantees that not only is there a bigger mob in to watch (hundreds of schoolkids when I was there, astonishingly silent, as well as me and the men in suits), but more MSPs bother to turn up. More like three-quarters this time, instead of the barely two-thirds of the previous day.

David Steel is back in the driving seat and propels the questions through as if he's only managed to put 50p in the parking meter, the wardens are busy and he needs to get back to his car (a classic Jag, by the way, showroom condition, parked outside). Still no Alex Salmond, but plenty of Dewar, who crumples himself up in his chair like a sheet of stiff grey paper wedged in a bin, only his nose, glasses and hair poking out of the top. He looks amazingly uncomfortable – not, I suspect, because of the pain of Question Time, which he handles either glibly or with forensic efficiency, depending on your point of view, but because he finds sitting down in a small executive chair for forty minutes of more-or-less pointless rhetorical exchanges to be a bit of a drag. 'Where's the question?' David Steel keeps sighing, as yet another MSP spirals out of control, nosediving into the desert of his own obsessions.

Everyone else seems to enjoy it, though. There is a lot more of the school-debating-society levity that one associates with the democratic process, along with taunts at the absent Salmond's expense ('How much easier it is to make progress without him,' as Dewar starchily notes) plus mild ritualised table-banging, mooing and bleating.

John Swinney (SNP) asks about the findings of the Bristol University report – the one which fingered Glasgow as the unhealthiest place in Britain. Dewar answers that the research is based on data going back to 1995 and that already things are much better – the stock evasionary tactic. A Tory MSP bores on about motoring, and whether the notorious Skye Bridge toll is going to go up to incorporate the VAT being levied by the EU: two typical Tory manias parcelled up in one question.

While the body of the Parliament is busy looking busy for the crowds, there are those who respond to the axiom that a boring Parliament is an authentic Parliament by getting bored. I am quite bored, again. And there is one MSP, seated at the back, on the furthermost tier of horseshoes, who is not only bored but appears to have strayed out of the ambit of rationality altogether. Whereas all the other MSPs have important piles of documents and papers to shuffle around and interfere with, he has nothing save what appears to be a heap of pizza flyers on his desk. In the absence of anything better, he pushes these around for a while before giving up trying to make sense of them and shoving them together in a messy sprawl, like autumn leaves. Then he starts muttering to himself, leaning back in his chair and scratching his waist and armpits and talking under his breath. Then he closes his eyes and essays a nap. Then he wakes up and spends a long time examining the maker's label on his tie, passing comments to himself as he does so. Eventually Question Time ends and he leaps to his feet (along with most of the other MSPs) and hurls himself towards the door. I have the feeling that maybe he is going to spend the night roaming through the Parliament corridors, fingering his tie and dropping pizza restaurant hand-outs on the floor.

And the rest? The more high-minded ones, obviously, stay behind to take part in a debate on an equal-opportunities strategy. The less high-minded shuffle out in a distinctly demob-happy frame of mind, earning themselves a rebuke from the Presiding Officer for chattering while still in the debating chamber. Either course of action – staying for a worthy debate or giggling and chattering at the exits – can be taken as proof of the Parliament's growing maturity. Does it matter that one MSP spent Question Time monomaniacally interfering with his own clothing? Does it matter that there is no Alex Salmond? The Scottish parliamentary system is big enough for people to take it seriously or fuck around in. The schoolkids start to leave, apparently satisfied with what they've seen.

And it *is* something, is it not, to see a Parliament where there wasn't one before? Even though this Parliament still has to defer to Westminster in matters of defence, foreign affairs, central economic policy, social security and immigration? For heaven's sake, it still has tax-varying powers, the health, education, transport, legal, agricultural, environment and *sports* portfolios. It looks like a Parliament and acts like a Parliament. And it doesn't require an enormous imaginative leap to see it – a few years hence – going all the way, out there, ultimately head-to-head with the *Folketing* of Denmark, the *Dàil* of the Republic of Ireland, or the National Assembly of Burundi.

Scottish Parliament, Official Report, Thursday 23 September 1999:

The Presiding Officer (Sir David Steel): 'The first item of business is a debate on motion S1M-163, in the name of Angus MacKay, on crime prevention. There is also an amendment to that motion.'

Tommy Sheridan (Scottish Socialist Party): 'On a point of order, Presiding Officer. Do you not agree that the lack of members in the chamber is criminal?'

The Presiding Officer: 'That is not a point of order.'

In the middle of all this, of course, Donald Dewar died. On 10 October he was taken to the Edinburgh Royal Infirmary after suffering a fall outside his official residence in Edinburgh. By midday, 11 October in the year 2000, he was dead as the result of a sudden catastrophic brain haemorrhage. And that was that. It was completely shocking, just as the death of Labour leader John Smith, in 1994, was much more than merely the death of a politician. When John Smith died, our local newsagent was so distraught he actually scrawled up a notice on the *Evening Standard* sandwich board outside his newsagent's, before the official flyer had come in: the news was that dreadful. I'd left Edinburgh when Dewar actually died, and so I can only guess at the mood of the place. The most striking thing about both Smith and Dewar was that they were politicians with that oddest of things: integrity. Normally, this combination is as likely as a car-dealer with a conscience or a moose with perfect pitch. But they both had it, and it hurt when they left the scene so abruptly. Which leaves you with the unaccountable intuition that of all the British, only the Scots have a properly tight grasp on probity and what it means to serve in a public democracy.

Came out of the Parliament building warmer and drier than I'd been for a long time and got lost trying to find my way back to my morbid hotel.

Not that it worried me to start with. In fact, I took it as yet another good sign that Edinburgh went on in all kinds of other directions, still being Edinburgh, but not Edinburgh the tourist honeypot. You go to somewhere like Bradford, or Ipswich, and you can walk across it in about twenty minutes. But not here. You walk across Edinburgh for twenty minutes and you'll be lucky to get as far as Meadowbank. What really drove the point home to me was going in search of a haggis shop down towards Merchiston – south-west of the centre – in the pouring rain, in the dark, with a street map that I could only just read on account of the torrential wetness and the absence of light. It was exactly the right set of circumstances to emphasise the scale of the place.

I was looking for Macsween's haggis shop. Best in Edinburgh, I was told. I wanted to buy the Chieftain, a huge eighteen-pound haggis, named – I guessed – after the lines in Burns' poem 'The Address to the Haggis':

> Fair fa' your honest sonsie face,
> Great chieftain o' the puddin' race!

The Chieftain was reputedly so big that if you tried to take it back on a plane, you had to buy it its own ticket and strap it in and give it beer and peanuts on the journey. Down Bruntsfield Place, they said, you can't miss it. I completely misjudged the scale of my Edinburgh Easyfold Map and started walking. By the time I got there, soaked and refrigerated, Macsween's had gone, and had been replaced by a wine store. I mean, it had obviously happened months before, not in the time it took to walk from the Parliament building. But the effect was the same.

I was miles from anywhere, half-past five in the evening, in the dark, my mouth opening and closing, fish-like, at the wine store that stood where Macsween's should have. There were office workers and shop people crowding the pavements. They had that statutory pissed-off, seen-it-all city look on their faces, the big-town slump of the shoulders, the long trudge back home. Could have been Londoners, but for the fact that they were heavily wrapped up in sweaters and waterproofs. They walked quickly and angrily through the rain. Well, I told myself, making the best of a bad job, this is when cities truly reveal themselves. Anyone can make their way up and down Princes Street and the Royal Mile and end up footsore but doltishly satisfied. The hard part is to make your way with the evening mob down the Lothian Road, across Earl Grey Street and Home Street and along Bruntsfield Place to the point at which it turns into Morningside Road. There you find out that the thing you specifically came in search of no longer exists, turn back up Merchiston Park, past the McEwan's brewery, over the Union Canal, up Grove Street in a two-pronged assault (up, lose faith, double back, study map under ineffectual yellow street lamp, go north again) and then by a sleight of hand through crunchy Hay Market and back towards the centre.

So I waded along black streets lined with archetypal Edinburgh six-storey buildings, villa-tenement hybrids built like cliffs. They were incredibly tall and dark, German Expressionist buildings, the kind of buildings F. W. Murnau might have approved of. The McEwan's brewery was equally vast and had a single great chimney floodlit blue at its centre, not that there was anyone there to see it apart from me, by that stage: all the office workers had gradually dwindled in numbers, thinning out as they slipped into the tenement villas, until I was the last lone figure on the pavements. The only shop (for half a mile in any direction) in the centre of the brewery complex was a massage parlour. The landscape plunged up and down. A building shaped like a drum loomed up to my right and disappeared again. The map flapped uselessly in my hand. For a couple of minutes I really wondered if I was ever going to see civilisation again, or if I was going to be found face down and blue outside the brewery massage parlour next morning.

Ironically, what a stroke of luck! This way, you get that feeling that only a really authoritative city can give you: the feeling of being completely lost, a speck of life drifting in the teeming indifference of someone else's town. Out in Merchiston, you can't even sense where the city centre might be. For a Londoner, this is all the proof he needs. And Merchiston is only halfway out. There are yet more horrible places like Corstorphine, Duddingston, Craigmillar, Muirhouse, Sighthill, Drylaw, Dean, Granton, Pilton, all of which constitute parts of greater Edinburgh and which are absolutely thousands of miles away.

I got back to my tarry hotel numb with cold and awe. I limped into the downstairs bar.

I was surrounded entirely by afterwork men, chewing on cigs and drinking hard. I stared up at the ceiling. The room, like my nuthouse bedroom, was taller than it was wide. The walls were rouged in colours of dried blood and ochre, while the ceiling – where whatever heat there was promptly migrated to – was a deep holly green. But it was at least somewhere near the centre of town, and I suddenly felt that I had been on a very, very long journey.

I asked for a whisky.

'You want ice with that?' the barman replied sarcastically.

My day had come full circle, bar to bar. I sat at a dark, sticky table for a long time, nursing my whisky and debating with myself whether to nip up and put on an extra vest before finishing my drink, or leave it as a treat for later.

I have to get out of Edinburgh, I told myself. You want it to be everything, but in reality, it's a separate world of its own. Edinburgh is dangerous, particularly for the English. Its refinement, its completeness, its arrogation of power, are all traps for the unwary English foreigner. England nowadays tends more and more to divide itself into a simple opposition between London and the rest of England. London patronises the rest of the country; the rest of the country despises and fears London. But Scotland, though smaller, has a more varied dynamic. Edinburgh is kept in tension by Glasgow, no more than thirty miles due west and bigger, too. The two big cities are distinct from but not *necessarily* superior to the little chain of east-coast centres, Aberdeen, Dundee, Inverness. The entire mainland is spiritually beholden to the Islands. And the Highlands are every Scotsman's Zion, from which he draws his spiritual inspiration and to which, given half a chance, his soul will return.

There is a more difficult network of relationships, in other words; a different jostling for the Scottish heart. Therefore I had to escape Din Eidyn and get away to its philosophical opposite, before I got badly twisted by the capital city's self-absorption and started to believe, as Londoners in particular will, that the Capital really was the capital.

I wondered if they ever caught Jason/Dyson/Tyson the dog.

SIX

I once saw George Melly in a pub in North Finchley. I mean, I saw him do his act. This was in the '70s, when he'd got bored writing for the *Observer* and had decided to revive his original career as a Jazz & Blues vocalist – the one he pursued in the 1950s with the Mick Mulligan band and about which he writes so zestfully in *Owning Up*. The gig was in the back room of a drab boozer called the Torrington, into which a midget stage had been inserted as well as a couple of dim stage lights. The place was heaving: the audience was monumentally drunk and since we were in the audience, me and my pimply teenage schoolmates were necessarily gassed on schoolboy vodka'n'limes. Mr Geo. Melly also appeared to be imbibing freely from a brandy bottle while onstage. He wore a hat, baggy pants held up by braces and a T-shirt. He kept picking at his teeth between numbers. 'I had a lamb curry just up the road before coming on,' he explained. 'Now I can't get rid of it.'

He was wonderful. He managed to be camp, avuncular, authoritative and salacious at the same time. He did 'Nuts',

'Frankie and Johnnie' (in which he did the oral sex pantomime by slinging his shoes – a pair of gilded pumps – over his shoulders and gobbling an imaginary lover) plus any number of Bessie Smith/whorehouse numbers involving sugar in bowls, hotdogs in rolls, and numerous hambones being boiled. He also did one which had some astoundingly memorable lines about nipples as big as thumbs and something between the legs sufficient to induce orgasm in a corpse.

For a fifteen-year-old suburban boy like me, this was beyond heavenly. This displayed artistry of the highest order – gleeful, passionate, hilarious, riotous. John Chilton's Feetwarmers (one of those quintessential New Orleans jazz combos made up of grizzled old white blokes with beards who cackle their arses off on the bandstand and shout obscenities from time to time) were backing him and played a blinder, completely impervious to their squalid surroundings. Melly was obliged to do several encores, audience participation was spontaneous and lively, I fell over a few times but finally made it home after the gig had ended and the whole night was sweaty and triumphant. I'm sorry if all this sounds too good to be true, and maybe time has overlaid it with a patina of brilliance which it doesn't deserve, but that's how it seemed to me.

So when Geo. Melly, backed by John Chilton, turned up in Edinburgh when I was up for the festival with my student girlfriend, what did I do but rush around announcing that this was the greatest event in showbiz music history since the Beatles played the Cavern and that everyone was to get tickets at once. We did that and turned up at this big city-centre cinema at midnight, high with excitement. I was busy giving Melly & Chilton a startlingly over-enthusiastic write-up even as we settled ourselves in our seats, wondering why the place seemed so big and chilly and free from salacity.

Something was wrong. What was wrong was that it was a cinema, and it was in Edinburgh. These were the days just before the licensing laws were relaxed, so everyone had stopped drinking at least an hour before the start. What's more, plenty of local citizens, not just us scabby students, had turned out. They were rich in fawn suits and high-necked blouses. They wore ties and slip-on shoes and in no sense unwashed jeans or pullovers with holes in them and food stains. The place filled up and we all crouched in our plush cinema armchairs, whispering. Morningside accents drifted through the air like the smell of camphorated oil. There was a lot of throat-clearing and leg-crossing. It felt like the AGM of some big company with a load of tight-arsed Scots share-holders in the main seats.

And when Geo. Melly himself came onstage, plus the Feetwarmers, I was clutched by horror as I realised that they too were tricked out in lounge suits and had evidently washed their hands and faces before coming on. They had ties spread across their shirt fronts like chains of office. Not that they didn't play their damnedest once the house lights dimmed and the stage had been bathed in a pink glow, but all the pleasure seemed to have gone out of it by the time Melly's 'Nuts' and Bessie Smith appropriations got to where we were seated. I'm not even sure he didn't trim some of the more engaging filth out of his act and replace it with tasteful homages to W. C. Handy and *The Birth of the Blues*. It got so bad that I started to feel as if I was out on a hot date to which the girl's parents had been mistakenly invited. Afterwards I spent days trying to paint a satisfactory word-picture of Melly's north London bacchanal, attempting to obliterate the memory of the Scottish cinema, but with no success. I felt like a fraud.

I also hunted around for someone to blame. I had promised intense rhythmic lubricity but delivered milktoast. Not

Melly's fault: he was just being professional, trimming his act to the crowd. So I blamed Edinburgh. I blamed Scottish Presbyterian prissiness. I knew that it was because the Scots (and especially the ones in Edinburgh) were the most up-tight and unfunky people in Europe that they'd conspired to bleach Geo. Melly of all his colour. And the thing is, the feeling sort of persists, even now. You could never, *never* conceive of a jazz-obsessed, ambisexual, hedonistic, Surrealist, free-wheeling, superliterate, drink-friendly Scotsman who pretended to give himself a blowjob while singing *I sure will be disgusted if your dog ain't full o' mustard*. There is no funk in Scotland. There's not much in North Finchley, but North Finchley is Beale Street in comparison with Stockbridge.

SEVEN

So I left the London-like security and complexity of the big city. After quite a lot of byzantine farting around, I went via sleeper train to Inverness and then on to Wester Ross in a rented car, to be where every Scotsman's heart tends, Walter Scott's 'Land of brown heath and shaggy wood/Land of the mountain and the flood'. And when I got there, then I could say that *this* is where the land and everything on it is clean with the insane cleanliness that comes from being hosed with 200 inches of precipitation per annum. *This* is where some of the highest mountains in the UK are (such as they are). *This* is where Gaelic is extant. *This* is where I am in a Seat rent-a-car, the low English enemy, prowling around waiting for a pungent Scotsman to jump out at me with a dirk. *These* are the Highlands.

I woke up on my train to find that Inverness, the capital of the Highlands and Macbeth's eleventh-century stronghold ('Think of somewhere the size and interest of Chiswick,' a London-based Scotswoman told me), is actually Inbhir Nis according to the little green Gaelic footnotes stuck to the station platform signs. In fact, there are green-lettered alternatives all around here on the roadsigns (Portree, on Skye, for example, turns out to be Port Rìgh), sometimes with the Anglo equivalent painted out by an angry hand. Severely Gaelic place names, when written, not read out musically on the BBC, are full of redundant and misplaced n's, b's, h's, words with permanent migraines: Lòndubh, Meall an Fhuarain, Beinn Liath Mhòr a' Ghiubhais Li. The reduced Gaelic names, the Scottish-sounding ones – Lochluichart, Aultguish, Achinduich – sound like sneezes, or someone hawking into a washbasin. Such is the air of difference, of conscious disjunction from everything southern, I vaguely expected the clocks to read a different time from London, just as all clocks used to keep local time before the wholesale imposition of Greenwich Mean Time. I felt I needed one of those nineteenth-century Vulliamy watches with two independent minute hands – one for London, one for the provinces.

This is even one of the last great wildernesses of western Europe, where roads only arrived in the eighteenth century, thanks to the English general George Wade. This is where Bonnie Prince Charlie, the man on the shortbread tins and whisky labels, wound up after the catastrophe of the '45 Rebellion, shortly before fleeing to Skye. This is the gnarled bit that faces out over The Minch – the stretch of water which separates mainland Scotland from the Outer Hebrides. And the Outer Hebrides signifies to us southerners the ends of the earth, the Nome of Great Britain. This is the furthest north I have ever been and if I headed due west without stopping (and this is really panic-inducing) I would end up in Frobisher Bay.

I'd got fairly close twenty-odd years earlier, some way down in the Grampian region, by Loch Tay. I was in a tent with my mate Phil, who'd got a student summer vacation job interfering with the trees around the loch. He'd been on his own for about two weeks when I joined him, and had slightly crazily pitched the tent on a thirty-degree slope at the loch's edge. He'd worked out a way not to slide down into the waters when asleep in his sleeping bag by lodging himself in a tree root. I could never get the hang of it though, and would wake up in the mornings halfway to drowning. That was one of the drawbacks, along with the midges and having to crap by holding on to a thistle and leaning backwards. And the disgusting food.

On the other hand, it only rained sometimes, and the scenery was astonishing, easily good enough to knock anything English into a ditch. There were mountains, there were icy freshets and brooks splashing down the mountainsides, there were deciduous woodlands where oak trees and birches were covered in thick grey frilly mosses. It bore the same relationship to English scenery that Edinburgh bears to English cities. It was awesome.

One evening, Phil and I went out on to the waters of the loch in a canoe. We took with us a bottle of whisky. Halfway through the bottle, we started one of those student conversations about the light from the nearest star and how many millions of years old it was when it got to us. Then we had the Students' Special Theory of Relativity conversation. Then we rowed confusedly back and lay on the narrow shore, staring up at the now revolving heavens and had another conversation about the terrible majesty of deep space. Then we found that we'd drunk the whisky. It was some time after midnight.

'We get,' Phil said, 'another bottle.'

He stumbled off to where his car was parked in a bush and started revving the engine. The car lights came on and he backed sinuously out towards a gate which led on to the track running up one side of the loch.

'Get in,' he shouted, as the passenger door fell open.

Then we had a journey that was like the end of *2001* – odd, errant lights flashing towards and past us, immense speeds, blots of colour distorted into crazy looking-glass shapes by the velocity. Then we were in this boozer in the middle of absolutely nowhere. It was nearly one in the morning and the place was full of other drunks, including two uniformed policemen. Phil paid for a fresh bottle of single malt over the counter, we staggered back to the car, drove at lightning speed back down the track, very nearly straight through the parking bush and into the lake, and started on the second bottle.

A few days later we went up Ben Lawers, not quite the highest mountain in Scotland at 3,984 feet. We took with us a large Fruit & Nut bar, some cigs and a bottle of whisky. No climbing skills were needed. Scottish grandmas were walking briskly up and down Ben Lawers' sides in sensible shoes. We took several hours to make it to the top, though, as we had to stop every hundred feet or so for a cigarette and a pull of whisky. I was also having trouble getting over the previous night but one, the two-bottle night, having woken up forty-eight hours earlier, crushingly hungover in a drizzle-damp sleeping bag at an angle of thirty degrees to the horizontal with a tree root in the small of my back and my eyes red with pain and my stomach lying dead in the undergrowth.

Two decades later, I made a ropey start out of Inverness, unable to find an unlocked public toilet. When I tried to get into the toilets at nearby Strathpeffer – a nice, wrecky old spa town, whose sulphur-and-chalybeate waters reputedly contain more hydrogen than any other waters in Britain – and found them locked, what did one of the two municipal gardeners leaning on their spades nearby say? 'No, closed last Friday,' he said. Then he gave a scornful laugh. 'Ridiculous, isn't it?'

After that I was terrified by the huge articulated trucks which came at me from the opposite direction like the invading German army, pounding in from Ullapool along a twisty, wet and slippery road. *Stornoway* they had mythically written on their sides. Also, a bloke (Scottish, wispy white beard, unhinged smile, in his sixties) had talked to me as I gathered myself up on the station platform at Inverness, stale from the sleeper train. He was keen to point out that they were doubling the size of the plug-ugly downtown Inverness shopping precinct by annexing a piece of land by the station car park and throwing up a huge new supermarket. They were also building three hundred and fifty new homes: 'Don't know where they'll find the people to put in them, though.'

He also told me that the old Inverness Airport used to be where the industrial estate now is; five minutes from the station, in the middle of town. Which meant that planes must once have taken off and landed down Academy Street, or Strothers Lane if the wind was from the east.

On the cheapish-slow-train-versus-fast-expensive-plane-to-Scotland argument, he was quite clear.

'Oh, you've got to watch the pennies,' he actually said, like Harry Lauder.

Then I pointed out the rain, which had been tipping down since dawn, foaming floodwater torrents rushing past the TV-sized window of my sleeper compartment, and which was still going at 9 a.m.

'Aye, it's set to do this all day.'

Elsewhere in the world, you normally look on rain as a drawback, something which detracts from whatever you're doing. But the rain out here is necessary for the aesthetic of the thing. The rain is inextricable from the beauty, even though it rains with almost sarcastic violence. Edinburgh rain is still city rain, still a kind of pollution. In the Highlands, on the other hand, it is the ground against which everything else is set. It shapes the way everything looks; and it shapes the way you think about the space you're presently occupying.

It even fills up Queen Victoria's *Highland Journals*, steady and insistent. 'A misty, rainy morning,' she writes at one stage in 1860. Later on, 'It became cold and windy with occasional rain,' followed by 'A thoroughly wet day.' This gives way, by 1873, to 'Mist on all the hills and continuous rain!', after which there was 'A heavy shower.' On 17 September 1877, she suddenly sees that it is a 'Splendid bright morning, like July!' But on the 18th, we are back to 'A wet, misty morning, no hills whatever to be seen.' The rain is the given, against which all Her Majesty's pleasurable activities (watching Albert kill stags, having meals, erecting cairns) stand out.

It also forces you to assess your relationship with the countryside in general, the countryside as a concept. To be brutally frank, the countryside really doesn't do much for me. Given the choice between an interesting cityscape and an interesting landscape, I go for the former without even pausing to pack a clean pair of socks. The problem with landscapes – one of the many problems with landscapes – is that you have to *be in* them to get anything back from them. You have to smell, touch, hear and feel the nature all around you. You have to experience it with all your senses. Otherwise you're left with nothing but tiresome picturesque, just an arrangement of folds and clefts and sprouts of vegetation, nothing really satisfying to get your mind round.

But what if you *can't* relate to it in that semi-sensual way? What if you can't *be in* it? What if it's raining so hard, all you can be in is a car or a room, looking out? If it's dull to start with, how much duller is it once all the peripheral stimulation's been taken away? Thus I worked my way in a bubble across the centre of northern Scotland from Inverness to Ullapool, the wipers on monsoon, quizzing myself, my teeth gnashing with boredom and irritation. There was every probability that I was never going to get out of my car. The Highlands would be things only seen through glass, like museum pieces or paintings in stately homes.

And then it happened as I bore off from Kinlochewe, south-west towards Torridon, on the A896. The clouds had thickened from dark grey to midnight black and the rain was baling out all down the road. Most of the scenery had vanished. Another downpour in the seventeen-feet-per-annum rainfall total. A dopey voice on the local radio was warning of poor driving conditions. I couldn't have been more in the Highlands if I tried, but I felt detached from the experience, trapped on a ribbon of wet tarmac. Then – no warning, no literal-minded announcement – the clouds parted as if being broken up by a pair of hands. Purse-lipped, I muttered an ironical prayer of thanks and switched off the wipers. And a waterfall of brilliant golden sunshine cascaded down on a mountain called Sgurr Dubh. I skidded to the side of the road and my mouth collapsed open with shock and amazement.

Sgurr Dubh is 2,566 feet high, a huge lump of 750-million-year-old sandstone. That moment it was also a mass of golds and browns, with a glittering curtain of fine spray drifting in front and across; and with the lowering dark peaks of Beinn Eighe to the right, a foil to Sgurr Dubh's terrifying brilliance. It looked about the biggest thing I had ever seen, and was shaped like a titanic pile of builder's sand. Even the continual jabbering interior monologue which passes as my idea of intellection was silenced.

Then the clouds and rain closed in again. Sgurr Dubh had been alight for all of a minute. I inched forward in my Seat. Now the mountain was no more than a massive grey outline, or something from a Japanese woodcut. And then – look! before it vanishes! – the sun re-emerged from another angle, over the shoulder of the mountain this time, silhouetting the pine trees on its slopes and the bare peak, curving round in a burst of luminosity – was that part of the mountain, or a bank of cloud rearing up?

In bright sunshine, of course, it would have been only half as theatrically entertaining. What's more, in bright sunshine, I might have got out and walked around and then been caught out by the ruthless Highland climate. In the conditions as they were, I was humbled and grateful that I wasn't lost somewhere on the slopes in a cheap anorak. Crouched in my car this way, I had my revelation and I didn't even get damp. It was, just, perfect in a way that almost never happens – even though I didn't smell, touch or hear the world I suddenly found myself in. It was big enough to transcend those requirements. Perhaps it was because it was my first real revelatory moment that it resonates so much. Or maybe Sgurr Dubh seen in a downpour from the A896 really is one of the great experiences of the Highlands.

But here's the real trick. Right round Sgurr Dubh I went and on towards Torridon and yet another epiphany. *Torridon* doesn't sound like anything, much – maybe a board game, or a muscle rub, in much the same way that Inverinate, on the Inverness–Kyle road, sounds like a treatment for a kidney infection – but the low-key banality of the name is a front. What happened as I came over a pass that led down towards the little settlement of Torridon itself? The sun burst through again, illuminating Upper Loch Torridon, a huge expanse of water, lightly topped with a shawl of mist. The sky ahead of me was blue and the hills at the western end of the loch were lit up as if for summer. The ones at the eastern end, my end, were hidden in rain, no more than cardboard shapes. Here the loch waters were iron grey and choppy. But at the far end was a Shangri-La, a Pisgah prospect.

And then, another dramatic inversion: the rain stopped

and a rainbow came out and lay seductively at my feet as I started descending towards the sea. The whole world seemed to be spread in front of me. It was like looking at one of those National Gallery landscape paintings, a Koninck or a Claude (only without the pricey buildings dotted around the vista), painted with a fake, godlike perspective engineered by the clever artist. Only this was real, the perspective was just the way the topography panned out, and the only artist was me and my capacity to take the scene in.

Oh, well, I thought. Now I've seen it. Now I know what the fuss is all about. The lexicon of admiration just opens up of its own accord: romantic, awe-inspiring, majestic, breath-taking, whatever you want to say, in fact. What's more, the Highlands live up to their own billing, in a way which most tourist landscapes rarely do. They are just how you hope they will be; and consistently so, which makes them even more impressive an achievement. Yes, there were moments of bore-dom leading up to my first great revelation, but, as I now know, these lacunae are there to urge you on. You can't have the transcendent moment without being softened up before-hand by a period of frustration and disappointment.

Pictorial England, by way of contrast, is easier and less rewarding, a typical southern dilettante. England gives you a taste of something before losing interest and moving on, the perpetual novelty-seeker, to something else essentially unrelated. Seaside cliffs turn into moors, which give way to cities, which haphazardly devolve into crap-caked farmland, which thoughtlessly yields to modest hills, and so on. England also prompts you to wonder idly, when you look at a particularly rugged piece of landscape, could I survive in this? If I got stuck here for a night, is there any way I could keep myself alive? The answer's usually a complacent *yes* from me. Just about anywhere south of Carlisle, the ruggedness will run out eventually and I will get (I see myself in my mind's eye, the struggling lone hiker) to some building or habitation where at the very least I can call a cab to the nearest hotel.

But here in the Highlands, once it gets into its stride, the scenery is obsessive, monomaniacal, as if it's got a point to prove. It never stops being Highland: it finds ways to do the same majestic, brutal things over and over again. The peaks are snow-capped even though winter hasn't arrived. The tree cover comes and goes erratically, apparently at the whim of the Scottish Forestry Commission. They have tall spindles on either side of the roads here to indicate where the roads actually are when covered in deep snow. And if you find yourself lost on a mountaintop in bad weather, there will be no bolt-hole cottage; no hamlet to escape to. You will probably die.

So the epiphanies, once started, happened again and again. Heading east up the Great Glen, constant vistas opened up around Loch Ness (so vast, as the tourist trade keeps pointing out, that you could fit the entire population of the planet into it, three times over) with another rainbow at the loch's northern end. The same magic happened when I first glimpsed Skye from the mainland. It happened in a domesticated form at Fort Augustus – a picturesque nineteenth-century tourists' waypoint at the west end of Loch Ness with a ladder of four locks in the town centre, where the Caledonian Canal drops into the loch. It was peeing with rain when I was there, inevitably, but it was still ravishing, in a puritanically irresistible manner. It happened at Ullapool: blacks and whites, low buildings, leaden sky behind – then, just beyond the harbour, the sun broke through, creating a white steely shimmer on the surface of the waters of Loch Broom as it emerges into The Minch. It happened when I realised that I had gone so far north that there was only one more grid square left in my road atlas before it turned into the Shetlands. I had indeed escaped the clutches of the city.

But, then.

It may be a question of utility, the twenty-first-century question, an American question, but: what are the Highlands *for*? What they do, they do unimprovably well. They do it, as I now know, almost on demand, which is efficient, too. But is it enough just to be big, tough and gorgeous? In this day and age? Are you surprised that with an area of nearly 6.5 million acres, the Unitary Authority of the Highlands none the less only supports some 200,000 inhabitants? Somewhat less than the population of Aberdeen? Or Wolverhampton? Indeed, the population density stands at around twenty people per square mile – less than the Orkneys, less, even, than the Shetland Islands; about twice that of the Saharan Republic of Chad. The Highlands are a mixed bag, a poisoned chalice, a whited sepulchre: beautiful, awe-inspiring, more or less useless. Holland is useful. The Highlands not.

That we yearn to visit them at all is partly thanks to the unending jaded hunger of the modern tourist, partly because the Scots tell us to, partly because part of us just really wants to and partly because of the Germans. The Germans are, of course, the Royal Family – Victoria and Albert in particular. They it was who fell in love with the Highlands and who made this part of the world central to our consciousness of Great Britain as a whole.

Sir Walter Scott is to blame. His novels (to say nothing of the poems) are now unreadable unless you're in prison or just fantastically old, but in his day, he was a towering literary prodigy, a colossus of the early nineteenth century, so blind-ingly industrious that he used to time his literary output with an hourglass (more exactly, a half-hourglass; but either way, appalling). He it was whose writing so touched Victoria and

Albert that they could recite his verse by heart. He it was who got them up there, directly or indirectly, and revealed the joy of the wilderness to them.

Victoria and Albert, being German, responded immediately to the Romantic landscape in front of them. They could afford to: minus the violence and crushing deprivations which Highlanders had had to endure for centuries, and with plenty of food, drink and attendants to make things comfy, they could have fun, apart from the rain and the midges. They could do for the Highlands what King Maximilian of Bavaria was doing for the Alps. While Maximilian remodelled the Bavarian castle Hohenschwangau in a mixture of the cod-medieval and the *gemütlich*, V & A remodelled a 'pretty little castle in the old Scottish style' at Balmoral in a mixture of the cod-baronial and the *gemütlich*.

At which point history unravels like a red carpet thrown down in front of a royal train. Thanks to Victoria and Albert, all of us Brits have grown up with images of the royals watching bagpipe matches, fishing in streams, relishing the Highland reels and the caber-tossing: the shortbread Highland life, the Highlands compressed into postcard form, embossed with royal patronage. Thanks to them, we have potent convictions about the Highlands in a way that we could never have about central Wales, for example, or, for that matter, the Kielder Forest. Not to beat about the bush, the Highlands are not just every Scot's homeland, but an elaborate Scottish–Anglo-Windsor–Teutonic construction. Which may help to explain why – however incredibly beautiful they are – they refuse to make much sense, when viewed by a suburban Londoner stuck at the edge of the known world.

I did the Highland thing for a bit, and ended up on the far side, in Kyle of Lochalsh, wandering its emptiness last thing at night. Kyle of Lochalsh is a downbeat place nowadays, ever since they opened the road bridge to Skye in 1995. At a stroke this deprived Kyle, with its Victorian railway terminus at the water's edge for the old five-minute ferry trip to the island, of its principal reason for being. At the same time, the bridge seems to have deprived Skye of *its* reason for being. Now you can get there in one continuous drive – paying an insane £4.70 each time you cross the bridge – Skye has become just another piece of mainland, not more or less remarkable. It's ravishing seen from a boat or from a distance. From the bridge, it's just more of that Highland experience, a New England fall all year round, never having to try harder.

So Kyle is now a place without philosophical justification. It used to be full of people waiting to catch the ferry. Now, it's so small and quiet that I overheard a bloke in the corridor of my hotel refusing to eat in the morbidly deserted expanse of the hotel restaurant. 'I'll just go down to the restaurant and order it there,' he said. 'Then I'll come right back up.'

Indeed, things were so slack in Kyle that I went to neighbouring Plockton, laid out as a planned Highland Village in 1794 and now allegedly a top tourist attraction. As it transpired, the most excitement you can have in Plockton on a marginally off-peak weekday evening is to watch a mechanical digger on the shorefront working while the tide's out; or to ride your bike on the slope in front of E. J. Mackenzie's Plockton Craft Shop. I went in search of nightlife, much as you would in Polperro or Burnham Market, also top tourist villages, and ended up eating hake in solitary magnificence in a restaurant which had a CD of Scottish war songs constantly playing.

The thrills only really started when I prepared to drive back down the hill to Kyle, to discover that I was down to my last teaspoon of petrol. I then made the mistake of thinking that because Plockton apparently has an aerodrome (at least, it's got a sign for an aerodrome) it would also have a petrol station. This meant that I wasted twenty minutes crawling around the outskirts of the village, my eyes bulging with stress as I peered into the darkness for a welcoming BP or Esso. I never found one, so, with only half a teaspoon of gas remaining, I let out the clutch and rolled off in the direction of Kyle.

No one *wants* to run out of petrol. But if I am going to run out of petrol at all, then I would rather do it in a fairly busy town centre, no more than, say, a quarter of a mile from the nearest petrol station/convenience store. What I did not want to do was run out on the fringes of the Scottish Highlands, in the pitch dark of a moonless night, miles from anywhere (with petrol), a gale blowing and rain expected. Wincing at every hiccup from my wee Seat and flashing up spectacular visions of myself pushing the car into a black eternity of howling rain and twigs snapped off by the wind, I crawled back into Kyle and filled up at the town BP, giggling with relief.

It was still fairly early, so having got shot of my car, I quartered the streets, drifting down to the pierhead station. Cute Edwardian detailing, like something out of *Thomas the Tank Engine*, statutory national railways patina of neglect, a sea of night beyond, only me and one other hunched person patrolling the platforms. The last train came and went and then silence fell like a bomb.

I went back into town. Outside, in the darkened High Street, a bunch of teenagers were scuffling around in the doorway of a newsagent's. A bespectacled fat boy sat on the step. A girl accosted him: 'You're not Scottish, are you?'

'I'm from England,' he said.

'Boo,' she replied and turned her back to where some less English boys were climbing over the scaffolding of a building which was in mid-renovation. With a lot of profanities, they squeezed through a security fence, unearthed a pile of traffic cones and started lobbing them across the road.

The girl who didn't like the English put her hands on her hips and shouted, 'Shut up, shut up, shut up. I've got a new game. You've all got to hit each other with poles.'

Fat Boy shifted on his stoop. He clearly didn't want to be hit with a pole, especially since – as an English fat boy – he was candidate No. 1 for hitting.

'I dunno,' he said.

'*Shut up*,' said the girl.

I left him to his fate. Back at my hotel, a solitary couple was eating a meal in the colossal untenanted expanse of the dining room. They looked like party invitees who realise they've turned up a week early. I went upstairs and watched an advert on Grampian TV for a special kind of Scottish tea bag.

This is the underside of the Highlands. This is the price paid: *there really isn't much happening here.* Kyle is just a particular exemplar of a general truth. The startling romanticism of the landscape distracts you from the fact that the Highlands and Islands are running out of life, and have been ever since the Highland Clearances began at the end of the eighteenth century. (The Clearances – from the end of the 1700s to the mid-1800s – is one of those historical topics which cannot be mentioned without provoking rage, pity and horror, particularly among a Scottish audience. A mixture of religious and political persecutions, post the Jacobite Rising, combined with the collapse of a rural economy which could no longer sustain the numbers of people dependent on it. Highland landowners began to evict their tenants – the *clearances* themselves – and replace them with more profitable sheep. The kelp industry, which for years had seemed like a long-term money-spinner, also collapsed when the import duty on cheap foreign kelp was abandoned. The potato famine of 1846 arrived from Ireland and starved out many of the remaining Highlanders and Islanders. In essence, a few decades saw a wholesale

destruction of a branch of the Scottish peasantry, the barbarous suppression of a way of life, the forced expatriation of
thousands, and their replacement by hundreds of thousands of
sheep. The upshot was that, by the end of the nineteenth century, most of the Highlands was deserted.)

So what do you reach for in the twentieth and twenty-first
centuries when there is a yawning physiographic and economic void like this one to fill? Tourism. The sheep now
aren't worth a dime and look appalling anyway – a sheep
wandering across the road looks somewhere between a big
dirty hairy dog and a maggot on stilts – and the fishing isn't
what it was. Ullapool has a workmanlike ferry terminal and
fishing boat harbour, but the only active boat I saw when I
was there was one large trawler flying a Spanish flag. The
little black-and-white town was thus forced to make the most
of two demented hikers, dressed as for a Force 7 at sea,
stomping off towards a distant hill. What the Highlands
mainly has to offer, now, is the unique large-scale tourist
attraction of a stunning glacier-scoured Precambrian massif
somewhere north of Carlisle. And that's it.

What they want you to be, up here, is a foreign tourist
driving around in a hire car, looking at things and stopping to
spend money on Highland crafts. Road signs are in five languages. The Scottish Road Safety Campaign has a little
pamphlet, 'Driving in Scotland': *No aparque en Lugares de
paso*, it says; *Lassen Sie bergauffahrenden Fahrzeugen Vorfarht*;
Conduisez à gauche. You can't go more than three miles without hitting a roadside Highland craft shop tricked out in an
avalanche of warring tartans, plus thick-knit sweaters, tam-o'-
shanters, whisky miniatures, bits of emblazoned chocolate;
notices in five languages outside entreating you to enter. You
find these gifties in all the obvious places and in places that
are scarcely places. I remember passing through Glen
Docherty, a nothing between Dingwall and Kinlochewe, and

even as I wondered why such a non-place had been donated a name, I nearly collided with an immense souvenir shop the size of a hovercraft hangar, its lights blazing, the noticeboard outside flapping madly in the wind, open for all business first thing on a streaming Monday morning.

Of course, by saying this, I am putting myself on dangerous ground, as if you hadn't already guessed. As an Englishman, I am prohibited on moral grounds from criticising Scotland or any part thereof. There is an ethical contract between the two countries which affirms that England may not pass judgement on Scotland any more than it may pass judgement on Belgium, New Zealand, Tunisia, Surinam or indeed any country which is smaller and has a less exploitative past. To put it another way, had we English been subjugated to the French for this length of time, how would I take to some dreadful Parisian trampling all over my carefully conserved national identity? The answer, I think, is plain.

Besides, I am too cowardly to do a Dr Johnson – who was quite cowardly enough in his own way. Johnson, you will remember, went to Scotland in 1773, was wined, dined and fêted. He found much there that was both admirable and charming and said so, including Flora Macdonald, the Highlands, Dunvegan, the Laird of Lochbuy, Iona and the Duke of Argyll. Then he got back to London and, as if ashamed of a weakness, went back to his old habit of opprobriating Scotland like a bastard: 'Seeing Scotland, Madam, is only seeing a worse England.' Or, 'Their learning [the Scots'] is like bread in a besieged town: every man gets a little, but no man gets a full meal.' Or, cutting short Adam Smith's song of praise to Glasgow, 'Pray, Sir, have you ever seen Brentford?'

This is not a pattern I want to follow, and, quite apart from the dictates of conscience and reason, here's one very good reason why not: picking through the *Press and Journal* ('The

Voice of the North') as I drifted across the Highland rain-scape, I found a piece about another writer – Ian Rankin, the top crime writer from Fife, even, not England – who dared to compare the town of Macduff, near Aberdeen, with the Bronx in New York City. Broken glass in Macduff, he'd said. Free-range dogs, ghetto music, atmosphere of simmering violence, NYC in the Grampian region. This was so insulting to the *Press and Journal* and its readers that the paper gave over its main comment page to a detailed and furious counter-attack against the slander and the man who'd committed it.

This defence was so thorough that it not only quoted a soldier who'd served in Northern Ireland as well as a spokes-woman for the Grampian Tourist Board, but also Mickey Spillane, veteran crime writer, speaking from his home in South Carolina: 'I don't think I've heard of this Mr Rankin. Is he any good?'

They had a picture of some nice Macduff people to prove how wrong Rankin was. They quoted a spokesman from the NYPD. It must have been a 1,500-word piece, easy. It was awesome in its thoroughness and vituperation. It was a philippic with no stone unturned and four-wheel drive. I thought: this is what they do to a Scottish assessment of Scotland. What would they do to me?

There are times – when loitering in the Highlands, reading the *Press and Journal*, let's say – when I actually feel the need to pretend that I'm German or Dutch. This, I like to think, would account for my presence there in the middle of the week, driving around Scotland in a rented car, or wandering up and down the streets, not in work clothes and with appar-ently nothing better to do than try to find an open lavatory between Inverness and Ullapool, or hide from the pouring rain. It would also mean that I wasn't English and would not need to be beaten up. I think I could manage that North European look of tall apprehensive bemusement.

EIGHT

So I was listening to Scottish radio as I drove around, and on came a programme about Scottish troops serving in the Korean War, that forgotten war in which 3 million people none the less lost their lives. The Scots regiments – as opposed to the North Koreans, South Koreans, Chinese and US troops – had no real investment in the war, and found themselves stuck in this Godforsaken nullity of a country, thousands of miles from home, being shelled by Chinamen. It was evidently a deeply depressing experience.

How did they keep their spirits up? Scottish country dancing and the skirl of the bagpipes is how. When the troops found themselves enjoying some temporary R & R, what did they do but break out into 'The Flowers of Edinburgh' or 'Lady Catherine Bruce's Reel'? A fruity commanding officer reminisced that the genius of these dances – the sort where you form lines opposite each other and zoom in and out, grabbing the person opposite, twirling, spinning, dislocating your wrists and bruising yourself but not actually cosying up with a specific partner – was that 'you didn't need women, you see. It was just country dancing.'

The pipers, on the other hand, injected fire and pride into the poor Scots bastards whenever they had to kit up and go off to the front line to get shot at. For the few minutes that the pipes skirled and brought back memories of their homeland, they all felt invincible. This is a tactic still in use today on the sports field, not least when some bunch of Scotsmen called the Claymores (who play American football) use a piper called Jimmy McRae to Dutch them up before a game with his bagpipe music. McRae also intimidates the opposition by playing loudly outside their dressing room.

'I march up and down,' he is quoted as saying, 'outside the away-team dressing room, gien' it laldie before the game. Let's say it unsettles them a wee bit.'

Scotland has this extraordinarily compact, portable culture, compressed into a handful of potent images and concepts and flogged the world over: the skirling music, the whisky, the tartan, the heritage of oppression and inventiveness, the lowering beauty of the landscape (captured in picture and verse), the adamantine handsomeness of the cities (in video and guidebook form), the wonderfully simple and memorable Saltire waving untainted over all. At the same time Scotland seems to be able to exist anywhere, like the Catholic Church, provided that whisky, tartan and a man called Ewan are present. Scotland does not have to be located on a specific block of land north of the 55th parallel. You can do Scotland wherever Scottish expats are.

Hence, we all think we know Scotland because Scotland has spent the last two hundred years packaging up and transporting and selling this vision of itself, much as Jaguar Cars sells a vision of leather and walnut with a big, wasteful engine, or Disneyland sells a vision of mind-frothing, limitless fun. And when you don't get it, delivered straight to your door with a full guarantee and a tank of petrol, or shoved remorselessly in your face in the broiling Florida sun, you feel cheated and resentful. It works in the Highlands, uncannily so. When I got to Aberdeen, on the other hand, I found that the metaphysical Scots quality control department had somehow failed to take sufficient interest in the product. I was in Scotland, but Scotland wasn't living up to its own packaging.

But then again, compare the Scots package – omissions, faults, shortcomings and all – with the speculative void that is presently Englishness, and you can only conclude that the Scots hold all the aces while the English are somehow the residual stub of the United Kingdom, the destitute colonialists reduced to a confused twilit existence in the bedsit of the world.

Englishness, unlike Scottishness, is baffling, diffuse. It begs questions which are fundamental and which the English are occasionally alert enough to ask but habitually too tired to bother to answer. What common culture do we, the English, hold dear? Can we even make a conspectus of our land and point out things or practices which are uniquely ours? Why is the Queen of England not the Queen of Britain? Why is the Union Jack so unnecessarily complicated that most English people can't tell whether it's upside-down or not? Are we a cultural mish-mash, a nation whose vitality has always depended on the interventions of people from other countries? Or a bunch of white-skinned Anglo-Saxon bigots whose truest desire is to disappear up our own ideological arseholes?

Viewed sympathetically, Scotland manages the neat trick of appearing to look simultaneously backwards to a mythic past and forwards to a mildly radical future. The arrival of devolution is just the start. The logic has to propel Scotland further and further towards complete sovereign independence – trad, but anticipating the new Europe and an exciting world of small, intelligent, prosperous economic units operating within the bigger global picture. Unlike England, yes, which is erratically bogged down in the past, Victoria's funeral cortège caught out by mudslides, rockfalls, diverted cataracts.

Of course cultural portability as the Scots enjoy it is one of the by-products of oppression, so one reason why the English can't summon up *Heimat* cultural resonances in the same way is that our culture hasn't been repressed for around a thousand years; we haven't been obliged to boil Englishness down to a handful of superpotent transportable objective correlatives.

But what if the Bourbon French had overrun us in the eighteenth century and somehow Napoleon had taken charge in the nineteenth? What if we'd had to go underground, while Roman Law, the metric system, curly French handwriting, the persistent use of wines and spirits, the French language, *La Gloire*, had spread over us like a powerfully savoury duvet? What if posh Englishmen spoke English with a pronounced French accent, while the proles spoke in a native English accent (a situation that obtains with regard to the Scottish voice in Edinburgh and the Armed Forces)? This is assuming that English was still spoken and we hadn't gone wholly Francophone, of course.

There are, it has to be said, moments when it seems that Scotland is to England as England is to Continental Europe: always three decades behind the times, always looking back over its shoulder, always the last to see the value of European co-operation. To put it another way, to the rest of Europe, we must look like the Isle of Man. But what if that difference had ceased to be two centuries ago? What if we'd had generations to nurture our idiosyncratic resistance in the face of suave theoretical centrist French conformity? What would the English have clung to as visible tokens of their covert nationhood?

– Maybe Shakespeare, in the way that surprising numbers of Scots seem to be familiar with all that terrible Burns poetry, or anything by Sir Walter Scott.

– A cup of tea? When American dentists and orthodontists are unlucky enough to peer into our mouths, they say *Ah, British teeth*. It's not just the zoo of snaggles, chips, dents, gaps and old fillings made of lead, arsenic and mercury which tip them off. It's the tea stains, the tides of brown which lap against our gums. Even the most swinging of us cannot resist tea the way we like it, murky as an untended lake and topped up with cow juice.

– The rolling countryside. Hard to say where, especially for a Londoner who doesn't really care how much rolling the countryside does provided he can still get the tube home. But I suppose things like the Yorkshire Dales, South Downs, Dartmoor, bits of Shropshire, all that might make us shed a furtive tear when we see a picture of it in the drab Toulouse suburbs where we've had to come to find work because the further north you go, as everyone knows, the worse the job prospects.

– The flag. Slightly depends on how the French have left it. Do we get a Union Jack, or a St George's Cross? Do we care?

– Music. Purcell? I doubt it. We wouldn't have had the Beatles or Gilbert and Sullivan, so that's most of our post-eighteenth-century repertoire gone. Perhaps we might have evolved some kind of homespun mouth music or vernacular oral tradition and be crooning laments to each other like Hebridean fishermen staring out over The Minch. But minus that essential Celtic lyricism, the chances are not. More likely doggerel directed against the French and using as many profanities as possible. My God! We'd all be listening to Johnny Halliday!

– Heroic resistance leader. A real possibility, but obviously you can't speculate as to who it could be. Odds-on that he or she wouldn't be slim and fey like B. P. Charlie. More likely thuggishly purposeful, Churchill-style, with a strong streak of that head-down philistinism which always stirs our blood.

– Apart from that? This is a pretty scant collection, after all. Tea, Shakespeare, the Norfolk Broads. Naturally, I am open to suggestions, but it does make you wonder exactly what it is we've got to show for two centuries of raging imperialism and at one time the greatest economy on the face of the globe. This residual cultural non-specificity that's baffled everyone from Orwell down looks a bit meagre up against porridge and tartan sashes.

Well, what would you include? Beer? Crown bowls? The English legal system?

NINE

I left Kyle first thing. It had rained all through the night and was still keen to rain some more. I passed a woman walking her dog along the cold, soaking pavements. She was kitted out as if about to go on the deck of a trawler somewhere out in the Malin or Bailey fishing grounds. I headed east, towards Loch Ness, past some more places that sounded like people sneezing or hoiking, through the ineffably pretty Fort Augustus with its rising locks (the central point of General Wade's road system) and Loch Lochy (yes) to the south-west, before whizzing past the little stone cairn erected to the late 1950s speed ace, John Cobb, who bought it at 206 m.p.h. in a jet-propelled speedboat on the waters of Loch Ness. 'In Memory Of A Gallant Gentleman' it says on the cairn, which looks touchingly like a sentry-box made of pebbles.

And then I got to the Loch Ness Visitor Centre in Drumnadrochit, where I found – hardly surprisingly – that I could scarcely move for visitors' treats. The need for the tourist dollar is so urgent here that there are actually two visitors' centres – The Original Loch Ness Visitor Centre, and The Official Loch Ness Monster Centre. The latter is nice and new and full of sinister *son et lumière* environments containing bathyspheres and dummies in diving gear. It has a plaque at the door announcing that it was opened in 1999 by Sir Ranulph Fiennes OBE, Explorer, and in one room it cleverly gives you the impression that you are underwater. It also has a nicely sceptical line on the monster itself, with a surprise ending which I won't give away here.

The former, The Original Loch Ness Visitor Centre, is, conversely, a rickety nuthouse in which the only thing to do is stare at a collection of murky old snapshots of bits of car tyre, reflections of cormorants, twigs, all of which are tremulously deemed to be Nessie, before watching a crazed, credulity-threatening home-made documentary called *We Believe in the Loch Ness Monster*.

This is shown in a green Nissen hut with plywood walls into which 120 old cinema seats, covered with a generous 1950s moquette, have been stuffed. The sixth-century St Columba appears in the form of an artist's impression, calming the monster on film. You get a monk as well, plus a drawing of what might have been Nessie crossing the road some time before the last war, and a flotilla of boats using echo-location devices which may or may not have found something. A voice, growling with awe and superstition, makes one inescapable point after another. You know how it is: by the end, I wanted to believe, much as Bertram Mills, the circus owner, must have wanted to believe when he offered £20,000 to have the Loch Ness Monster scooped up in a net and delivered to his circus.

More importantly, outside they are selling The World's Smallest Bottle of Whisky at 99p as well as racks of *Braveheart* T-shirts and heritage postcards to the ambient Japanese coachloads. This is the real point of the day, and no worse, as it happens, than The Official Loch Ness Monster Centre, whose similarly ballroom-vast giftshop is piled to the ceiling with stuffed green nylon cartoon Cool Nessies, shortbread and postcards. In either place, your strongest lingering memory is of the pure hunger for cash transactions. As a result of this hunger, The Original Loch Ness Visitor Centre is about 30 per cent video film, 10 per cent whiskery old photos and about 60 per cent frenzied consumer come-on. The good news is that if you're English, you don't have to worry about your origins too much. This is pure touristland, where your antecedents are irrelevant and the only currency is financial. At no point do you have to pretend to be Dutch so as to avoid the contumely of the people working there.

This would, however, have been a good plan at the Culloden Visitors' Centre, where I went after Loch Ness. The English aren't good at feeling guilty, it's not one of our gifts, but the Culloden Visitors' Centre makes you – makes me – feel like a Nazi. This is the motherlode for so much of that antagonism, that endless friction between us and them. It is also typical of the Scottish love of glorious loser melancholy, the national desire to draw attention to defeat. What are the two most celebrated scenes of conflict in tourist Scotland? Culloden and Glencoe, disasters both. Can you imagine the French making such a big thing out of Crecy? Do we dwell endlessly on the shambles that was the Battle of Jutland? Of course what the Scots would really like would be for us to rename, say, Waterloo Station as Culloden Station. That would without a doubt be the cherry on the top of the cake.

The first thing you see as you enter the kempt low-build exhibition and information complex just off the A96 to Nairn, is a life-size mannequin of the Duke of Cumberland. William Augustus 'Butcher' Cumberland was the second son of George II and had been sent up north to squash the Jacobite Rebellion of 1745. Fort Augustus was named after him while he was still a schoolboy. If the Visitors' Centre dummy is any-thing to go by, the Butcher was as fat as a Sumo wrestler, with a dangling lower lip (just right to park a cig on), pig eyes and dangerously imperfect posture. Bonnie Prince Charlie, the Young Pretender, Charles Edward Louis Philip Casimir Stuart, leader of the '45 Rebellion, faces him across the approach to the ticket desk. Charlie is the Duke's obverse: slim, lithe, youthful, alert of mien and wearing a jaunty plaid suit, in contrast to the Butcher's wearisome redcoat. Really, you don't need to go any further than that. You don't have to pay for the audio-visual lecture, the historical background display, or the self-guided walk around the battlefield. You can leave it there. We are pigs; the Jacobite Scots, proud and free.

Well, yes, but some compulsion to nod towards historical balance makes me record the observation that Bonnie Prince Charlie was not only the doomed hero of the Scottish resist-ance and leader of the last great blow against the English – a heady conflation of Paul Revere, Che Guevara and Giuseppe Mazzini – but also a typical brainless aristocratic waster. I know, this is about as bad as fingering the Queen Mother as a child molester or the late Sir Stanley Matthews as a junkie, but how else do you interpret the facts?

Brought up in Rome to believe that the Crown of Scotland was his, not King George's (which it had been since the 1707 Act of Union), he got backing from the French in 1743 to invade Scotland and destabilise the whole British scene. 'Backing' actually turned out to be a couple of nervy French naval vessels, one of which met a British warship en route and retreated to France, taking with it most of the invading force's supplies and weapons. The one with Prince Charlie on board made it to the island of Eriskay in the Outer Hebrides. There, he was advised by the locals to give up and go home. But he used plausible aristocratic rhetoric to win over doubters and gather the clans, then marched east to Invergarry and Blair

Atholl. Numbers grew, he seized Edinburgh in the name of King James VIII and beat the English at the Battle of Prestonpans. By now, he had an army of about 5,500 behind him, and, not content with the throne of Scotland, headed south to London to seize the throne of everywhere else.

Londoners were panicking at the thought of all these mud-spattered Highlanders descending on them, but when the Jacobite army got as far as Derby, the Young Pretender (after some lobbying from his chieftains) thought better of it and marched all the way back again to Scotland, ending up at Inverness at the start of 1746. Here he waited for the showdown with a freshly raised English army of 9,000 soldiers, roused for battle by this time and led by the Duke of Cumberland.

Well, this is heroism in the classic mould, a lone figure laughing at destiny and the odds. This is Bonnie Prince Charlie, blithe, fearless and gay, the Young Chevalier single-handedly goosing the Auld Enemy. But then he screwed it up. All the time he was quartered at Inverness, the Prince neglected the needs of his exhausted, hungry and poorly equipped troops. He diddled around, embroiling himself in predictable upper-class pursuits, namely drinking, partying and chasing the local women. Many of his Highland warriors quietly left and went home. The rest got hungrier and more ragged.

Fat Cumberland, on the other hand, was busy training and feeding up his forces, so that they were in prime condition, like a bunch of Dobermanns. The Jacobites launched a night raid on 15 April which failed utterly and which meant that when the day of battle dawned on 16 April, they were even more exhausted and dispirited than before. As every Scotsman knows, it was a massacre. All over in forty minutes, it saw the deaths of around 1,000 Highlanders in exchange for around 50 redcoats. Cumberland earned his 'Butcher' cognomen by ordering his men to despatch by bayonet any wounded Scotsmen they found lying around, before spending the next few weeks hunting down a further 1,000 escapees. It was the last battle ever fought on the British mainland.

So Bonnie Prince Charlie ran off to generate chapter three of the legend. This entailed hiding in the Highlands and Islands for five months with a £30,000 bounty on his head. No one betrayed him, amazingly enough, although you'd have thought that it might have crossed Flora Macdonald's mind. After all, what did he ever do for her? *She* famously disguised him as her serving woman 'Betty Burke' and rowed him over the sea to Skye, under the noses of the English, before hiding him some more, risking her life and the lives of her nearest and dearest and finally giving him a bottle of whisky and a chicken before he took his leave.

What did he do in return? He ponced around the islands, striking heroic poses and kissing people, before giving Flora a miniature of himself, then shoving off, saying, 'I hope, Madam, we shall meet in St James's yet.' Did he ever thank her for saving his life once he found his way to safety? No. Did he ever communicate with her again, in any way? No. Did he ever commiserate with her on her subsequent imprisonment by the English? No. He took her help, her bravery, her chicken, used them up and carelessly spat them out. Then he devoted the rest of his life to becoming an embittered lush, dying, leaking with drink, in Rome in 1788. And this was after he had nearly bankrupted the entire city of Glasgow with the levies imposed by his army of insurgents. There you go: incompetent, venal, inconsiderate and shameless in one move. In the end he was no more than the King of Shortbread, the Prince of the Whisky Bottle Label, and his legacy was the butchery of thousands of Scotsmen.

But back at the Visitors' Centre, this arrogance and incompetence elides into the awfulness of the Culloden bloodbath and the vicious repressions that flowed from it: including the suppression of the clans and clan tartans, the elimination of Gaelic, the prohibition of the playing of bagpipes and the carrying of arms. After Culloden and the failure of the rebellion, English was imposed throughout and Scottish nationhood was obliterated in the calculated subjugation of one culture to another. The Highland Clearances followed.

Given this horrible litany, the Young Pretender's failings tend to get lost in the fog of history. Events overtake causes. Another cardinal Scottish moment comes into being, with the result that in the corridor of my hotel in Skye, two large historically charged watercolours – Bannockburn and Culloden – could hang, brooding, a clenched fist of freedom for sympathetic foreign tourists to admire, a glassy-eyed intimidation for any passing Sassenach resident.

And here I am, having shuffled past the big plaster dummy Butcher by the ticket desk and having bought my ticket in as neutral and pan-European a voice as possible. I am sitting in the audio-visual auditorium, yearning to be Dutch or Danish and not English, waiting for the infotainment to start. I am surrounded by doleful Swedes and Germans who are already infected by the terrible burden of what they're about to watch, judging by their slumped shoulders and the way they talk in whispers, as at a funeral. The good news is, our auditorium is much nicer than the one where I watched *We Believe in the Loch Ness Monster*. It is airy, beige, like a businessman's hotel, and has a respectable turn-out, maybe thirty of us. *We Believe* had just me and a young English couple who kept giggling and playfully fighting over a ginger tam-o'-shanter throughout the film.

Both Culloden and *We Believe* share the same crack-of-doom Scottish narrative, though. Thus the Culloden movie opens with the promise of disaster (stormy skies, grasses waving in gales, bits of stone) and keens away for about twenty minutes with noises of death and murder coming and going like trains passing a window. A line traces the Jacobites' futile route south and then north again. The Highlanders wipe their knives clean on a bit of moss. The English eat well and tend their state-of-the-art cannonry, smirking grimly. The watching Germans and Swedes stiffen in their seats.

For the Swedes, this must represent final confirmation (after football fans and package holiday tours) that the English are the most disgusting people in Europe; while the Germans must find it a relief that for once someone else is on the receiving end of the burden of moral shame. Pictures flash up of leering redcoats bayoneting wild-eyed Highlanders who bravely but pointlessly fight back with primitive studded shields. The soundtrack yells and barks. The Young Pretender appears in watercolour, striking a stupid attitude. He would have been all of twenty-six, so fair, so unfat. Music plays, a pibroch to lament the passing of Scotland's finest. Heather tosses in the wind. It is the death of a culture. The Young Chevalier is seen legging it, east to west. The lights come back up. We all shuffle mournfully outside to the area around the ticket desk, where Butcher Cumberland's dummy porkily awaits, spoiling for a fight. '*Ontstellend*,' I say to myself, haggard.

Outside, it's raining again, but I button up and go to atone for my sins in the battlefield. This has been restored to something like the condition it must have been in for the battle – marshy, overgrown with spiky vegetation, almost impossible to move across without falling over. The Young Pretender was counselled against having the fight there in the first place as it was soggy and flat as a pancake – neither of which suited his Highland warriors' style of assault, which involved starting at the top of a hill and running down, screaming. But he insisted on doing it in this bog between Inverness and Nairn and so put himself in the wrong once again.

I peer at the little stones which betoken the resting places of the clansmen who died and watch the traffic pound past on the A96. The Swedes and Germans are also picking their way along the paths which lead through the scene of the crime, but it's freezing cold, the rain is just turning to sleet, and, besides, the heritage battlefield is both too small (neatly delineated by a square of flags indicating who stood where) and too close to the main road to match the meaning of the event with a suitable grandeur. The sleet gets into its stride, now, and I turn up my collar and join the North European retreat to the car park.

This hatred thing: you don't know it's there, down in London. Scottish people who move down south like to play up their Scottishness for effect, but they don't *usually* wander around calling us cunts to our faces. You can't tell that they hate us, just by looking. An aura of puritanical mistrust is usually about as bad as it gets. Scots Londoners are apt to look a little more scrubbed, a little more straight-in-the-eye than the English variety. Friendly but basically disgusted seems to be the ethos.

But the Anglo-Scottish relationship is a dark mixture. It's rhetorical as well as sinister; theatrical but bitter; a kind of sibling rivalry involving alcoholism and death. And outside politics and the history books, when is it most clearly articulated? At a football match.

Just as I was cranking up to start this book at the end of 1999, England and Scotland had their first match for ten years as part of the Euro 2000 play-offs. Once again it turned out that the English were the *Auld Enemy*, and that the Scots wanted to dismember us on and off the pitch. At the time I was mildly surprised. Why were *we* the enemy? The *French* – now, I could understand anyone wanting to hate the French. But taken overall, what was so wrong with us? Apart from a long and bloody history of oppression and exploitation? And why was it so hard for anyone north or south of the border to get a ticket? What did the authorities think would happen?

Clearly, they thought that what happened a decade earlier would happen again. May 1989 was the last time England had played Scotland at football, in an annual tournament known as the Rous Cup. This was the oldest international fixture in the world and had been going for 117 years. The England team went up to Hampden Park, in Glasgow, and beat the Scots 2–0 while their supporters – who had turned up particularly early for this very purpose – got pissed and then started a riot outside the ground. Some 250 people were arrested, most of them English. Subsequently, the Scots asked for the game not to be played again and for the Rous Cup to be left to die in peace. This, then, would make us the greatest Barbarians of all: so awful that even the Scots can't stand us.

Except that it's a two-way street, as is often the case. The English, by way of contrast, like to recall the notorious pitch-invasion/goal-mangling incident of 1977, which took place when Scotland played England at Wembley. A load of bladdered Jocks pulled the Wembley pitch apart and smashed up the goalposts in their excitement at having beaten England 2–1. This event so seared its way into the collective head of Middle England that just before the Euro 2000 game, the *Daily Mail* went and dug up one of the Wembley perpetrators, twenty-two years on. The one they got was the skinny, bare-chested Bay City Roller lookalike who'd been pictured with his arms aloft and spread all over the sheets back in '77, a one-man shorthand for the Scottish condition, a pictogram of Scottishness. 'In 1977,' ran the caption, 'he and his tartan clad pals ripped Wembley to bits.'

It turned out that this monster was called Alex, had become a millionaire in the house renovation business, grown a beard and moved out to Jersey. 'I still see a few of the lads from that day,' he said from his beachside retreat, 'and we reminisce about what went on. It was all high spirits.'

Nevertheless, for the first leg of the encounter, Scotland was Brave and we were the *Auld Enemy* and feelings were going to run high. The England team went back up to Hampden Park. Thousands of Scotsmen put on tam-o'-shanters the size of family-feast pizzas and painted the Saltire on their faces. Glasgow's *Daily Record* pointed out that the behaviour of the England fans in Marseilles during the previous World Cup was an abomination among civilised peoples and went on to list twenty reasons why the Scots had to beat England, among which (reasonably enough) were Jeffrey Archer and Tara Palmer-Tomkinson. Then the Scottish supporters made a small piece of history by booing loudly and clearly through the British national anthem. They carried on booing through part of 'Flower of Scotland' too, the nearest thing Scotland has to its own national anthem, until they realised what was going on. Then the Tartan Army chanted, 'If you hate the fucking English, clap your hands.' Then they lost the game 2–0. This allowed the London *Observer* to remark that 'Hampden brings out the worst in the Scots' and that the place 'remains at heart envious, small-minded, suspicious of strangers'.

A week or so later, the Scottish team came down to play the second leg. Nothing much happened, except that England played more like they usually did and Scotland won 1–0. This meant that the Tartan Army could go home full of woeful dignity and contempt, beaten by fortune rather than the better side. Thus the classic Scottish position of delicious failure, which Gavin Esler called 'the national anthem of whining'.

There you go. We meet, we eyeball one another and snarl, we part. What I cannot quite understand is why the English always manage to come out as the savages. The

Scots are famous not only for moaning and being tight-fisted, but also for being the most intimidating fighters in the world. If a Scotsman can't find anyone else to fight, he will make do with fighting another Scotsman, and so on. Glasgow may well be the toughest city in the UK. And yet Scots football supporters can travel across Europe in amity and high spirits, while the English crew is clapped in irons the moment it gets off the ferry. Is this anything to do with the fact that the Scots are essentially Celts, whereas the English are essentially a mish-mash of German, Norse and Norman blood, a mixture of the most belligerent races in Continental Europe?

But then again, I found myself talking to this Scottish bloke in a Scottish pub, quite a bit later, after the Scottish and English teams had both been eliminated from Euro 2000 (the English, naturally, in the traditional orgy of vandalism, hooliganism and tabloid-baiting). I wondered if all good Scotsmen would be rooting for the French, the *auld alliance* and that.

'Definitely not,' he said, swirling the McEwan's around in his glass. 'There's a lot of anti-French feeling around here. It used to be the auld alliance, but not any more.'

I feigned surprise and a sense of loss that this should be so. Why? What had happened?

'Well . . . all the beef bans, the air traffic controllers' strike' (they'd just had another one), 'the port blockades . . . Lots of people around here' – a rural community, this was – 'don't like the French at all. You know, in this district, they even stopped selling French wines in protest for a while. The Dutch are more likely to get our support.'

Well, the Dutch were about to play Italy that night. Okay, we all like the Dutch, but why so much more than we like the French or Italians?

''Cos Rangers have got a Dutch manager, that's why,' he said, mustering a degree of self-control. Later on I found out that the fearsome Glasgow team are indeed (or are indeed at the time of writing) managed by Dick Advocaat, late of PSV Eindhoven.

'Quite a lot of Rangers supporters have started turning up wearing orange in support of the Dutch players.'

Bert Konterman, Ronald de Boer, Giovanni van Bronckhorst, Arthur Numan, Michael Mols and Fernando Ricksen, since you ask. I was on the brink of blurting out something about how a sea of Protestant orange must piss off Rangers' old enemy Celtic something remarkable, but then I thought better of it. You never know how these boozer encounters are going to work out.

So the Euro 2000 play-off was the collective confrontation, the symbolic public enactment of antagonisms. The intensification of Scots sensibilities around the time of the 1997 referendum also made hay with a lot of the old bitternesses. But it was happening more privately, too. Not long before I turned up at latitude 55° North, there had been much discussion about the plight of a couple from Liverpool who had retired to a place called Clarencefield, near Dumfries. This is actually so close to the border with England, you wonder why they bothered. But they did anyway.

Once there, they were swiftly banned from the Clarencefield local, the Farmers' Inn, for being English. So they took their grievance to the Dumfries Sheriff Court, backed by the Commission for Racial Equality, and claimed damages from the publican who'd barred them. They added that not only had they been barred from the pub, but that rubbish had been dumped on their front doorstep, placards had been placed around the village reading 'English Out' and that on one of the scant occasions when they *had* been able to visit the Farmers' Inn, local teenagers had played 'Flower of Scotland' sixteen times on the jukebox.

'Flower of Scotland' is a terrible dirge all about Robert the Bruce, who defeated King Edward II of England most famously at Bannockburn in 1314. It is so much worse than 'Scotland the Brave' that it is hard to conceive why it should have become a de facto national anthem, but there it is. Robert the Bruce is arguably *the* Scottish hero, not only for driving out the English and establishing an independent Scotland in 1328 but also for avenging the murder of the previous Scottish hero William Wallace. (In 1305 Wallace was forcibly divided into four separate sections by Edward I – who sent the pieces to Newcastle, Berwick, Stirling and Perth, as a kind of yellow card to the troublesome Scots.)

Anyway, it was sixteen renditions of 'Flower of Scotland' in one drinking session, plus vandalism and abuse. In the end, the matter was settled out of court, with the complainants being paid a four-figure sum and having their legal costs met before they returned to England. The twist was that the publican himself turned out to be half-English, as did 50 per cent of the entire village.

The Commission for Racial Equality noted that since it began to keep records of anti-English racism in the mid-1990s, there had been twenty-two complaints originating in Scotland. Detective Chief Superintendent Tim McCulloch said that Dumfries and Galloway did not have a racism problem, although local people apparently agreed that low-level harassment of the English was common. Irvine Welsh allows one of his characters to pinpoint the status of an Englishman living in Scotland as that of 'a barely tolerated guest'. It was indeed worse, they said, after *Braveheart* came out.

I headed off towards Nairn to get away from the brooding resentments of the shared Anglo-Scottish past. I was greeted for an instant by a large and beautiful rainbow, which I would in normal conditions have cheerfully interpreted as a symbol of ethereal peace. But after a few days in the Highlands, I knew that rainbows were as commonplace up here as graffiti down south. So even though this rainbow appeared to end immediately in front of my car and I experienced that little surge of irrational hope on account of the pot of gold which I knew awaited me two hundred yards down the road, I quickly remembered where I was and discounted it straight thereafter.

Nairn is a seaside town which, unusually for a seaside town, has two fine beaches, a reputation for sunshine, a riverside and a museum, but no front. I wandered around the pleasant little concrete harbour for quite a while, trying to work out where the statutory Southend-style esplanade could have been (bomb-proof fairy lights, wrought-iron Edwardian wind shelters, crappy playtime steam train which is actually a diesel van pulling some GRP fake carriages and which may or may not run at all out of season, the conventional British seaside package) and after twenty-five minutes gave up, because there isn't one.

What there is is a long walk along a patch of rough greenery called the Links, with Nairn town huddling some way inland to protect itself from the unsurprisingly dreadful weather coming off the North Sea. The Victorian Dr John Grigor was a big fan of Nairn, promoting it as 'The Brighton of the North' and arguing that it was one of the healthiest places in Britain. Dr Grigor was also a great proponent of the use of cannabis in childbirth, so respect is due, but no one would ever set their sights so high as to anticipate pleasant weather when there's nothing between you and the Skagerrak except waves. Which may account for the absence of a traditional sea front.

They held the 1999 Walker Cup up here (a tournament for golf amateurs, United States v. Ireland & Britain) and the only surprise came on the morning of the first day's play, when the wind blowing across the course of the Nairn Golf Club, hard by the Moray Firth, actually dropped. In the days preceding the game, they'd experienced gusts up to 50 m.p.h.; and on the afternoon of the first day, normality reasserted itself with a succession of heavy squalling showers. Apparently, the only other surprise after that was that the British/Irish team won. They were pictured holding the cup, grinning their faces off, while indigo storm clouds and yet another deep depression from Scandinavia boiled up over their shoulders.

I paced around the High Street and Academy Street and bought some chips. In between showers, the sun came out. I feasted on it, working on my tan, still trying not to look like a Sassenach. I don't think my imposture worked. When I asked for the chips, the girl behind the counter looked at me warily and said, 'You're not from round here, are you?'

Not from round here is evidently a euphemism for *English*. I waggled my head and hitched up my eyebrows. She saw straight through me.

'Vinegar's over there,' she said. In *that* way.

TEN

You can't overstate the significance of *Braveheart*. This is the film directed by, and starring, Mel Gibson as William Wallace. William Wallace was the prototypical Scottish hero, who led a great uprising against King Edward I in 1297 before being trounced at the Battle of Falkirk in 1298. Then he was hunted down, hanged, drawn and quartered, thus becoming a martyr in the cause of Scots nationalism in 1305. After *Braveheart* came out, in 1995, sales of kilts rocketed, English immigrants got beaten up, the SNP got a shot in the arm and Scottish football supporters started to turn up at games with that blue poster paint sloshed over their faces *à la* Mel.

It also spawned about a million *Braveheart* T-shirts that you can buy in tartan gift shops, smaller numbers of none the less even more repulsive *Braveheart* mannequins of Mel in a kilt, and an insane website called *www.macbraveheart.co.uk*, dedicated to 'the best motion picture ever' and which notes in passing that 'We (John and Linda Anderson of Edinburgh, Scotland) have seen *Braveheart* 51 times.'

The rest of the website is too vast and multifarious to describe in any detail, but with its endless reiterations of *Braveheart* themes and its lengthy FAQ section (much of which grapples directly or indirectly with one of the film's central shortcomings, i.e., that it is more than 80 per cent made up, relying as it does on a deeply untrustworthy fifteenth-century romance written by Henry the Minstrel) it does at least indicate how much *Braveheart* – as opposed to its filmic contemporaries, *Rob Roy*, or *Loch Ness*, starring an unusually disorientated Ted Danson – stirred the Scottish consciousness.

Not just that of the Scots. It won a bunch of Oscars, including Best Film, Best Director, Best Make-up and Best Photography. It's taken the thick end of $200 million worldwide since it first appeared, and even the normally vinegary *Halliwell's Film Guide* tearfully describes it as 'a stirring nationalistic epic, acted and directed with great verve'. It admits that 'some of the history may be suspect', but fortunately for Mel, 'the film creates a sense of myth with its sweep and passion'. When the *Sunday Times* came to review it, it cried aloud, 'At last: a costume drama that wears its costumes with pride.'

There you go. As with his more recent *The Patriot*, it makes you wonder what it is that Mel Columcille Gerard Gibson (to give him his full name), of Peekskill, NY (he only went to Australia when he was twelve), has got against the English. I mean, what did we do to him? Bully him on account of his height and his second name? Or for the fact that his first name is more normally given to girls? But then, the loathing of the English he evinces in *Braveheart* is clearly a loathing that a lot of other people enjoy sharing. In the film, we occupy precisely the same conceptual space as that which used to be occupied by the Gestapo in movies about the Second World War. In other words, we rape, burn, torture, butcher, display every conceivable sign of a depraved and bestial cruelty and talk through thin hard lips as well as down our noses. This is a very popular dramatic framing of the English character nowadays and it clearly worked a treat for Mel.

Key moments in the film?

– A Highland warrior who has an arrow sticking out of him still manages to lift up an entire spiked wooden paling in order to get at the English troops on the other side.

– A Mel Gibson height joke, in which two mud-spattered men complain that Mel cannot be William Wallace on account of not being tall enough.

– The Highland braves greet one another by punching each other in the face. Not a moment, as such: more an endearing motif.

– They all lift up their kilts and expose themselves to the English army.

– William Wallace gets to snog the Princess of Wales. A topical allusion, of course, as Princess Diana was still alive when the film was made. Strictly speaking, the thirteenth/fourteenth-century Prince of Wales never married the Princess until after Wallace had died.

On the other hand, you really have to want to believe in the film very badly to get much else out of it. This is supposed to be thirteenth-century Scotland, and while the rain pisses down medievally in many of the scenes, and the mud has that wholly realistic cloying Scottish appearance – the kind of mud that lodges in your corduroys and sometimes in your ears – the cast have unconvincingly excellent skin, mainly, and good teeth. They do not look as if they might be in line for the Black Death or smallpox. Many of the battlefield extras have got authentic tough schemie coupons but even so, the worst they look is like Ginger Baker.

This is especially true of Mel and the various beautiful girls who fall helplessly in love with him. Mel does wear a wig like a dead dog on his head but, despite adhering to the principle that dirty, mud-bemired characters are virtuous, while clean characters are bad, he has no problem avoiding a beard or keeping his teeth white. Robert the Bruce starts off enormously well-washed, but as he grows in stature throughout the course of the film, he becomes dirtier and dirtier until he is quite virtuous, but nowhere near as filthy as Mel. The inverse of this rule applies to beautiful girls, of course, whose hygiene is an index of their lovability.

The dialogue, by way of contrast, is spun-dried polyester, but at least there isn't too much of it. Actually, Mel's Scottish accent is equally the product of purely artificial ingredients, and whenever he opens his mouth you tense in your seat, wondering which part of the pan-Celtic universe he'll be inhabiting this time.

If the lack of period physical degradation is one drawback, the lack of any interest in sticking vaguely to the historical facts insofar as they are known is another. The movie starts with the stricture that history is always written by the conquerors, lest we rush too eagerly to any English history books to find out what really happened. And it is also the case that the events of William Wallace's life are only scantily documented. Plenty of scope for invention, in other words. But – as even *macbraveheart.co.uk* sometimes acknowledges – Mel does play fast and loose with whatever we think we do know. When the English Nazis kill his beautiful wife, this act becomes the trigger to set off the rebellion and the chain of events which ensues; even though it has been observed that in reality, Wallace was already harrying the English, who then murdered his wife as a punishment.

Equally, we get the strong impression that Wallace's army took York from the English and sacked it, when in actual fact, the Scots didn't have the resources to achieve such a thing. Even Henry the Minstrel only has him staging a kind of protest there for a couple of weeks before leaving again. Oh, and the Battle of Stirling Bridge? The great set-piece of the film, the bit where Wallace rouses all the extras into fighting for him against the numerically superior and infinitely better-equipped English? Yes, it was a major strategic loss for the English, a springboard for the Scottish uprising, no question. On the other hand, it's not known as the Battle of Stirling Bridge for nothing. It was fought across the bridge at Stirling which spanned the River Forth. History, for what it's worth, claims that the English made a huge tactical mistake by rushing across the bridge like maniacs, while the Scots stood on the far side and slaughtered them as they crossed. Then they took Stirling.

Where is the bridge in *Braveheart*? There is no bridge. What there is is Wallace (a) demonstrating his awesome powers of oratory and (b) using his cunning (a theme of the film) to trick the English into charging on to a wall of pointed spikes. The upshot may be the same, but the process is different.

From a purely directorial point of view, merely showing the English trampling one another in their eagerness to get butchered on the other side of the bridge wouldn't have made much cinema, I have to admit. By telling the story it does, *Braveheart* at least gets to stage a terrific primitive battle, in which the English Nazis (led, naturally enough, by a couple of well-washed cod-medieval stooges straight out of *Blackadder*) get chopped, hacked, bludgeoned, stabbed, impaled and mangled in a real welter of blood'n'guts. Your most atavistic impulses, the sort that centuries of civilisation have done their best to divert and repress, boil up and you find yourself hissing *yes* every time an Anglo-Nazi loses his nuts to some screaming Pict. Even if you're English, watching in the grey suburbs of London.

So why should I complain? After all, for years, people (especially the British) believed that the first man to fly faster than the speed of sound was Brit Nigel Patrick in David Lean's *The Sound Barrier*, from 1952. It wasn't until Tom Wolfe rehabilitated Chuck Yeager's reputation in 1979 with *The Right Stuff* that we bothered to think any different. Why shouldn't someone other than Shakespeare play fast and loose with *our* history? Not that anyone's going to bother to rehabilitate 'Longshanks' Edward I's reputation or demote that of William Wallace in the twenty-first century. But either way, the symbolism and the drama are what matter. If Mel Gibson wants his entrails pulled out on screen by a jobbing actor in the cause of the larger moral gesture, then fine.

No, authenticity isn't quite the big problem. The big problem is how much of yourself you invest in a propagandist piece of art, and how long before what seems inspirational now collapses on its own rhetoric and becomes completely hollow, an embarrassment, like the poems of Sir Henry Newbolt ('Play up! play up! and play the game!'). Even as Mel adds to his fortune and the *Braveheart* figurines multiply like the terracotta army of X'ian, so the context in which *Braveheart* makes sense slowly descends into the vaults of history itself and those who cleave to it find that they are cleaving to a joke, rather than a political manifesto.

And what steps forward to replace it? Why, none other than the scary *Ratcatcher*, written and directed by the talented young Scots *auteur* Lynne Ramsay. This came out in 1999 and promptly picked up Best New Director at the Edinburgh International Film Festival, Best Debut Feature at the British Independent Film Awards, and a Silver Hugo at the Chicago International Film Festival. Not five Oscars, no, but not bad for someone who wasn't yet thirty when she made what is her first feature movie.

So what is *Ratcatcher*, anyway? *Ratcatcher* is the shatteringly depressing account of a boy growing up in Glasgow in the 1970s during a dustmen's strike, befriending the school slut and having a bath with her and dreaming of escape from his feckless dad, his trashy sisters and their clammy tenement building, delivering himself into a world where you can have a nice toilet and run through a cornfield and be happy for once with your shitty family. Drowning in a canal (purpose-dug for the movie, as it turns out) plus the routine casual abuse of people and animals feature largely.

Key moments in the film?

– As the rubbish sacks pile up outside the tenement, we observe two scabby blokes poking around for interesting items of refuse. One of them pulls a large dead Alsatian from a plastic garbage bag. 'Aw, look,' he says, 'someone's thrown away a perfectly good dog.'

– The hero's dad (played by Tommy Flanagan, who fleetingly appears as a stooge in *Braveheart*) sports not one but *two* Glasgow Smiles, which I would have thought the absolute limit for Glasgow Smiles on the human face.

– The sunlit cornfield through which you can run next to the house with the nice toilet symbolises the persistent Scottish dream of escape: from rain, cold and stone, into a land of sunshine, dry heat and cereals. From Scotland to Australia, in fact.

If *Braveheart* is the way the Scots would like to see themselves, then *Ratcatcher* is the way quite a lot of them actually are, allowing in both cases for the distortions imposed by the creative process. Neither, it has to be pointed out, is the way the Scots saw themselves in *Whisky Galore!*, courtesy of Compton Mackenzie: sly, whimsical, slightly wild, living on Barra in the Hebrides. Nor, for that matter, the way Bill Forsyth portrayed Scotland in either *Gregory's Girl* or *Local Hero*: both of which trade successfully on a distinctively Scottish admixture of cuteness and asperity – much like *Whisky Galore!* – advertising Scottishness without overselling it.

In comparison with these, you can't help but notice that not only is Mel Gibson not Scottish, but that he is using the dialogue of Anglo-Scots historical relations to make a point about oppression and liberation in any and all contexts. The film speaks to millions not necessarily because of its Scottishness but because of its verities about freedom and justice. If it *had* been made by a Scottish director, of course, then it would have been just one long whinge. The fact that Mel made it removes the taint of special pleading. But it's hard not to suspect that Mel would have been happy enough to have made a film about Anglo-Irish history, or even Anglo-Australian history, if the resonances had been right and he'd been comfortable with the accent. In fact, he just has, in *The Patriot*. It's all business for Mel.

Which leaves one wondering why so many Scotsmen have invested so much yearning, so much faith, in a non-Scottish product, made by a smart opportunistic movie king from America, whose passion for Scottish freedom must be some way below his dislike of the English and his eagerness to keep his place at Hollywood's top table. I suppose you take your inspiration where you find it and don't complain – any more than the English worry that, among their more revered national figures, Alexander Fleming was Scottish or that the Duke of Wellington was Irish or that the Queen is German.

ELEVEN

Terrible news – Alex Salmond has resigned as leader of the Scottish National Party after ten stupendous years! As with the Kennedy assassinations and the death of John Lennon, I can recall exactly where I was when I discovered the news. I was sitting here, tapping away, when I opened a newspaper and Salmond's cheerfully cracked grin sprang out at me, followed by the news that he had quit. 'It has been a privilege to head the party,' he said. 'SOLO ACT WILL LEAVE A VACUUM', said the neighbouring headline which clearly implied more than it meant to.

I was shocked. I had banked so much spiritual capital with him. To give you an idea of how hung up on Salmond I had become, let me confess that I even spent money on the SNP, in a bid to reduce their notorious £400,000 cash deficit and somehow to connect myself ethereally to my hero. A while back, the party released a CD of patriotic Scottish music. This was called *A New Sang: 12 Songs of Scottish Independence*, a cunning way to boost its funds and, at the same time, keep the party's profile high (always surprisingly prominent, unlike that of, say, Plaid Cymru, but a profile which never quite garners the votes the party thinks it deserves).

The clincher, of course, was that Salmond himself had committed to sing on the CD. This is bravery to an astonishing degree, braver even than when he criticised the British involvement in the Kosovo crisis of 1999. So Salmond was all over the news – claiming that vital media exposure, those column inches – wearing headphones in the studio and making a spectacle of himself. *This*, I thought, *is too good to miss*.

Quick as a flash I was down to the Princes Street HMV, looking for the CD. No sign of the disc on the racks, so I risked making myself appear to be a nasty-minded southern crank by asking the guy behind the HMV desk for a copy.

'I've heard of it,' he said, stroking his beard. 'Wasn't it on the telly?'

He dived below the level of the counter for a wad of docketing. Came back up frowning.

'We should have it. But the SNP have decided to do the distribution themselves. And we have to go through our usual distributors, not the SNP. So we can't stock it even if we want to. You could try the SNP if you like.'

Well, I didn't have time for that. So I left, cursing the SNP silently, and started a long and fruitless search for it somewhere – anywhere – else. The search only ended months later when a friend up in Edinburgh called in specially at the SNP offices in Charlotte Street and got a copy. But was it worth the wait?

It is rich in songs of yearning – 'When the People Speak', 'Theme for Scottish Independence', 'Freedom Come All Ye' – interspersed with shouters such as 'Gie's a Drink' and 'The De'il's Awa Wi' the Exciseman', plus the odd provocation such as 'Scottish MP'. Performers include Dr Winifred Ewing MSP, Mother of the House; Andrew Wilson, the SNP's financial spokesman; some of the members of Gaelic folk favourites

Capercaillie; a group called Deaf Shepherd; and the then National Convenor himself, Alex Salmond MSP.

Folk music of any kind is difficult to find the right approach to, given its customary mixture of po-faced wankiness and belligerent hilarity. In this case, the problem is doubled by having politicians weaving nervously through their chosen melodies like drunks making their way the length of a bus, just grateful to get off when it stops. However, by alternating rank amateurs with fervent professionals (or pairing them up on the same track, sometimes) *A New Sang* avoids the ever-present danger of forcing the listener to switch off completely when faced with a pile-up of pub backroom crooning. It still has that irksome folkie haze hanging over it, though – well-meaning, anti-progressive, fundamentally evangelical at heart.

Salmond's number is 'The Rowan Tree', written by Lady Nairne, the late-eighteenth/early-nineteenth-century songwriter and collector who, under the pseudonym of 'Mrs Bogan of Bogan', corralled together 'The Rowan Tree', 'The Auld Hoose', 'The Land o' the Leal' and many others in a book called *The Scottish Minstrel*.

'The Rowan Tree' begins: 'Oh! rowan tree, oh! rowan tree, thou'lt aye be dear to me, / En twin'd thou art wi' mony ties o' hame and infancy.' Salmond pronounces the first syllable of *rowan* to rhyme with *cow* rather than *show* (second option would seem more normal, but then I'm not from Linlithgow), but otherwise lays into the melody with what sounds like plaintive sincerity. The sleevenotes describe him as 'the one-time child chorister' – at Linlithgow Academy, one presumes – and he still has that chorister's reverence for articulation, as well as that old itch to sing in a key slightly higher than you can comfortably manage. The fact that he can do it at all is impressive – but the fact that he's *prepared* to do it is even more arresting.

What would the southern equivalent be? Michael Howard doing stand-up comedy? Clare Short cooking a meal for twenty lobby correspondents? Something naked and potentially irretrievable, at any rate – something which exposes you to the world, and which, because revelatory in this way, could go terribly, uncontrollably wrong. But he gets through it without catastrophe – allowing for the fact that in authentic folk-song fashion, it turns into a pious dirge at the end ('Now a'are gane! We meet nae mair aneath the rowan tree'), inviting winsome reflectiveness, tears, sorrowing drams round the peat fire. Still. This is ballsy behaviour, and it subtly shifts one's understanding of the crinkle-cut pontificator. Now, he's a risk-taker, a politician with a vulnerable tenor voice, an MSP with a handle on music, that most daring, unpredictable and democratic of all the arts.

The fact that it's a music CD – rather than a volume of poems or essays, or a video of speeches – also confirms the Scottishness of the enterprise. It's all of a piece with that near-Jesuitical truth that all you have to do is summon up a few cultural essences and you have Scotland re-created where you stand. In this case, through the medium of some minor chords, a morose Scots voice, a couple of dialect words (*hame*, *mither*, *Jeanie*), an atmosphere of homesickness and *sehnsucht*. Just put it together in a bowl and stir, and *voilà*! You have instant Caledonia!

Being Scotland, of course, it also plays the old trick on you. Just as you're getting ready to ridicule such stuff as cheap, formulaic, maudlin, bad art, stuff for the tourists, in fact – out comes another song, 'Battle of Waterloo', sung by Jim Malcolm. Despite adhering to all the conventions of Scottish balladry (a footsoldier from Kirriemuir reflects on the futility of war as he dies on the battlefield), this is none the less so poignant, so heartfelt, that even I can't listen to it without bursting into tears. You can fight against the tartan and the bagpipes and the endless references to Jeanie and the broom blossoming in the springtime all you like; but eventually a stray phrase or sequence of notes creeps under your defences and there you are, helpless.

Only now Salmond himself is *gane*. Maybe they'll write a dirge about the loss of Prince Alex, *wabbit* by the cares of leadership, his *gyte*, *pawky* expression all peely-wally and lined by woe, his *blethering* all *forfochen* and his *douce* voice reduced to a *shilpit greet*. Because without him, who cares?

TWELVE

By now, I was thirsting for a proper city again. Enough of all that parochialism, that backwoods barrenness. Go for something big. What's more, I had an agenda. It all seemed plausible enough at the time. Go down to Aberdeen, catch the Bank of Scotland Scottish Mixed Curling Championships, that crazy bowls-on-ice the Scots love (and are world champions at), sink myself in the culture, get inspired by the third biggest city in Scotland. So I fell out of the train at Aberdeen Station, stupidly early in the day, and was greeted by an array of local graffiti:

SCOTLAND ON DRUGS
BONG ON
FOR SEX PHONE BETTY

The usual cavalcade of crap, but with a couple of spicy moments:

ENGLISH SCUM

and

. FUCK THE ENGLISH.

Welcome to Aberdeen, I thought, as I went round the corner to the tourist office to check the time and location of the Curling Championship.

'Oh, yes,' cried a nice lady in plaid behind the counter. 'I know about that. It's at Dyce.' Dyce is an outlying satellite of Aberdeen. On a bus route, no distance. 'My son's taking part! Are you interested in curling?'

I waggled my head and smirked and did my best to intimate that, yes, I was quite hot for some curling in the free moments my busy schedule would allow. I didn't want her to get the impression that I was so parched for stimulation that I'd come all the way up to Aberdeen just to watch a bunch of locals push a forty-pound stone around a sheet of ice.

'Well, it starts on Friday. Do you know how to get there? You go out to Bankhead and it's right at the roundabout then straight on. That's where the rink is.'

So I was nodding and grinning and shooting my eyebrows up and down like roller-blinds, but what I couldn't bring myself to tell her was that I'd completely fucked up the dates. Today was Tuesday and I wasn't going to be in Aberdeen on Friday. I had to be somewhere else on Friday. I had, in fact, come up especially to see something which I was now not going to be able to see, because I couldn't read my own diary properly. I smiled and cackled a bit more, thanked the lady, went outside and debated whether or not to hang myself there and then, or get a drink first and then hang myself. I now had forty-eight hours (or myself) to kill in Aberdeen and almost no idea of how to kill them. I had also forgotten to pack any pyjamas.

*

I blame the guidebook copywriters. They took advantage of my credulity. They made it all sound so big and lively. Well, Aberdeen *is* the third largest city in Scotland and the key to Scotland's exploitation of North Sea oil. This is where support ships hang about, and where vast lumps of equipment are fabricated and repaired. It's not – apparently – as good as it was in the 1980s, when the place was a mass of brawling Norwegians and Texans, the American Club opened and property prices went through the ceiling.

Actually, it wasn't even that good in the 1980s. When the journo Robert Chesshyre got up there in the mid-'80s for his look-what-Thatcherism-is-doing-to-us-all conspectus of Britain, *The Return of a Native Reporter*, the boom had already fizzled out. 'By the time I got to Aberdeen,' he intones, 'the "oil capital" of Europe, the good times were over.' A bit later on he wonders if 'Aberdeen would then be another of our industrial museums like north of England smokestack towns and the Welsh valleys, a further landmark on the road to national bankruptcy'.

In fact (once I got there fifteen years on), I would have said the place has reverted to an earlier, simpler type – university town/regional centre/fishing – but for the heavy rig metalware penned up in yards and compounds on the north side of the city's harbour, plus outbreaks of specialist engineering companies (The Pipeline Center: US spelling) lining the drab roads which stretch down to Footdee at the mouth of the River Dee. But it is still a big place by UK standards, huge by Scottish standards, and at the time of writing, the North Sea oil business is experiencing a revival as the price of crude goes up and the ingenious engineers find new ways to extract oil reserves from previously inaccessible areas. Prosperity is on the up, it does have museums and restaurants and it is the famous Granite City on account of the fact that any building constructed before World War II will have been made out of suspiciously blatant granite chunks that look like breeze-blocks or compressed coke bricks in the morning light.

What's more, it's not Edinburgh. It is deeply Scottish. Aberdeen is rich and raw. Inverness is refreshing. Dundee is where *The Beano* comes from. These are real places, places which have to live with the day-to-day perplexities of modern Scotland; whereas Edinburgh is a rancid stew of lawyers, bankers, politicos, journalists, arty types, friends of the English, educationalists, soft bastards and priests, lost in a private world of intrigue and futile self-advancement.

Aberdeen, by way of contrast, owes nothing to anyone, being far too far north for the English to affect it greatly, except when they sacked it in 1644 (or rather, got General Montrose to sack it on behalf of Charles I) and then put General Monck there (on behalf of Oliver Cromwell) a bit later. Aberdeen is all about fishing and being the regional capital of north-east Scotland and having a toehold in the Highlands while facing out to the brutish North Sea and trading with Scandinavia and the Baltic.

On the other hand, it's not quite the 'Simply somewhere else' that the Aberdeen & Grampian Tourist Board word-paints. 'In sunshine, the granite's embedded mica chips act like millions of tiny mirrors . . . Who could have guessed that, amid the hard granite, the city would prove so conducive to rose growing . . . Aberdeen is a prosperous city . . . wears a cosmopolitan air . . . One of the finest Edwardian theatres in Scotland . . . Its elegant crown spire . . . The second-largest granite building in the world . . . Aberdeen once claimed the title as Scotland's largest seaside holiday resort . . . spectacularly upgraded . . .'

All this quality embellishment ormolu prose, alongside the usual album of carefully tinted and manhandled pro photos, got me to thinking that what with it being the third largest city and the centre of the North Sea oil industry and full of fish, Aberdeen was an undiscovered treat. Oh, for sure, the *British Journal of Psychiatry* had recently named it the worst place in Britain for SAD – Seasonal Affective Disorder – the depression that overtakes many people in the winter months on account of lack of daylight. Twenty per cent of its population was thought to suffer from SAD, allowing the tabloids gleefully to characterise Aberdeen as the 'UK's Saddest City' and all that. Move to Eastbourne or the Isle of Wight was the advice. But I knew that not all Aberdonians were dragging their possessions down to Ventnor or Pevensey Bay just so they could cheer up. Something was keeping them in Aberdeen. And I was going to be the clever swine who went all the way up and found it to be a Hibernian Boston or, failing that, a funky crossbreed of Manchester and Penzance.

What I actually found, once I'd got over the stupefying shock of learning that my principal reason for being there was no longer viable, was that Aberdeen has got its good moments (Union Street, the pretty little streets leading off to the north of Union Street, the roads to the west of Union Street) and quite a lot of bad or, at best, indifferent ones (the knuckle-head savagery of the road system around Guild Street, Bridge Street and Market Street, the air of penetrating dismalness around the harbour, the cold and grey, the dull Bridge of Don, the sad late-night Union Street vagrants). Which doesn't make it much worse than, say, Bristol, but does make it less of a draw than, say, Inverness, just up the road.

Actually, I was intuiting as much even before the curling crisis. Coming out of the station, I staggered around the harbour for a while and found a boozer (handy for Market Street) open at 7.30 a.m., already well briefed with early-morning alcoholics. I went to fix up my hotel and came back two hours later to find that the bar was still open, still full of pensive drunks. Beyond that stretched a hinterland of tenement buildings, shrunken offices with no inhabitants, broken shops and yet more boozers, these so small, black, ruined and wrecky that they looked like the kind of drink-holes you'd expect to see hastily cobbled together in the aftermath of a nuclear strike.

And then it was out to the warehouses and oil supply companies, with the wind roaring in off the North Sea and herring gulls skidding through the air or walking around self-importantly, picking at trash. It was now about ten o'clock. I'd heard the bad news about the tournament and was feeling painfully sorry for myself, debating whether or not to nerve up and see Aberdeen's award-winning Maritime Museum – *but if I did that, how was I going to fill the remaining day and a half?*

Then I walked into Footdee, and things started to brighten up. Literally, because the sun came out enough to let me undo a button on my coat. The wind was still howling, but the sky was as blue as a baby's romper, and there were strong shadows on the ground to confirm the strength of the daylight. And there was Footdee – pronounced *Fittie* – a weird little fishing village at the point where the Dee exits into the awful leaping sea.

Generally speaking, Footdee is overlooked by fuel containers and gas cylinders from the maritime refitting and repair depots next door. But if you look the other way, you can see the alternative to this quotidian world, the real Footdee, the place that was designed in the first half of the nineteenth century by the villagers themselves. It is sobering to stare at the most easterly row of cottages, the ones that face straight out to sea, and note that their sea frontages have no windows, doors nor any other kind of opening. What they have is a lower section of toughened stone wall, topped by a completely hermetic slate roof to keep the North Sea out. All the openings are on the lee side. They are more like cave

dwellings than houses. And the doors and windows themselves are so tiny and sparse, you wonder how much light
ever gets in and how much claustrophobia you must be able
to put up with to live there.

Further inshore from these unburstable little homes is a
kind of garden square, surrounded by insane sheds. Some are
well painted and obviously in use – weather-vanes shaped
like boats on the eaves, sections of wrought-iron decoration,
plastic tulips, numbers – while others are semi-derelict or
frankly past dereliction. Some are as black and tattered as if
they've been burnt down and then reassembled from the
remains. Some have got bent chimneys up which tramps must
send the smoke of their billy-can fires.

As I stared at these structures, an extremely short, almost
cubic man worked his way round the corner of the square,
leaning over against the gale, and headed off towards the
main road. Thanking God that I'd had the foresight to put on
some longjohns under my regulation suburbanite's jeans'n'-
jacket drag, I followed him. This took me up a short slope
and then, in the sudden blast of the north-westerly gale, on to
the sea wall that leads up to Fun Beach (a 'Fun, sport and
leisure menu for everyone').

Astonishing! My spirits soared like a cormorant on a cross-
current of air. There was sun, immense white clouds,
occasional blizzards when it all went black and three minutes
of snow whipped your face; and then the sun came out again.
People were marching along the esplanade as if this were perfectly normal. They were walking dogs and holding
conversations. It was as much as I could do not to be whisked
out towards Norway like an empty carrier bag. There were
purposeful boats out at sea, riding the whitecaps, as well as an
oversized infernal-looking piece of floating machinery about
a mile out: some kind of dredger or borer or scourer, plugging
away in the water.

So I experienced a complete manic-depressive reversal of mood. Instead of wrenching my hair and loathing myself and Aberdeen, I fell wildly in love with this two-mile bit of Scottish coastline, for no real reason other than that it was not bad and it was not where I'd just come from. Yes, there was a lot of trashy new building going on in the teeth of the blast, Lego-style fabrications set a road's width back from the strand with a cinema complex and a branch of the ubiquitous Harry Ramsden's, that guarantor of thickwit style. But just beyond the cement mixers and thuggish men in Kangol hats was a parade of jaded seaside cafés, all completely full of people tucking into snacks and late breakfasts.

I gave a yelp and darted into the most distant and cheesiest-looking caff. It was beautiful. Family parties sat crushed into leatherette banquettes. Elvis was singing 'The Wonder of You' on the radio. A superhumanly helpful man in an apron shoved tea and muffins at me before leaping to meet the needs of two geezers in Kangol hats at the table behind me.

'Gie's a pot o' tea and some mair toast,' they said. 'Aye, same again!'

Round the corner, out in the sun and snow, was a sand-papery golf course in the Scottish style. There was no way anyone could have played golf there unless they were happy to watch their golf balls either shoot out to sea like ground-to-air missiles or swerve off furiously a hundred miles inland, depending on which way the mad wind took them. It was good just to sit in the steamy blanket of the caff and laugh at golf's futility.

In fact it was so good that I hit on a way of staying in Aberdeen for two days without going entirely tonto: I'd leave Aberdeen and go somewhere else. No, not *leave* Aberdeen entirely. After all, I'd checked in at a hotel near the station which (it was keen to let me know) had been highly regarded by Margaret Thatcher, the Princesses Margaret and Anne, and where Ramsay MacDonald used to have breakfast. Also, there were still things to learn about Aberdeen as a whole. Wherever I went there were huge posters about the controversial Section 28 of the 1988 Local Government Act. The Aberdonians, being Scottish and thus members of the 'most repressed people in Europe', according to the *Independent on Sunday*, wanted the clause to be retained and to make the promotion of homosexuality in schools a punishable offence. There were pictures of Scottish grandmas and concerned Scottish dads and endless exhortations to Keep the Clause lest Scotland be overrun by an invasion of predatory sexual inverts.

Furthermore, as I was trying to cross Market Street – four lanes of killer traffic mashing your toes as you stand like a dummy on the edge of the pavement – I saw a large man in a Crombie overcoat and beret on the other side. He was shouting terrible, incoherent things above the roar of the cars and lorries. He waved his arms. He had a beard. I felt in my waters that the moment the lights changed and the walk/don't walk man turned to green, he would march straight across and punch me or throw me over his shoulder on to the concrete of Albert Quay.

But I didn't even have to wait that long. He simply marched out into the stream of traffic, laughing and bellowing. The cars screeched to a standstill as he sauntered across the central reservation. He looked so big and insane that no one dared so much as toot their horn. Three lanes gone and all of five feet away from me, he turned to blow a kiss at the nearest car (smoke still issuing from its shredded tyres). Then he faced me and shouted, '*Nae worries, bonny lad!*'

A long half-second passed before he idled off in the direction of the fish market. Still holding my breath, I scampered away in the opposite direction, wondering whether this was typical Aberdonian gutsiness or just a chance outbreak of dementia. I thought: I'll go back to that boozer full of early-morning pissheads later on. That'll be full of geezers bellowing *Nae worries, bonny lad.*

I also determined to do the fish market itself, first thing next day, catch the arcane fury of the auctions, the tang of the sea, the granitic self-reliance of the hardy fishermen. 'The earlier you go, the more impressive it is,' it said confidently in my guide. This is what happens when your mood swings uncontrollably from despair to elation. You find stupid and ill-considered ways to occupy your time. So, with all that waiting for me in the Granite City, I caught the bus to Peterhead, because Peterhead is even more of a fishing town than Aberdeen, and while sitting in the caff at Fun Beach I had this dazzling insight that Peterhead would either be like something on the Atlantic coast of France, or like something out of *Whisky Galore!*: quintessential heritage fishing community stuff.

I got on the bus, settled in my seat like a schoolboy on a trip, tried to look out of the windows, but found they were so covered in crap and silt from the wee roads of the Grampians that it was almost impossible to see anything through them. I'm pretty sure I spotted a field full of people playing shinty, the Scottish variant of hurling. There were hockey sticks threshing through the air and awful barks and yells like the soundtrack of the Culloden film distantly penetrating the glass. Then they were gone and I gave up trying to interpret the scenery going past. Instead I stared at the back of the driver's head and tried to suppress my excitement.

So this is Peterhead, the most easterly town in Scotland: a mob of incredibly fierce schoolkids eating chips in the town centre; warehouses with TUBE ICE and CRUSHED ICE and FLAKE ICE in vast signs on their sides; an enormous power station on the edge of town, as big as a city (Bolton, maybe) and draped in billowing steam clouds; kids spitting to pass the time; a proper hardcore trawlerman's chandlery, selling heavy plastic dungarees, lots of string, sweets and oil filters, renting out videos, not your conventional yacht-owner's sissified place full of deck polish and hull dusters; Scoobies Plaice chip shop; a virile old trawler in dry dock, massive-keeled and armour-plated; some yobs kicking a plastic chip tray to death; the largest white-fish port in Europe; electricity sockets on the quay carrying 32 amps for the trawlermen to plug their welding sets into; a Highlanders mobile recruitment van with no one much taking an interest in it; a whole fleet of breathtakingly tough fishing trawlers, roped and lashed together in the inner harbour, bigger ships further out; pink granite, although locally known as the Blue Toon; blizzards; hard, freezing; concrete, stone and tar; almost entirely unlike, say, Polperro; back on the bus, sleet-blasted, forgetting not to bother to try to look out of the mud windows.

I got back to Aberdeen. Now it was dark and still blizzarding. Still a full twenty-four hours to go, and then some more. What, I wondered, was all *that* about? What good, exactly, had a trip to Peterhead done me, other than to suggest that there were places on the north-east coast which one might want to holiday in even less than Aberdeen? Although this was a useful insight in itself. And I'd escaped a day of foot-slogging up and down the leafless streets of central Aberdeen, dodging traffic and peering in frank consternation and disbelief into bars.

But all the bug-eyed euphoria of the morning was gone. The place I thought Peterhead would turn out to be had in fact always been Footdee, just up the road, not an hour's bus-ride away.

Oh, but of course, I do a disservice to Union Street, the Union Terrace Gardens, the Music Hall, Thistle Street and Duthie

Park. They should have lifted me back up. In the gloaming, when the sky cleared, all of these are just fine, undemonstrative but mature in their charms. And without the usual thunderous graffiti and loser vandalisms of suburban London. But with the characteristic Scottish discretion (amounting to furtiveness) with regard to restaurant and pub exteriors: I'd look at a horrible, ruined doorway, the paintwork done in, the glazing defiled and cracked, sense the hogo of involuntary emissions coming off it, only for the thing to crack open and reveal a shimmering, brilliant interior full of chrome and halogen lights and young people laughing outrageously at one another's jokes. Or I might find that a disease-laden flight of stairs, crammed with old newspapers and splashed with puke, would turn out to have a fully air-conditioned curry house at the top, complete with smoked glass, surgical white tablecloths, suave staff ('Are you in town on business, sir?'), mirrors, halogen lights, enormous helpings.

But while Union Street is the centre of town, the rest isn't; and Union Street is so long and so wide and ideal for tunnelling gales down that I really didn't feel like walking along it for more than two or three minutes at a time to get to any of the other things. Which meant turning off, one way or another, only to find that if I turned off to the south, the ground would plunge away towards the harbour, leaving me freewheeling helplessly down to sea level. There I was faced with the prospect of killing myself to get back up to the city lights or staying put in a feeble, enervated way, down by the docks where everything is bleak and battered.

But: at least I could go back to the pub of derelicts. I wanted rough, *pur sang* Scotland? I wanted something urban and the opposite of Wester Ross? I wanted to escape the beguiling lies of Edinburgh? I was there, right then, somewhere in some heart of perceived Scottishness and light years from sitting around with a load of Anarchist Libertarians at the Edinburgh Festival, thinking how really rather fucking clever I was. It was like a terrific piece of offal after days of boneless chicken breast.

At nine in the evening, the boozer had the same – or equivalent to the same – complement of alcoholics as at nine in the morning. That is: two wrecky geezers on one side of the U-shaped bar nearest the door, one slouched figure in an anorak in the centre, a fourth guy wearing an orange reflective waterproof on the other side. A bag lady with a whimpering dog sat at one of the tables. Two ruined barmaids – one fair-haired, thin and battered; the other with dark hair and a face like the late Ernest Thesiger – wandered around shouting at the punters. Sometimes these barmaids would let themselves round to the customers' side of the bar and sit and drink and smoke before ambling back to the business of pulling pints of Tennent's. Decor? Second World War lino, vinyl banquettes with tears and fag burns, some amber ceiling lights and a bit of lager bunting. Red and brown and black the key colours, late Rembrandt. Meat Loaf played at the kind of volume that gets into your sinuses and the nerves in your teeth. And there was me, slumped in a vinyl booth, staring alternately at the drinkers and out of the window at dark Aberdeen.

Across the way I could see a red neon display on top of the Regent Centre by the harbour. It showed the temperature steadfastly dropping as the night dragged on. I was there for an elastic period of time, somewhere between fifteen minutes and seven hours. I had a newspaper with me, but was unable to concentrate on it. My gaze kept swivelling around the room and out through the glass as I waited for something to happen. I was sure it would. There was a pent-up belligerence in there – or at least, a kind of pent-up anarchy. Things could go any way. I could get glassed; one of the regulars could die on his stool; it was good odds that someone would puke.

As I stared out at the red display, something did indeed happen. A second bag lady came into view on the street outside. She pressed her face to the glass and smiled right through me. The guy in the orange reflective waterproof saw her, at once fell gracefully from his bar stool – his fall turning into a run as he hit the lino – skittled across the pub, past my knees and into the window-pane. He stuck his lips to the glass and transmitted a frenzied and graphic kiss to the bag lady who went on smiling distantly. The orange waterproof man then fell back off the glass with a sucking noise, stomped over my feet again and went back to his stool, cackling.

The second bag lady wandered in and joined the two drunks on the side of the bar nearest the door. Everyone knew everyone else except me. They shouted at each other across the battered wood vinyl and lino space which separated them. Time paused while Meat Loaf carried on bawling until a little geezer came in with a carrier bag containing a pair of trousers. He offered this to the orange waterproof guy who fell on these same trousers, crying, 'Excellent! *Excellent!*'

This was about the only word of his that I understood in the whole evening. I would have said that he suffered unusually from some kind of Attention Deficit Syndrome, a tricky five-year-old's reflectiveness, such were his galvanic leaps from his bar stool to go and kiss the window, or go for a piss, or nip out to transact a piece of business. These were accompanied by an equivalent rasping torrent of hectic language, machine-gun speech.

But then, it seemed that soon enough everyone was talking this way. Tough Scotsmen in run-down pubs seem – verbally, at least – vastly more speedy, more animated than their London equivalents. There's a Celtic frenzy about their speech which meant that I could penetrate none of it apart from the profanities which sprayed around the room like shrapnel. Even when Meat Loaf finally shut up and calm descended, I might as well have been in Warsaw or Shanghai for all the sense I could wring out of the dialogues I was so painstakingly trying to tune into.

Hence, a conversation between the orange coat guy and the guy with the trousers in a bag (who had immediately made himself comfy on a bar stool and accepted a pint of McEwan's off the Ernest Thesiger barmaid) would go like this:

'Illatoolafuckingaeusafuckindee.'

'Ahfuckofyafuckincunt.'

'Issnothafuckalltoodlefuckinwhoahsadoonshitfurcunt?'

'Aye.'

'Izno?Amahgiezahdeefurthafuckinduin.'

'Whozacunt.'

'Aye. Cunt.'

Now and again the boys would get into a tremendous belching contest, earning themselves a rap on the knuckles from one of the barmaids. This was better for me, because the barmaids had higher, clearer voices, and spoke a bit slower. When one of them said *fuck off* it sounded like *fuck off* rather than *fkoffyateedledintayeaaaaaaaaarrrrrpp*. Indeed, when the phone rang behind the bar and the fair-haired one answered it, I really got into the swing of her backchat with one of the near-the-door guys who tried to nab the phone while her back was turned.

'Piss off and leave it alone,' she snapped.

'Iwizawnlytryin—'

'Fuck off ya fuckin' liar.'

Or, talking about a pair of cord slacks she'd bought – this after trousers man had revealed his prize – 'Oh aye, they're very nice. I got them at the Heart Foundation. You know the one in Union Street?'

'Aye.'

They paused and nodded and drank, thinking about trousers.

The first bag lady's dog whimpered in the hiatus. The outside temperature hit freezing.

The trousers were good, if only because I managed to get a vague handle on what the boys were going on about once they'd uncovered some visual aids. It happened again, with a mobile phone. One of the near-the-door guys (by now fully loaded and only just in contact with his bar stool) was wrestling with a mobile.

The orange jacket maniac, naturally, sprang into life and started shouting a conversation about – I'm pretty sure – which mobile phone network to go with.

'Zitoarunj?' he queried.

'Noah,' said the guy with the phone. 'Swuntywan.'

'Wuntywan?'

'Wunty*you*.'

(Laughter.)

'Yacunt.'

(More laughter.)

'Snoarunjtheyn?'

The drunk on the bar stool with the mobile phone decided that, no, it wasn't on the Orange network. The maniac gave a serious, confirmatory nod, left the bar, exited the pub, weaving like a man ducking gunfire, and came back after three minutes with a paycard which he gave to the drunk.

'Oah,' the drunk said. 'Chirz. Chirzpal.'

The drunk then started screwing around with his phone, burbling into it, caressing it, muttering at it, as if talking familiarly to it would make it talk back to him. Then he slumped semi-conscious on the bar, drawing the dark ruined barmaid to him.

'No?' she asked.

He woke up and started pressing the buttons on the phone once more. Gargling noises, the sounds of the farmyard, came from his lips.

The orange jacket maniac shouted across the room: 'Zitwuntywan?'

'Ayefuckiniz.'

'Wuntywan?'

'Aye.'

'Ah. Fuck.'

My head was going round in circles. Maybe it was the Tennent's lager. Maybe it was the Vicoesque nature of the conversations. I unstuck myself from my banquette and tottered out into the dark and cold.

'Chirzpal,' said a barmaid as I returned my glass. I blessed her with a fuddled wave. Twenty minutes later, I found myself outside a chip shop. I was terribly hungry. There was something on the menu called a Mock Chop. I went in and asked what it was, exactly. The girl serving said, 'I don't really know.'

But I had it anyway. And I don't know what it is any more than she did.

I got up at half-past four the next morning to catch the return of the fishing fleet and the mad excitement of the catch being off-loaded from the trawlers. Yes, I thought as I prised my eyes open with fingers and thumbs, I can see it: the cigarette smoke in the lights, the clamour of the fish auction, the breath steaming in the dawn air, the catch hurled into refrigerated lorries and the 5.30 a.m. express train ready to hurry the produce down to London for all the rich folks' evening meals, standing sombre and oily in the shunting yard down by the water's edge.

Awful time of day, pitch black, cold, a light sleet. Fully longjohnned, I crept out of the hotel so highly regarded by Margaret Thatcher and made my way down towards Market Street. I hadn't been going more than a couple of minutes before I realised that there was no one else around. I mean, not another soul. Not even any traffic on the roads, no post vans or courier trucks or shift workers making their way home or off to work. That post-Anthrax stillness that you normally only find in rural French towns at any time of the week except Fridays.

It didn't take me long to work out that this was not right. There should have been fish operatives, cod professionals hurrying down to the market. There should have been lorries revving and grinding as they jostled into place in the parking compound. As it was, every time I coughed it sounded like a mortar going off in the stillness.

More long minutes went by, in which time I still clung to the hope of suddenly coming across a bunch of large unshaven middle-aged men done up in quilted anoraks and dragging fiercely on get-you-started morning cigs: men I'd already pictured as the sort of guys who'd turn up at fish auctions in Aberdeen. I really did – I could see all the way down the road and knew perfectly well that there was no one else there; and yet the small stupid voice of blind faith kept shrilling in my ear that at any moment the harbour would come to life and all my efforts would be justified.

Eventually, there was no further for me to go. I was right outside the big boring shed which is the Aberdeen fish market. A door had slid open about halfway along its side. Light poured out, but no people. I walked round past the barrier which forbad the public to go any further, as far as the actual quay against which the fishing boats tied up. And how many boats were there, lashed to the quay next to the fish market? One. One boat, frantically hurling its catch into the hands of a couple of guys with one lorry waiting in the park on the other side. I walked round to the other side again, where the door had been slid back. Then I walked round to the harbour once more. There was no auction, just tired men chucking stuff around in plastic containers. The slap of box on concrete; the rasp of crushed ice being flung from the hold. An occasional shout of instruction. The lorry started its engine, running its refrigeration unit to keep the fish quiet and cold.

So I walked down the length of Albert Quay in the freezing morning air to see if the fleet was somewhere else, coming in off the sea, perhaps, foregathering at the harbour entrance. I counted a further eighteen fishing boats tied up, silent and sleeping. The awesome oil support vessels lay on the far side of the harbour, their security lights blazing down on the inky water, their superstructures thick forests of electronics and gear-handling equipment. But the fishing fleet had evidently gone nowhere.

I made it to the end of the quay before turning back, trying at the same time to look to any pre-dawn passer-by as if I had important real business there, undercover police work or environmental protection issues. By now, one or two early risers had appeared and were letting themselves into the marine support companies and P&O back-up services which framed the harbours. A woman marched past me clutching a huge bouquet of roses. She gave me a nod, which I returned in a businesslike manner. Indeed, that little gesture almost made me feel as if I *had* business there, and wasn't a complete time-waster. It didn't last. Another ten minutes went by, in which the dawn finally announced itself, before I returned to the hotel, peeled off all the clothing I'd laboriously forced myself into at 4.35 and went back to bed, wondering exactly what horrible thing I'd done to Aberdeen in an earlier existence to make it want to piss me off so much this time around.

THIRTEEN

I was told this second-hand. It is allegedly a true story. It involves the colleague of a friend of mine. Colleague is called Dave.

Dave, who is Scottish, finds himself talking to a tramp outside King's Cross Station in London. The tramp asks for money in guttural Glaswegian. Dave walks on, tramp curses, Dave responds in kind. The tramp picks up Dave's Scottish tones. Moderates his language. Gradually a conversation begins.

'Oh, I'm from there too. Do you know so-and-so?'

'Know her? She's my cousin.'

'Really? And did you go to that little primary school?'

'Oh aye, where . . .' Etc.

A rapport develops.

'Sorry to swear at ye, son, but y'know how it is, people hear the accent and assume you're a drunk.'

'I know, I know . . .'

Finally, the tramp says, 'And which football team d'ye support?'

'Well,' says Dave, 'I'm not really a football fan, but me Da' brought me up to support Rangers.'

'Well,' says the tramp, 'then your Da' brought y'up to be a *cunt*.'

End of conversation.

FOURTEEN

It's the standard tourist's dilemma, but with a twist. When you go somewhere, you want it to be something you've plotted in advance. You have a preconception of what it ought to be before you get there; and then spend your time hunting down experiences which confirm the preconception. If (a) you're lucky, you are then fruitfully challenged by the unexpected while delighting in the anticipated. If (b) you're unlucky, you find nothing that matches your expectations but only experiences that depress or appal you. This is travel, today.

Scotland being part of the country I live in, but at the same time not part of it, has this characteristic to an advanced degree. It's not Cambodia, it's part of Britain. I should know it. I should have a clearer idea of what it is I think I'll find when I get up there than if it were, say, Cambodia, and tailor my aspirations accordingly. So when I get to Aberdeen and do nothing but work myself up into a low-key rage of frustration and thwartedness, whose fault is that?

*

Eight a.m. came round. I woke up again. It was like giving myself a whole other day in Aberdeen, on top of the two that were already quite enough. I was on the brink of *Groundhog Day*.

After a long period of sighing and head-shaking in my lugubrious bathroom, I got a grip and decided that if Scotland's third biggest city was killing me then perhaps I should give the fourth biggest a try. This is Dundee, a place whose reputation for parochial Scottish backwardness hangs around it like halitosis. This is where the scary DC Thomson turns out *The Beano* and *The Dandy*, as well as the *Sunday Post* and *Dundee Courier*.

If you look at the cartoon streets in which many of Desperate Dan's stories are played out in the bestselling *Dandy*, you'll see that they're a weird mix of between-the-wars semis, placid residential roads and Arizona. This psychotropic interfusion of two worlds only starts to make sense when you discover that it's the unchanging outer streets of modern Dundee which are providing half the background to Dan's japes. These are also the milieu for Oor Wullie, the cartoon scamp from Dundee's *Sunday Post*, who exists even now in fastidiously preserved late-1940s suburban Dundee hinterland, where the streets are clean and the language is ration-book icebound. *Nae chance*, say the characters, *that's soft!* Also *Mair chins than a Chinese phone book!* So far as it's possible to tell, there is no irony involved.

And then there's (*Wheesht*) the Three J's of Dundee – Jam, Jute and Journalism. The jam being that made by the Keiller preserves factory, the journalism being DC Thomson again and the jute no longer an issue since the whole jute industry fell over and died some forty years ago. To say nothing of the whaling industry, in which Dundee was another world leader until that, too, fell apart.

*

I got to Dundee. Straight off, CONFECTIONS AND SMOKING ACCESSORIES above a newsagent's.

SIT DOWN, a terrifyingly bold directive in enormous letters outside a caff.

CHEAPEST MASKS IN SCOTLAND over a joke shop.

SWEETIE SHOPPIE.

Well, you can see how hard it would be to keep your intolerances alive in the face of *that*. Already, I was starting to get a taste for Dundee, ten minutes off the train. Not only that, but the stands at the main bus station were actually called stances, in the fastidious Scottish colloquial style. Back in Aberdeen, they're just called platforms. But here in Dundee they were striving to maintain the difference.

Oh, and there was more – the nicely mildewed docks with a couple of old tubs floating around – one a decommissioned lightship, another the now-mastless frigate *Unicorn*, the oldest British-built warship still afloat. Both of these gave me a thrill – as did the whole placidly crusty atmosphere of the place, with gangs of workmen tinkering away on the quayside to build refurbished warehouse offices for design companies and software compositors. Seagulls stomped across the stones, scattered lengths of chain and warp amusingly interfered with my feet. And then the Tay Bridge, marching across the river: at over two miles long the longest bridge in the world when it opened in 1878, before collapsing in the middle in December 1879, seventy-five souls lost. 'For the stronger we our houses do build,' McGonagall wrote, 'the less chance we have of being killed.' They reused bits of the old bridge to construct the new one, the one that's still there. They salvaged the locomotive from the bottom of the Tay and reused that, too. It was known as 'The Diver' for the rest of its life.

Or there's the town centre – handsome grey stuff, nice size, sensibly pedestrianised, nice City Square, a thing called the

Howf (which many towns have, actually), a very slightly indifferent museum display built around the preserved (and contrastingly fine) research ship *Discovery* used by Captain Scott on one of his Antarctic expeditions, you don't need me to go on, only with the Tay steely and sombre on one side, some loose hills on the other, it was precisely what I'd hoped Aberdeen would be but wasn't.

Yes, I drew the line at buying a model of Desperate Dan in the Dennis the Menace Shop for £25, but other than that, Dundee was right on the money. People were walking around in that tut-tutting way that middle-aged Scots have, pressing their hands together and adjusting their necks in their shirt collars. The younger ones, reasonably enough, were stumbling around spitting and sparking up fags like youngsters do. But even they had a kind of sham propriety about them, imposed by the need to keep their clothes wrapped tight around them on account of the penetratingly damp air coming off the Tay.

And the streets up from the river – they had precisely that well-made, grey, ashlared solidity that Scottish cities need to have, without going to the brutal extremes of Aberdeen. I mean, the hills weren't nearly so bad, for a start. And everything was that bit cleaner. All along Crichton Street, Commercial Street, Reform Street, Marketgait and the Perth Road, Dundee sat in a kind of neat stodginess of its own devising.

In fact, it even makes Aberdeen bearable. In this context, Aberdeen becomes a failed Dundee, a bigger, rougher sibling, a Dundee that's let itself go by consorting with oil men, raw cash, fish, road schemes, vomit, unwashed windows. You can picture Dundee trying to get a bendy-kneed Aberdeen to pull itself together, *Yer Da's going tae ding ye*, trying to show it a better way, *Look, the Queen Victoria's given us a Royal Charter in 1892*, but no luck. Aberdeen goes its own way, the two siblings growing apart, Dundee hitching up its slacks in disapproval and ultimately nipping off to join the Freemasons or get the curtains fixed.

Dundee cake, I muttered appreciatively under my breath as I roamed around, trying to sound like Cary Grant in *Arsenic and Old Lace*.

I even find a kind of confirmation of all this as I bumble around Dundee's off-High Street streets. For no clear reason, I blunder on up the hill that leads through the university district, past Scottish cake shops of death and newsagents selling the *Dundee Courier* ('Raith Rovers Must Return to Winning Ways'), past enormously old ladies waiting at bus stops ('Not be long now, dear') until eventually I run out of energy by a quiet, dark-timbered boozer in the sombre Victorian residential area on the western side of town. I slip in through an oaken door and equip myself with a pint of heavy.

There are two well-turned-out old bags having a noisy Scottish conversation with a middle-aged guy who looks like a sales rep or roaming business operative – loud tie, shiny shoes, packet of Lambert & Butler shuttling anxiously between his fingers. And what are they discussing? They are discussing the provocative new £9 million Dundee contemporary arts building, just down the road, which looks like a cinema and indeed is a cinema, or rather, two cinemas, even though it used to be a car showroom.

One of the bags prods the table top with her finger.

'It's been up all this time, and they've not had a *single* Scottish picture in there.'

This is not true. The inaugural exhibition ran all the way from Andy Warhol (Czech) to Callum Innes (plainly Scottish). Thirty-four thousand people turned up to see it. Still. The rep purses his lip and nods.

'Really?'

'Half of Dundee,' pursues the other bag, 'is so disgusted with what they spent on it. And it was just for the university, for all the high-falutin' people in there.'

'Well, that's what they do, isn't it?'

'I've never set foot in there,' says the first bag, 'and I never will.'

Which is why she hasn't a clue what she's talking about. But then, truth is inevitably a hostage to rhetoric. What is important is the scarcely repressed xenophobia, blended with anti-intellectualism and a penetrating desire to watch the pennies. It is like a breath of the *Daily Mail* delivered in a crisp, Dundee cadence.

It also inspires the rep guy, after some fumbling with his rotten Lambert & Butlers, to weigh in against the Scottish educational system. As everyone knows, this has recently been made a laughing-stock at the hands of the Scottish Executive and their exam results screw-up, but this is not on my man's agenda. Instead, his plaint turns out to be the conventional south-east Englander's diatribe against the state system, shifted hundreds of miles north.

'I put my kids into private school,' he confesses, firing up a Lambert. 'It went totally against the grain. But I put them into the Dollar Academy because I'm so terrified about what's happening in the state schools.'

Dollar Academy? Clackmannanshire? A little out of the way for Dundee, I would have said. Maybe he is from Perth. Either way, this is hard to take. It's an article of faith down here that while the English tit around for decade after decade with their schools and universities and fail to make any appreciable difference, the Scots, with their baffling Highers and Standards and their four-year degree courses, have always managed to affect that *de haut en bas* look when the subject of English education comes up. Much as they do in matters of jurisprudence. Only now they too, it seems, suffer from the modern world when it comes to crap schooling. Oh, and in hygiene regulations, as well, as the rep guy swerves off-piste and starts in on a fresh topic.

'There's too much regulation! I was in a butcher's shop in Spain, and he was smoking a cigarette and serving behind the counter! And no one minded! He wouldn't have lasted five minutes over here. Why can't people be left to do what they want? Why can't you smoke a cigarette in a butcher's shop?'

He takes a heave at his gasper.

'Very true,' says a bag. 'Too many rules from Brussels.'

I'm back in the state I was in in the Edinburgh boozer with the sad barmaid and the Billy Crystal impersonator with the parcel of biology textbooks. I have an intense desire to interject something in the debate, outweighed by a greater desire not to look like an English bastard. In a perfect world, I would cry out, 'Now, look here, people. How come it says in my *Guide to the Scottish Parliament* that "Nowhere is the reliance of the whole devolution package on compromise, goodwill and reasonableness so apparent as in respect of relations with the EU"? How about the professed vision of the SNP that "We see in the future that Scotland will move on from devolution to full membership of the European Union"? Isn't it a cornerstone of Scotland's new view of itself that, unlike up-its-arse England, the nation will engage constructively with the EU, use Europe's resources and exploit the presence membership will give small Scotland in the big world? Or is this a difference between Dundee and the rest of Scotland? Or between this bit of Dundee and the rest of Dundee?'

I can feel the words trembling on my lips, but even as I wrestle with the problem, an uptight Dundee voice rattles through the smoky air.

'We should never have joined,' offers a bag.

'Well, I'm with you there,' says rep guy, smoothing the ale from his lip. 'Another pint, please. I've got the time.'

I sat on a bench in the City Square, wondering to what extent Dundee was the quintessential Scottish town. It had to be, in some ways: muted, stony, short of cosmopolitan flash, conservative to the point of reactionary, but at the same time pragmatic. For the first time in a long time, I found myself just sitting around not having to make an issue of anything much. *Relaxed* is a word you don't normally attach to anything in Scotland, but it was getting close here. *Nicely inert*, maybe, with all the stonework and the quiet provincial decencies. And I could even understand what people said. Oh, and dull, of course. Edinburgh is stupendous, but only Glasgow is allowed to be exciting. Like the boringness of the Scottish Parliament which confirms its democratic sense of purpose, the boringness of Dundee confirms its fundamental Scottishness. It could have been so much worse.

Then I wondered about possible titles for this book. *This Is Scotland: How Can You Tell?* strick me as clumsy, but appealingly direct. Or, *I Thought I Was in Scotland* – nice unresolved note of suspense in there. Or, with a nod to a cult group called the Orphans of Babylon, *Pinch Me, I Think I'm in Scotland*. Although somehow that lacked the punch of the original, *Pinch Me, I Think I'm in Kent. Sitting in a Succession of Scottish Pubs* was clear and factually accurate, as was *Trying to Keep Warm*. Not exactly pulse-racing, though.

Much later on, *Kilts, Curling and Crap* volunteered itself from the back row, the cheap seats of my mind, but even I could see that one wasn't going to work. And in answer to the question facing both Scotland *and* England – what *is* a country now, exactly? – it lacked, well, it lacked deliberativeness, I thought.

FIFTEEN

My, how you've changed! It seems like only yesterday (but was, in fact, nearly two centuries ago) that Scottish literature was defined by the proprieties of Walter Scott and Robert Louis Stevenson. This is stuff that your Grandma kept on the shelves: *Waverley*, *Guy Mannering*, *Kidnapped*, *The Bride of Lammermoor*, *The Master of Ballantrae*, *Weir of Hermiston*. Nothing wrong with all this, if you're in the mood for literature with that solid oak feel to it, literature with lots of drawers in it, plenty of handles, well-turned legs, perhaps some doors at the front, the whole thing stained and polished a solemn brown. The fact that *Kidnapped* and *Waverley* both heavily feature the '45 Rebellion, plus quantities of Highland scenery, wetness and terrible vegetation, just confirms one's tendency to shove Scott and Stevenson up at the far end of the bookshelf and leave them until another day.

Because, anyway, we jump across the void of Time, flying over the sleeping form of John Buchan, and arrive with an awful fright at New Scottish Writing. This has as much to do with Scott and Stevenson as the Marquis de Sade's *120 Days of Sodom* has with the *Mr Men* books. This is where we are at, now. Scottish writing has exploded across the scene like a big sweaty firework. From Alan Warner to Duncan McLean; from Booker-winner James Kelman to Christopher Brookmyre, who created a stir with his first novel *Quite Ugly One Morning* by kicking off chapter one with a corpse that had severed fingers stuffed up its nose and a huge turd on the mantelpiece. You've got your anthologies of New Scottish Writing such as *Acid Plaid* and *Children of Albion Rovers*. You've got this weird coinage which I've come across once or twice, to parcel them all up: 'The Scottish Beats', they've been called.

And at the head of them all, the Godfather of new urban Scottish fiction, is Irvine Welsh, who, with the collusion of actors Ewan McGregor and Robert Carlyle in the film version of *Trainspotting*, introduced us to a phantasmagoric new world of Scottish puke and heroin addiction. Everybody knows who Irvine Welsh is, even though they may not know how curiously reflective and tender some bits of *Trainspotting* can be. It is definitely a masterpiece of some kind.

What they think they know is more likely to be found coursing through his bestselling *Filth*. In this, one of the world's most disgusting and degenerate policemen shares centre-stage with a tapeworm, a mass of drugs, endless pornography and abuse of the self as well as third parties: 'I withdraw my cock from her miserable torn face, stuff it in my troosers, zip up and leave her to her tears . . . We go to the bog and give our arse, thighs and genitals a good clawing, then we cut up a line of coke . . . I want to punch his face and deck him and then stomp that smirking posh face into the ground under the heel of my boot and keep doing it until his skull explodes over the lino . . .' And so forth. This is a *tour de force*, no question, 'A snarling epic of a book' as the *Scotsman* put it. But God, what a pathology it suggests – and which, by association, attaches to the whole of the rest of urban Scotland.

Gone is the twinkling heroism of Scott's Waverley – 'His person promised firmness and agility, to which the ample folds of the tartan added an air of dignity' – to say nothing of John Buchan's brick-chinned xenophobe Richard Hannay – 'I may be sending you to your death, Hannay – Good God, what a damned task-mistress duty is!' In its place lies the full loathsome dystopia of modern urban life, peopled by junkies, craven idiots, psychopaths, rapists, human ruins, fucked-up coppers, parasitic worms, sadists. There's also a tendency to use the word *Tory* as a lazy shorthand for *incorrigible villainous arsehole*, the cancer in the body of Scottish society. I've nothing against this practice philosophically, mark you (and Iain Banks is apt to do it, too); it's just that once you've come across it once or twice, it does get a bit transparent. But, anyway, there you have it: the transformation of Scotland from an Edenic wilderness populated by bright-eyed action heroes to a full-scale urban catastrophe, the mass disintegration of a people, crushed by the violent exigencies of twenty-first-century living.

Except for a couple of things. First, the world of Scott and Stevenson is actually pretty torrid. Instead of the gentility of Queen Victoria's Highlands and towns, you get a good bit of bloody action, plus endless squabbling Scotsmen bitching at each other. Stevenson in particular likes to turn up the heat, either in the form of a character such as the furiously bad-tempered Alan Breck from *Kidnapped* ('If the day comes, David man, that I can find time and leisure for a bit of hunting, there grows not enough heather in all Scotland to hide him from my vengeance!') or in the moral fury of what's supposed to be his masterpiece, the unfinished *Weir of Hermiston* ('Then followed the brutal instant of extinction, and the paltry dangling of the remains like a broken jumping-jack'). This is hardly Jane Austen, or even Anthony Trollope.

The second thing, by way of contradistinction, is that even coarse modernity has a certain literary gilding to it. Return to Irvine Welsh and what do you find? A verbal jostling for space between the refined and the disgusting, only cranked up to maximum pitch for that full *épater les bourgeois* horror. 'I let the spunk drip on to my thighs,' explains the hero of *Filth*, DS Bruce Robertson. 'Its alkaline properties might do the rash good.' Renton from *Trainspotting* eloquently disparages some old bag on the bus: 'Get the fuck oan or fuck off and die ya foostie auld cunt. Ah almost choked in silent rage at her selfish pettiness and the bus driver's pathetic indulgence of the cunt.' Detective Sergeant Robertson again: 'These, however, pale into insignificance beside his greatest and most damaging conceit, namely that he's fuckin polis.'

This kind of stuff is eye-popping, rollercoaster language. It's gangster language, the sort of mind-your-manners stuff that Harry Flowers (the Ronnie Kray character in *Performance*) comes out with immediately before the extreme violence. It makes you deliciously, sordidly uneasy.

In fact, literary gilding may be a Scottish characteristic generally. I was in this pub (yes, I'm sorry, yet again in a pub, let's just say it was in the Dumfries and Galloway region) listening to a bunch of very large hairy men having a discussion at the bar. The four of them were all sporting full beer-guts plus half-mast jeans, shattered sweatshirts, cigs on the go, nicotined working men's fingers the size of bananas, vermilion faces. Big rough blokes enjoying a quiet jar and a swear about the follies of the world about them. Except that among the low-level persistent grunting and cussing, there were these verbal refinements that kept popping out. One guy, talking about some kind of building development that he'd been to see, scratched his Cinemascope gut and announced, 'It was like a wee village. I was fuckin' *enchanted* with it.' A bit later on, another one confessed to being 'fucking surprised. No, really, I was fair *taken aback*.' And later still, when there was a bit of good-natured joshing about whose glass was whose and whether someone was trying to nick a full glass that wasn't his own, 'Are you showing *burglarious intent*?'

Line this up against your average London pub interlocution ('Nuffink but a load a fackin' crap, innit?') and it sounds like Henry James. Here's another thing. You get something of that fastidiousness, those formulations, in Billy Connolly's act – *I've a mind to call a CONSTABLE* – he shouts when a proctologist disappears up his arse. Or, *I do enjoy the occasional libation*, as he once said in a Parkinson interview (in his pre-teetotal days) – which echoes the common genteel Glaswegian euphemism of '*refreshment*' for '*drink*'. Which is one reason why his act is so successful and so durable: this mixture of gross-out and refinement which allows him to offend without causing offence.

And what do we infer from it? That the Scottish ear has a healthy respect for the formalities of speech, only subverting them for effect? That this clever juggling of tonal register indicates a deep-rooted reverence for learning? That, like the Irish and Americans, the Scots can do English better than the English?

SIXTEEN

Then I went to Gretna, to see if I could spot the difference. The difference, I mean, between England and Scotland, right on the margin, the border at which one turns into the other. At what point, exactly, does this happen? Or does it happen gradually? Does Englishness elide into Scottishness in a sidling sort of way, like a pint of milk on the turn? Would it happen blatantly at Gretna, where all the Scottishness would appear (kilts, raised voices, rain)? Or would it happen at Gretna in strange indefinable ways (something in the light, sense of mystical partisanship, smell)?

I leapt resourcefully into a car and jinked down to the south side of the line, where the legendary M6 spears north, and waited for something to happen. Soon there was just me, some dogged maniacs towing caravans, the voice of Radio Cumbria in my ear like a conversation in another room. There were little vistas of northern England peeping out: dry-stone walls, green knolls, swollen lumps of rocky matter in the background, shreds of white cloud swirling overhead. Even the motorway was something more like a steroidal A-road, rising and twisting between the folds of the landscape. It wasn't the England I know, *my* England, but it was pretty good, all the same.

And then it was unexpectedly Scotland. I knew it was Scotland because the road went a bit odd and I plunged off the motorway towards a sign reading *First House In Scotland*. As the motorway swept away over my head towards Motherwell and Glasgow, so I veered left into Caledonia with all the fanfare of someone nipping on to a garage forecourt. And the First House? This turned out to be a Victorian crap-hole with a Saltire like a tramp's hanky dangling from a shoddy pole. The time was 1.25 p.m. I had done a coruscat-ing 150 miles and was steaming with car foetor as if I'd been stuck in the airing cupboard overnight wearing a four-day-old shirt and my gardening trousers. Somewhere around here I had hoped to experience the mystical transformation of England into Scotland. Somewhere at this point I had hoped to find a Truth. Instead I got an up-your-arse road intersection followed by a house looking like a big dog kennel.

Indeed, the transition from England to Scotland couldn't have been plainer. The only strange thing about it was that it turned expectation on its head. This was because the English side of the border was the bare, romantic, rugged one, while the Scottish side at once collapsed into acres of flat, semi-coastal stuff, nothing big or strong or Caledonian about it. It was just level boggy fields interrupted by low trees, bushes, damp weeds, some thick-witted cattle. It was a bathetic inver-sion. It was like going down to Canvey Island.

Oh, and then we had Gretna Green.

Which is what? Gretna/Gretna Green (the Green lies on the other side of the main road, under a different name from Gretna, but part of the same philosophical whole) has no fea-tures of its own at all. The only thing about it is that Gretna is where people go to get married in a hurry. Insofar as I understand it, you can get married under Scottish law at the age of sixteen without parental consent, provided you give due notice and are not mad or already married. This must be why people still cross the border to do it.

At least, I think this is right. It certainly used to be the case – Gretna's fame is founded on it – that you could get married here without parental consent when such consent was still required. 'We were within a few hours of eloping for Scotland,' as one of Jane Austen's characters admits in *Sense and Sensibility*. The whole process was so informal that all that was needed was a declaration before a witness, while the union was 'forged' by a blacksmith over his anvil. One such blacksmith is reputed to have performed over 5,000 ceremonies.

Nowadays the Registrar's Office sits in the main street of Gretna, which, to look at, could be in Suffolk or Lincolnshire. But no matter, because there is this big modern low building done in the contemporary/retro civic fashion, and its front aspect is covered in notices of forthcoming marriages. Thousands of them, stretching months ahead. This is the Registrar's Office. There's even a free-for-one-hour parking space immediately opposite, so you can pull up, rush in, jump the broomstick and flee again in wedlock, without any kind of car payment or the inconvenience of parking your car in the entirely free car park twenty yards round the corner.

I sat in my own motor, watching with detached interest as a young couple pulled up in a Fiesta immediately outside the Registrar's building. He was wearing a smart shirt and trousers plus tie and a floral buttonhole but no jacket. She (sitting in the passenger seat, a bit harder to inspect, her face tight with disapproval) was done up in a cream-coloured gown, her hair permed nice. He leapt out of the driver's seat, rushed up to the front of the building and scanned the notices fiercely. Then he leapt back in and the two of them had a brief, violent argument before he drove off at speed towards Dumfries.

What conclusions do we draw? A screwed-up elopement? Best Man and Maid of Honour on wrong day? Best Man at wrong Registrar's Office? There's something persistently half-baked about the main street of Gretna, anyway: its succession of little shops selling wedding cakes, hiring out old cars (a Lanchester) for the trip to the Gretna Green Blacksmith's for the photos, renting wedding dresses, tartan wear for the groom, photographers and pipers wandering in from the A75 and the dank Dumfriesshire countryside to bestow Scotch Mist on the happy union.

I bought a four-day-old newspaper in the sweetshop and stationer's – the *Dumfries & Galloway Standard*, billed as 'South of Scotland's bestselling newspaper' – marvelling yet again at the boringness of the provincial press and at my susceptibility to its appeal. Top story was about a Tibetan monk jailed for indecent assault. The road stretched dully away towards nameless fields and newbuild residential plots. The sun came out for a minute and a dog walked by. I had that nervous feeling of being a long way from anywhere even faintly interesting and with no real prospect of things improving. I couldn't go back to Edinburgh and I wasn't ready for Glasgow (which I was scrupulously deferring until the moment was spiritually *à point*). It was just me and Dumfries and Galloway. Maybe this was what had infected the angry couple in the Fiesta: the sense that even though they were in the right place, they were obviously in the wrong place, too.

So it turned into a frenzied road trip. Still fidgeting over the apparent absence of meaning at the point where England becomes Scotland (and thus deprived of a chance to draw some quick, rich, insightful, specious conclusions) I decided somewhere fairly deep down that I was going to have to compensate by covering as much ground as possible in the time I was fully wheeled up. When it comes to lack of quality, quantity makes a very plausible substitute. This is the motive force behind a lot of travel writing anyway, and I was in that kind of mood. So I emptied all the sweetie wrappers out of the ashtray, filled up the tank, adjusted my seat belt and floored the accelerator, rocketing off towards the squalor and thrills of Dumfries at thirty miles an hour and at an angle of forty-five degrees from due west.

I thought at first I might stay in Dumfries on account of its being surrounded by 'woods and beautiful gardens' and the fact that 'its history is as bloodstained as that of any border town', according to my book. Being on the border like this meant that the whole Dumfries and Galloway region was constantly threatened by attack of one kind or another from the English. There are fortifications all over the place. Oh, and Burns lived for four and a half years in Dumfries, before dying there. And there is something called the 'Guid Nychburris Festival' in summer, when they crown a festival queen and several citizens walk around the shopping area in Nathan and Berman costumes. The full lively provincial panoply, in other words. At least, this is the story you sell yourself.

The reality is that it's quite like, say, Worksop. You wish it all the luck in the world, with its nicely pompous redstone buildings, its traffic and its generally low-key air, but you don't want to look for a hotel because it is just too depressing. After forty minutes of dolefully wandering about amid run-down retail outlets and dank boozers, forcing myself to try and like Dumfries enough to spend money there, my mind was finally made up the other way when I saw two laughing yobs being led across the road, handcuffed to two correspondingly but inversely granite-faced coppers. I took it as a sign that Dumfries was just another of those rough provincial towns (Salford, Llanelli, yes, Worksop) and that there was no point in hanging around. So I unleashed the thunderous urgency of my Volkswagen down the A75 in the direction of Stranraer.

Warbling contemporary folk music flooded from my car radio, music like someone gargling with cherry brandy. It was a lady folk singer, performing in a programme of mixed light classical favourites and Celtic folk. This was, in fact, a senseless hour of musical miscegenation introduced by one of *those* local radio voices: chuckling, obtuse, full of strange mid-sentence searches for thought followed by misplaced emphases, tangled periphrasis and litotes that end up hanging in space . . . *So . . . where was I? . . . it's one of those afternoons when you're just in the mood for the not INCONSIDERABLE talents of a voice . . . well, I've got her here! It's Katriona MacLean . . . who's BEEN working, I gather, in the Orkneys of all places . . . So tell me . . . where was I?*

Once in a while I have to do radio interviews with these fabulously ill-prepared people, in order to plug a book, or because I've written something controversial in a newspaper about self-assembly sheds or losing your socks. I go to a self-op studio in BBC Broadcasting House in London and sit in a room with the size, shape and even the aroma of a toilet cubicle, wearing headphones while a distant voice says *We'll just get to the end of this Bee Gees number and then I'll introduce you. Is that all right, Chris? So that was the Bee Gees, there, and with me down the line I've got a man for whom the expression Never Say Die can only mean one thing in the not unfamiliar context of SOCK dispersal. It's Chris Jennings and he's written an article about . . . well, what have you written an article about?*

A furtive detour took me through Kircudbright and some standard roughcast hutches, until I found the centre of town. This turned out to be an artists' community. Many of the trad stone Scottish houses had been painted in blithe Mediterranean colours and offered B&B just as if we were in the West Country. There were shops selling free-range daubs and modellings and there was a restaurant called Artie's to rub the point home. There was even a bloke posing as an artist by standing on the edge of the pavement, wearing black jeans, a black leather drape jacket and a white collarless shirt and goatee. On top of all this excitement, there was also MacLellan's ruined castle, a sweet little harbour and a tiny yachties' marina. You have to demonstrate how in the know you are by pronouncing the name as *Kircoobrie*.

The whole thing was saved from its own extravagant pretensions, though, by the presence of a nice big centrally sited warehouse for builders' skips immediately opposite the dieselly Texaco garage. These chimed in with a stupidly hideous bridge over the River Dee and, in the distance, a looming hydro-electric plant like a Church of Divine Ugliness. Seven out of ten, in other words.

Obscurely braced by Kircudbright, but not so braced that I wanted to spend any money there, other than on a Twix, I also inspected the pretty ruined abbey at nearby Dundrennan. For the first – and so far, only – time in my life, I was mistaken for a member of the Armed Forces. The guy who fronts the Abbey's ticket kiosk and mows the lawn into a snooker table of obsessional neatness asked if I was up on holiday. I couldn't think what to say, except that I was *sort of* working.

'Oh,' he said, straightening to attention, 'are you from the firing range?'

The Ministry of Defence firing range is next door and has notices on its perimeter warning ramblers that if they pick up anything interesting-looking which they find lying around, it will invariably turn out to be a piece of live ordnance which will blow them into pieces of mince.

'Certainly not,' I shouted back at him, fingering the acci-
dental Army Officer haircut and my unintentional chunky
Off-Duty Army Officer Pullover which I had somehow
assumed before driving up. This must never happen to me
again.

Everywhere, it seemed, the scenery was bafflingly south-west-
peninsula in character; not just in Kircudbright. I could have
been driving around Devon. Not necessarily when I got into
Castle Douglas (black and white, good-looking but Scottishly
resistant to intense prettification, unlike, say, Salcombe or
Buckfast, or, for that matter, Kircudbright) but south-west in
the climate, spurred on by the warm Gulf Stream and the
sheltering Mull of Galloway, and the damp green vegetation
all around.

It could also have been Devon on account of the English
voices everywhere. The place was full of women who had
obviously come straight from Barnes, shovelling children
across the road into hearse-like waiting estate cars. The thin-
faced bloke behind the counter of the newsagent's into which
I slunk was also English. Essex, maybe? He started in on the
tendency of the law courts to take a stern line with farmers
who used a degree of force to defend their properties against
criminal intruders (there'd been a rash of such stories over
the preceding weeks). Now there were two more (dairy farmers from Perthshire) who felt that the law had dealt meanly
with them, and the newsagent agreed.

'It isn't right, is it?' he demanded. 'They're made to feel like
criminals when they're cross-examined. You know how you
protect your property?'

I shrugged with as much harmless amiability as I could
manage. The guy was evidently nuts.

'You got to do what I do. Get a couple of Dobermanns.'

Expensive, though, isn't it?

'Yeah. It is that.'

I was going to ask if he used to run contraband cigarettes in through Ramsgate in a Ford van but bit my lip and shuffled out, tossing my head and murmuring *Dobermanns* hilariously and ostentatiously under my breath.

There was even an Englishman in the Castle Douglas curry house, later that evening. I climbed up this doomy flight of steps on the High Street and at once found myself in a world that could have been in Ealing or Bristol. There was low lighting, moquette, framed pictures of Indian ladies sitting in gazebos and summer houses watching limpid streams pass by and lilies grow. I was so baffled by the discontinuity – from pleasantly austere Castle Douglas outside, the cool of the evening, the empty main street, the fishing-tackle shop selling cans of Frenzied Hemp Seed next door to an Evangelical Christian stop'n'shop promoting a video called *Simply the Best of John Pantry*, to the crepuscular comforts of your traditional British curry restaurant – that I asked the boss what, frankly, on earth he was doing in Dumfriesshire.

He revealed that he'd been travelling around a few years earlier and had stumbled upon Castle Douglas by accident. He quoted the curry house adage that 'the first person to start a curry house in a town will always make it big'. So here he was. Business tended to be a bit slow in winter, but picked up in summer. 'Summer keeps you going. Winter, you just get by.' At this point the other Englishman appeared to collect a takeaway for himself and the rest of his holidaying family.

The proprietor asked where I was from and I grandly declared myself to be from south-west London. He replied that he was 'from the north-east'. I thought he meant Epping or Ponders End, but no: 'Whitley Bay.'

So there I was, sitting in a curry house in Castle Douglas in Scotland, run by an Asian guy from Tyneside, and eating a hybrid cuisine developed in the East End of London by immigrants from what was once India and what is now Bangladesh. Having realised this, I spent a lot of time staring anxiously out of the window, trying to reassure myself that I was still somewhere where I thought I was and not somewhere else where the person who I thought I was wasn't.

No worries, though, when I finally left the building. Castle Douglas was apparently as bare and deserted as any market town in Brittany. Five pimply kids hung around the entrance to the Spar on account of its being the only place open on the main road apart from some boozers. A bit further down the road, some more kids hung about a bench on a patch of open grass. Some boys from the Spar shouted at the girls on the bench: 'Ya fuckin' slag.'

The girls shouted back, 'Ya fuckin' wanker, fuckin' suck it.'

Then the boys joined the girls, one of whom got highly agitated.

'Yer a liar,' she shouted at one of the boys. 'Ya got fuck all to do wi' me. Get the fuck out of ma sight.'

Which he did, shrugging, while an astonishingly stupid man drove up and down the road, over and over again, in an old white Vauxhall Nova with trip-hop pouring out of the windows. I lost count of the number of times he did it, but was conscious of each one, since my hotel bedroom window overlooked the main drag along which he was cruising. Equally, I could hear the bickering girls, squabbling long into the darkness, in the intervals between the moron's return trips past the Spar.

This, I guess, was the big difference between Castle Douglas and a Brittany market town: for a place with nothing going on in it, it was noisier than King's Cross. Actually, the place it most closely reminded me of was Southwold, in Suffolk. This too is a pleasant little tourist town (closer to the sea than Castle Douglas, and a bit more financially loaded) whose fresh streets, parents'-generation shops and classily self-denying architecture gets a mob of visitors every year. The big difference is that Southwold gets its mob from nearby London, with the result that the pubs and hotels have grown more and more fashion-conscious and the pavements are littered with smart-arses from N1 wearing look-at-me country gear and driving the property prices up into the ionosphere. The papers run regular pieces in which the locals bitch about the loss of Southwold's quietly retro identity.

What would Castle Douglas make of that kind of popularity? It sounded as if it was having a brush with it, but at three and a half times the distance from the M25 that Southwold is, you could see that the weekend trade wasn't going to come from Highgate or Kensington. Was this good or bad news? Also, the weekend trade from London tends not to drive backwards and forwards and up and down the main drag of Southwold in a shagged Vauxhall playing house grooves to the Spar and keeping people like me awake. And I had to get some sleep because tomorrow I was driving, driving like a madman, west to Stranraer and then sharp right along the coast, as far as my capacity for sweets, instant coffee and local radio would take me.

Woke up later than I meant to, in a panic, tore through breakfast like a lorry-driver about to miss a ferry, jumped in my car and left Castle Douglas in a drifting blue haze of tyre smoke.

Before I knew it I was thrashing through scenery that was another Anglo-Scottish co-production, entirely English south-west peninsula in style but co-opted for this odd part of south-western Scotland. Friesian cows were grazing on the wet grass which grew by inlets. The hills were blue and I experienced the desire to come back for a holiday. This is always a misleading and dangerous thought, as almost any-where in the UK is not where you should go for a holiday. You spot somewhere, stash it away in the garage of your mind, dig it out much later and go and spend a week there and wonder how a place could either have changed so much in two years or have been so catastrophically misleading in the first place. Nicer than Cornwall and Devon, nevertheless, because not plastered with cream teas and gift rubbish; still touched with some of that benign austerity you get in the Norfolk/Suffolk coastal diaspora.

And then with a sudden lurch I was in Stranraer, which turned out to be a bit like Peterhead, north of Aberdeen, only much prettier, more geared for tourists, with no fishing fleet, but with a park and a view across the waters vaguely in the direction of the Mull of Kintyre. There was far more lush green vegetation growing in the humid microclimate – rho-dodendrons, palms – plus, as well as the natural roughcast/schemie utility buildings, some standard-stock British seaside late Victorian architecture. This looks like your great-grandmother's dining-room furniture, fiercely enlarged and pushed out into the street, and at Stranraer is built in the same bibulous red stone as the buildings in Dumfries.

On reflection, it resembled Peterhead only inasmuch as it was Scottish and by the sea. The difference between the east coast and the west is like the difference between a piece of hard tack and a scone. For God's sake (I heard myself mut-tering under my breath), people were even peeling off their clothes and walking around with their skin tentatively exposed to the air. I did as much myself, but only in the con-fines of my motor car. On the other hand, terrible ferries steam off to Northern Ireland from here: a place even more anxiety-making than Glasgow, a place the thought of which made my foot tap the accelerator just to get away from the possibility of meeting a chance Orangeman.

Only what was next up the coast as I arrowed north? A place called Cairnryan – a little settlement of almost no houses or cars or, for that matter, people. But it was dwarfed by a ferry terminal the size of a couple of DIY warehouses, with on the one hand a huge smouldering P&O ferry pouring smoke from its funnel, and on the other, one of those high-speed Supercats lounging in the waters of Loch Ryan like a special effect from *Stingray*. There was even a lighthouse – the whole thing a tableau of movement and drama dropped in an odd corner of north Britain and pointed towards Ireland. At the same time, there was a busyness around the place, which got more pronounced the further north I got – a visual interest which felt, candidly, Mediterranean. Those islands in the near-distance; those sleeping passages of water; those vistas closed off by wooded rocks; the boats plying between them all. You don't get that around the coast of England, where the shore meets the sea and the sea then stretches grey or snot-green non-stop out to the horizon a couple of miles away. This complexity was odd and nicely disturbing. Only the arrival of Ballantrae, as in R. L. Stevenson's novel, brings you back to the real world. Stevenson in fact set his book a bit further south, using the name alone. But there it is: a stone bridge and a roughcast hotel and the reminder that Scotland is not, as it turns out, southern Turkey or Nice. *Haste Ye Back* it says on a roadsign as you depart Ballantrae, accompanying the entreaty with a shattering smell of seaweed, powerful as eight-month-old trainers.

And then, just past that – oh, damn, I missed it: somewhere down there on this coastline is something called Sawney Bean's Cave. Almost impossible to get to, it's where a cannibal called Sawney Bean lived – in a cave – with a large inbred family, kidnapping wealthy passers-by, eating them and thieving their gold. According to some accounts, the Bean family even went as far as pickling the limbs of some of their victims to give them something to see them through lean patches. This was too good to miss, but of course the condition of driving around in a car means that you miss almost everything.

And then I found I couldn't stop for anything at all, caves full of cannibal Scotsmen notwithstanding. Idly wondering if all this looked nicer than Wales or about the same, I shot off towards Ayr, a big dump on the horizon. Girvan was a pretty little harbour to the south of Ayr. Ayr was a ringroad with a racecourse and Prestwick Airport. Irvine was a council estate, could have been anywhere but for the absence of trees. There were trees – palm trees, even – at Fairlie, which looked a bit like Ryde on the Isle of Wight. There was a place called Largs followed by the beautiful Cloch lighthouse, built in 1797, which devolved into the genial Victorian holiday resort of Gourock. Gourock was plainly to Glasgow as Blackpool to Manchester, only nicer. It still has smelly nineteenth-century hotels ranked up along the streets, an open-air swimming pool for anyone whose sense of cold has been surgically removed, and there were a couple of blokes in overalls repainting the crazy-golf course. This seedy British coastal charm, plus the bustle of the Caledonian MacBrayne ferry operations, almost made me stop and stay. I know that I made a mental note to buy myself a cup of tea and an ice-cream as soon as I brought the car to a halt. Not that I ever did bring the car to a halt. Following a brief mental struggle over whether or not to do Glasgow there and then (I decided I wasn't ready for it just at the moment: all that culture, the Glasgow smile, the ill-health, the grandeur; not quite), I let motion take over, banked left over Erskine Bridge (opened 1971) and made for Dunbarton and the verdant hills.

I was burping away at the wheel with a noise like a circus lion, I might point out, as I'd allowed myself the scant refreshment of a bottle of Irn-Bru a few minutes earlier. Irn-Bru is one of those vicious regional soft drinks (like Vimto) which (unlike Vimto) has made inroads into the southern consciousness by means of a gritty ad campaign involving doctored archive photos and bus-shelter humour, as well as offering Irn-Bru in chewable string form, very appealing to children. The actual drink, I now know, is like regular orange juice with something slightly kinky added – urine, maybe? It is also so supercharged with CO_2 that every mouthful is like a fire extinguisher going off in your head. The upshot was that for half an hour after I finished my bottle, I burped long, profligate, gargling burps, burps like the rattle of small-arms fire, burps which exploded in the confines of my car like landmines.

Thus I *braaaapped* my way up Loch Lomond, conscious of the fact that, unlike in the Highlands, there were signs of life and activity here. Until, that is, Loch Lomond started to look more like the Highlands at its northern end. At this point (quite consistently) economic progress started to dwindle and grow distant, while vital (and mercifully distant) Glasgow started to look more appealing. Did I stop? Did I (still burping away like a ruptured beer keg) say *Oh well fuck it, enough's enough*? No. I barged on.

Past Tarbet I drove, spotting two bent-backed hikers staggering up the face of a rock on the way. Less like Wales or the West Country, now, and more, oh, more like the Picos de Europa in northern Spain, only much less high, of course. And even rainier. I left the Rest And Be Thankful behind without even noticing it, let alone resting or being thankful, and swept magisterially on like the outrider for an invading army, towards Inverary. I paused here because Inverary is pretty to the point of being annoyingly so, and sheer prettiness (that most English of characteristics) is something you don't often get in Scotland. Oh, and because I remembered having passed through once before, years ago, when taking a break at the late Sir Fitzroy MacLean's hotel on the other side of Loch Fyne, in Strachur.

Sir Fitzroy's place was one of those wholly undemonstrative country hotels that looks like a well-to-do schemie project from the outside (low, whitewashed, pitched roof, hidden in trees) and turns out, in the Scottish manner, to offer the height of creature comforts and world-beating food. Very old retainers would sometimes emerge from hidden compartments in the wainscotting and sturdily heave bricks of peat on to the fire. They gave you a spoon made of horn to eat your porridge with. It even offered the late Sir Fitzroy, before he was late, I mean. He came stumping out of a side door one evening, dressed in fearsome plaid trews and frowning incredibly fiercely at his jabbering paying guests before disappearing into the kitchens. I only saw him for a few seconds, but even in that flash of time, you could tell that he was exactly the kind of man to journey illicitly into the heart of pre-war Stalinist Russia and then to liberate Yugoslavia from the Germans while also helping to found the SAS, before writing a series of bestselling memoirs, including *Eastern Approaches* and *Back from Bokhara*. There was even a piece of paper in the snug bar declaring the undying bond between the SAS and Sir Fitzroy, *signed in whisky and blood*.

Inverary, on the other hand, has all the formal restraint and gentility of a model town created in the eighteenth century by an enlightened laird. Which it was, in 1743, by the 3rd Duke of Argyll. Discreet black-and-white paint schemes abut tough but tasteful raw stone cottages (one of them with a Janice Unisex Hairdresser sign provocatively hanging outside). The fact that such a tiny place boasts two petrol stations indicates the levels of tourism the current Duke enjoys nowadays. A three-masted ship sat tied up in the baby harbour, its pennants fluttering. People marched purposefully from gift shop to gift shop, bickering over fudge and postcards.

The only blot on this scene comes when you try to walk around the lovely loch itself. The tumbling wooded hillsides look okay from sea level, but even as I drove around the fringes of the loch, I was reminded of the time my wife and I (when staying at the late Sir Fitzroy's) tried to go for a walk through the woods. Then, as now, all that you got was thick, damp afforestation, completely devoid of views. The higher we climbed, the worse it got. We ended up exhausted and still unable to see anything. The only time this situation changed was and still is when the tree-fellers have been round to slaughter some woodland. The gap they leave behind is your only chance of gazing down from on high at the limpid loch waters, across a shattered grey moonscape of devastation, naked tree trunks and branches lying heaped at all angles as if a comet's crashed there, or a crippled army helicopter. It is dismal and depressing, made worse by the fact that, wrapped up in your woollens and waterproofs you feel simultaneously cold and sweaty, like wearing a wetsuit while dipping in the Solent. It is one of those cheats you come across in life, one of those shills that nature tricks you into. The framing of mountains, water and wood looks so intelligible at a distance, so full of promise, that it's impossible to believe that when you get up close to it it won't unlock itself to you, conveniently sharing its more intimate loveliness with any passing stranger.

No matter. I was off before I had a chance to get too morose, just as the rain and mist started another assault on the human spirit. One or two bleak families were trudging along the A85 towards Killin with the traffic, some of which was me, roaring past them at 65 m.p.h. Being British (I could make out the odd yell from some of the younger kids as I courteously drove by at a mere 30 m.p.h.) they wore stupidly unquestioning holiday grins on their faces. Near Killin itself – cute, touristy – four foreigners toiled across a little bridge, conversely looking extremely unhappy. I could tell they were foreigners by their fractionally more attention-grabbing clothing and by the way one of the women in their party wiped her nose on a tissue, her face betraying a disillusionment, a resentment against the falling drizzle that no one from the British Isles would have bothered to express.

I, on the other hand, was secretly twitching with startled anticipation as Killin approached. Somewhere along here was the boozer where my mate Phil and I had blagged a bottle of whisky at one in the morning. It had suddenly dawned on me that I was now quite far north, starting to reach the southern approaches to the Highlands, unintentionally retracing my steps. Perhaps this was buried beneath the decision to bank left over the Erskine Bridge: the human compulsion to return to one's past, to make sense of it.

But then, twenty years had intervened between then and now. After a couple of minutes I realised that every boozer I passed could have been the historic one. I kept unexpectedly slowing down and speeding up on this damp narrow road, causing fear and rage in the cars behind me. I shot past a roadsign which said THANK YOU and nothing else, and gave up the struggle. And then I reached Taymouth Castle, and it all changed again.

SEVENTEEN

Taymouth Castle is the spookiest place I have ever been to. The building which now goes by that name was completed in around 1842, when the man who had commissioned the castle, Lord Breadalbane, ordered a vast new cube-shaped wing to be added in honour of a visit by Queen Victoria. The rest of the edifice is more or less early nineteenth-century, vast, grey granite, standing on the leftovers of the sixteenth-century Balloch Castle, built by one of Breadalbane's forebears.

It is one of the biggest castles in the country, a central section of four storeys with round towers at the corners and a massive inner square tower rising above the line of the main roof. To the right, as you face the building, is a long, low, castellated wing for the serfs. To the left is the marginally more Italianate guest HQ for Her Majesty, with a flight of wrought-iron steps leading up to the *piano nobile*. The whole structure sits in lush green hills with a golf course sprawling at its feet and the River Tay a little way away. According to the guides, it has one of the most opulent nineteenth-century interiors of any building in Scotland, and, indeed, in the United Kingdom. Its carvings, its wall decorations, its furnishings, all supposedly display – or displayed – the highest quality and the greatest extravagance. When Victoria wrote up her trip there in her diary, she was pleased to note that 'the firing of the guns, the cheering of the great crowd, the picturesqueness of the dresses, the beauty of the surrounding country with its rich background of wooded hills, altogether formed one of the finest scenes imaginable. It seemed as if a great chieftain in old and feudal times was receiving his sovereign.'

The real clincher, though, is that for the last few decades, this extraordinary, charismatic structure has been left semi-derelict because no one knows what the hell to do with it. Early in the last century, the Breadalbane estate was broken up, and the castle was taken on by the Taymouth Castle Hotel Company Ltd, who also turned the deer park into a golf course. Requisitioned during the Second World War, it was then used as a convalescent home, subsequently becoming a headquarters for Civil Defence Training in Scotland, and finally, briefly, a school for the children of American servicemen.

Which was more or less how Phil and I found it all those years ago, not long after the servicemen's kids must have left. I can't recall if this was before or after the whisky crisis, but I do remember driving up there, with him muttering, 'You have to see this place. It's just *unreal*.' He was right. When we reached it, the first thing we saw was a line of pink hairdryers in one of the prison-like upstairs windows, with a wig stand at one end. In another doom-laden stone corner were the fading traces of some brightly coloured curtains. It was so quiet you could hear our bowels whining. Moving away from the grey bulk of the castle, we found ourselves in some Nissen hut outbuildings. In one of these was a steel locker with the legend DO NOT DISTURB THE DEAD MAN INSIDE scrawled on it in white paint. And on one corner of the granite walls of the castle itself, PLEASE SAVE US, scratched at child height.

We hurried away from the outbuildings, making noisy excuses, and went back to the main building. Positively shouting at each other now with fright, we glimpsed through some of the larger windows a carpeted inner area, rich with turned and carved woodwork, finials and cusps everywhere, beautiful linenfold patterns on the panellings, a metal lantern hanging in the gloom. A faded handwritten notice just inside the entrance hall read THE CASTLE IS <u>NOT</u> OPEN TO THE PUBLIC. An even older notice from the Ministry of Works advised that the Ministry did not accept liability for loss of, or from, or damage to, vehicles.

Despite the golfers just a few hundred yards away, the sense of dread, of brooding abandon, was overpowering. Whenever a stray reflection or passing shadow created a shape in one of the windows, Phil and I jumped inches off the ground. When the wind creaked in the outbuildings, we fancied we heard the distressed cries of spotty American kids, marooned at the outer edge of the universe in a freezing Gothic Scots castle. When we accidentally wandered past the locker with DO NOT DISTURB THE DEAD MAN INSIDE once again, we legged it back to Phil's disgusting Austin Allegro like a couple of Olympic trackmen.

Had it changed much since then? Hardly a jot, except, if anything, to get weirder still. Sadly, someone had closed the shutters over the big windows so that I couldn't peer into the deathly hall. But then it did give me a better chance to admire the shutters' linenfold carving, the quatrefoils sprinkled about, the Gothic floral motifs. The Ministry of Works sign was still there, though, confirming the fact that I hadn't dreamt any of this. And there were still ragged curtains in the windows to add to the spectral drear. THE DEAD MAN INSIDE was gone, and a burglar alarm had been stuck to an outer wall: somebody must have scraped together enough bottle to vandalise or pillage the place. I forced myself to make a complete exterior tour of the buildings, passing a glass-fronted cupboard in the domestics' wing which must have held estate keys, and in front of which lay a sheet of paper with the words *Taxable Pay Table* printed on its head.

Round the back I found the old stables – which I'd never dared approach twenty years earlier – and discovered inside that (a) they still bore the painted decorative cornicework from the last century but one; and (b) that the golf club used them as garages for their electric buggies. Some wrecked bits of contemporary catering equipment lay in the courtyard outside – presumably the debris from some perverse attempt to turn part of Taymouth Castle into a Gothic greet'n'eat leisure paradise, a place for William Burroughs or the Munsters to relax in. The clock over the stableyard stood at 11.35, rusted into stillness.

Coming round to the front again, I realised how immense the chapel was in relation to the rest of the building (towering stained-glass windows casting purple shadows) and that Queen Victoria's cubic wing was covered in rendering, rather than the more wholly baronial granite of the main structure. And then I had to restrain myself from sprinting off into the distance yet again, trying to escape the fear.

But why is it so scary? Partly because it's so huge and so Gothic and so untenanted – it couldn't look more like a monster insane asylum for the hereditary peerage if it tried. Partly because, unlike most other heritage buildings in limbo in the UK, there's no fencing around it, no guard-dog perimeter. You can walk right up to it and squint inside, an activity affording you every opportunity to frighten the crap out of yourself when you catch sight of your own reflection staring back out, like that of some derelict architectural historian who crawled in there to die in 1988 and whose ghost you've now just awoken.

Partly it's because the nightmare sits in this placid golfers' glen, with trees and clipped putting greens all around it. The quiet, banal world of amateur golf goes on in the awful castle's shade. And the discrepancy between the two somehow points up Taymouth's horror more than if the building were in a more appropriate location, viz., beneath a stormy crag; at the end of a drowned village; on an island destroyed by anthrax.

And, of course, its uselessness drives the awfulness home. It compels you to look on it and ask, *What the hell could they do with it?* So ghastly and massive, it forces you to interrogate all the possibilities (hotel, conference centre, Scottish Executive regional centre, old people's home, themed shopping mall, film set, children's play area, start-up tech company multiplex, brothel, morgue). And in so doing, it forces you to think longer and harder about its characteristics than you would otherwise want to. It is a riddle, drawing you by hypnotic attraction in its dark, troubled world. It is, in fact, a sight you don't see every day and I recommend it to anyone of a *grand guignol* temperament.

What's more, the effect lingers even as you leave the castle behind. At the entrance to the golf course/castle nexus, there is a sign which reads BEWARE THESE GATES ARE LOCKED OVERNIGHT. If it had also said PEOPLE AROUND HERE DISAPPEAR FOR NO OBVIOUS REASON, I would merely have nodded and taken it at its word. The stone gateway at the entrance to the estate drive is pure Edgar Allan Poe, with three pencil-sharp Gothic spires (two of which are surmounted by spiked Maltese crosses) and a pair of turreted gates on either side.

Even Aberfeldy, the next medium-sized settlement along the way, has a vagrant cloud of spookiness hanging over it, cast by Taymouth. Its High Victorian stonework, the Gothic detailing on the wooden eaves along the main road, the Palace

Hotel like a dwarfish Caledonian, all conspire to lower the mood. It was only the sight of the Aberfeldy whisky distillery (founded by John Dewar & Sons of Perth in the nineteenth century) which got me back on track – and the prospect of getting away from the Highlands again.

But the symbolism, though: the symbolism was momentous. What I haven't let on, up to now, is that shortly before inspecting the corpse of Taymouth Castle, I went in as a paying punter to Inverary Castle, home of the Duke and Duchess of Argyll, just down the road. And the mixture of concordances and dissimilarities between the two castles can, without undue struggle, be read as a neat embodiment of the whole Scottish condition. Because while Taymouth lies brooding and mouldering at the end of Loch Tay, Inverary Castle is a hive of purposeful heritage-cash generation at the end of neighbouring Loch Fyne.

Not as large as Taymouth, but bearing a strong resemblance to it (Taymouth actually took Inverary as the model for its four-square central section), Inverary Castle (begun in 1746) has a sort of romantic, greenish, fairy-tale Scottish fastness. It has Disneyland spires on its four corner turrets and a king-size wrought-iron and glass porch from the Victorian era over the front door which makes the building look like a hotel and which, for some reason, does not feature in any of the pictures in the guidebook.

Fork out a princely £4.50 entrance fee and you will find that the interior is like a hotel, too. It is coated in bland, anti-septic apricot paint and has just enough trinkets and classy eighteenth-century interiors (Rob Roy's sporran, gilded ceiling in the drawing room by Dupasquier) to look like a stately home, while not quite enough of a thorough-going ruinous atmosphere to feel like one. There's too much that's fresh and impersonal about it. The unbaronial newness and relative tidiness of everything aren't helped by the fact that you can glimpse the lovely private gardens for the family, with the view down the loch, but can't enter them. Instead you get shunted off on a woodland walk miles away from the Argyll seat, so as not to bother anyone titled. And you can join the Clan Campbell just by signing a bit of paper and handing over some cash; like joining the AA.

This last affected me especially, because I am, after all, a member of the Clan Campbell myself. I am Scottish, you see. As I said to the lady in Kinloch Anderson, if I try hard enough, like any complete and utter Londoner, I can roust a bit of Scots blood. In my case, it's in the form of my great-grandmother, who was really born Jeannie Campbell, had red hair by all accounts, and certainly possessed a brooch in the colours of the Campbell tartan – now an heirloom of great distinction.

Do I worry about the fact that the Campbells were the villains at the Glencoe Massacre? Only a bit. Am I embarrassed by the fact that one of *the* great post-war society scandals involved the 11th Duke of Argyll and that notorious slapper, his wife, Margaret, Duchess of Argyll (their divorce in 1963 was the longest and costliest in British divorce history, and peaked with the revelation of a series of private pictures of the Duchess giving a blowjob to an unidentified male friend, known only as *the headless man*, no picture of her in the guide book)? Yes, of course.

Still. The past is the past, the Campbells were always the richest and most powerful of all the clans, and judging from the appearance of the present Duke (whom I saw on French TV not long ago, talking slow, drawling, aristocratic, but very good French to the interviewer) things could be worse. He is the Hereditary Master of the Queen's Household and gets woken up in the mornings by a bagpiper. And all I have to do to become a full participant in the world of the Campbells is complete an application leaflet (most of which is a Credit Card Payment chit or Banker's Order Form) and post it with payment details (£5 at the time of writing) to the Secretary of the Clan Campbell Society. I don't have to formally avow any particular relationship with the clan to get in. I don't even have to have an exact familial association with the name Campbell, as the application form provides a list of associated septs, so that if your surname (or that of your great-grandma) is MacPhun, Denune, Cattell, Hastings, Ochiltree or MacGubbin, you can still squeak in under the wire.

In return for this, you – I – get free admission to Inverary Castle, plus a copy of the *Clan Campbell Journal* (a compilation of articles and news of special interest to Campbells). And that seems to be it. No harm in visiting the castle once or twice a week for free, I guess, if you live in the area. Although the Clan Campbell Room inside is only slightly less disappointing than a lilo with a puncture, containing as it does not much more than a large map detailing the clan's dirty doings over the centuries plus examples of a couple of newsmags available to Canadians. And some drums. *Ne Obliviscaris* is the clan motto, 'do not forget', or rather, 'lest you forget', accompanied by a boar's head, burping. Perhaps I could get it on a tie or something.

And all this is no more than a few miles down the road from the ruined grandeur of Taymouth. Now, if you were to put the two estates side by side, you wouldn't have to be Chekhov to see them as parallel statements about Scotland's approach to changing times.

Which Scotland is it to be in the new century? Is it to share in the thought-through blatancy of the Duke of Argyll's clean touristical experience, heritage as a way of coining in investment for the future? Or is it to be several long decades of helpless decline and the dismembering of the Breadalbane estate (at one time covering well over

400,000 acres), resulting in a stupendous, ghastly monument to indecision, surrounded by golfers?

This is, in effect, the question posed by a study recently produced by St Andrews University. Called *Scenarios for Scotland*, this work postulated two options open to the nation. One was deemed a High Road for the newly independent Scotland: this envisaged, among other things, Scotland being the second wealthiest nation in Europe by 2015, enjoying the finest quality of life, massive inward investment and so on. The other was its obverse, the Low Road, in which Scotland, forever hidebound by – among other things – its mistrust of wealth creation and its obsessive loathing of the English, goes inexorably down the crapper. 'The Low Road scenario is an extrapolation of existing trends,' explained one of the report's authors, morosely.

Well, even the English don't want the Scots to vanish down the toilet of history. We want everyone to be happy and live in peace and harmony. What do the Scots want, though?

I open up my daily papers, looking for answers, and immediately spot two straws in the wind. In the *Herald*, a piece on the Op Ed pages starts, 'It is a quiet Sabbath evening' and unravels into a piece of gingery Presbyterian Bible-wrestling: 'There was Moses on Pisgah . . . the Judgement Seat . . . the land of Ephraim, and Mannaseh . . . a blood-soaked tree . . .' This makes the blood freeze. I mean, in this day and age: this is a secular country, for Christ's sake. Couple of days later, I'm patrolling the *Scotsman*'s Op Ed pages similarly, I spot a piece which kicks off, 'For a small nation huddled on the cold edge of Europe and frequently harassed by our neighbour, we have not done badly. Scotland has given the world television, the bicycle, the decimal point and penicillin, to name but a few. We have had more than our share of literary geniuses: Robert Burns, Edwin Muir, Hugh MacDiamid, Sir Walter Scott . . .' Then it spends the rest of its word-count belabouring itself

about the poet William McGonagall and what Scotland ought
to be remembered for, historically. There is no mention of
the future, only a brooding on the past.

Meanwhile, at about this time, the go-ahead *Los Angeles
Times* is fretting about the future and nothing but: nuclear
energy in the twenty-first century, Sino-Russian relationships, the new demography. Well, of course, they would in
LA. They haven't got a past. But back here, back in Europe,
even the conservative *Le Monde* is concentrating on the
upcoming World Social Forum and contemporary Las Vegas.
But hooray for Scotland! Getting its priorities lined up like
cans on a wall, it gives us hardcore Protestantism and the
William McGonagall Problem and hang the modern world!
Only William Deedes in the *Daily Telegraph* can do better
than that, and even he shows signs of a wayward modern-
minded adventurism from time to time.

So where will we all be in Scotland in twenty-five years'
time? Inverary or Taymouth? Ticking along soullessly but
nicely or sporting a notice that THE CASTLE IS <u>NOT</u> OPEN TO THE
PUBLIC? Peering concentratedly forwards or adjusting the rear-
view mirror of destiny?

I realised with horror at this point that I'd driven so far I was
practically in Perth. How the hell had I managed that? Perth
('The Fair City') is nearly as far up as Dundee, well north of
Edinburgh and an astronomically large distance from
Dumfries. Night was falling. The rain, having eased off
around Taymouth, was starting again.

I found myself on a motorway over which some thought-
ful Scots agency had placed big illuminated signs to keep me
safe: REMEMBER FRUSTRATION CAUSES ACCIDENTS. Another told me to
DRIVE CAREFULLY, while another rhymed IN TOWN SLOW DOWN. I
stopped at a motorway service area, stumbled out of my car
towards the gleaming plastic cafeteria, ended up forking in

kapok-flavoured chips while a TV screen played above my head.

From the border with England to Perth, from Inverness to Skye, everything sits close to everything else. It's like having Bristol, Leeds and Newcastle all together in West Sussex. I suddenly had the godlike sensation of being able to encompass the whole of Scotland in one effortless perspective, merely by standing on a motorway service restaurant table somewhere near Kinross. Of course, this may have been the result of too much time stuck in a car, or being freaked by old buildings.

Either way, it didn't last. Soon I was back at the wheel, hunting down a bed for the night and debating where I should head for next, perpetually on the rebound, forever reacting against whatever it was I thought I'd just experienced.

Back at the newsdesk, this just in from the *Herald*: in answer to the St Andrews University *Scenarios for Scotland*, High Road/Low Road what-shall-become-of-us-in-the-new-age, how-can-Scotland-prosper? research paper, the National Trust for Scotland has taken the bold and forward-looking move of surveying the battlefield at Culloden for things they might have missed last time they surveyed it. Radar, an electronic distance measurer and a metal detector are all lined up for the task, as well as some shovels. Survey leader Dr Tony Pollard, of Glasgow University, told the *Herald*, 'Prince Charles and the Jacobites will still have lost, much as we would have liked to reverse the decision.'

Two hundred and fifty years go by, empires rise and fall, world wars are won and lost, the silicon revolution is upon us, but we still need to know a bit more about the Battle of Culloden just in case the English ever feel like trying anything like that again. What is this? This is a peculiarly Celtic form of embracing the future.

EIGHTEEN

Let's talk about Denmark for a second. I would hope they talk about little else in New Scotland, because Denmark is the future and having been to Denmark I have seen the future and I bring back this eyewitness account of what Scotland could in all probability be like at some unspecified point in the next hundred years.

Why Denmark? It's glaringly obvious. Similar latitude to Scotland – it doesn't go much further north than Aberdeen, but then, who cares? Similar population to Scotland, at around 5 million. Similar well-tended sense of national identity and crucial defining social habits. Smaller land mass – something like 16,000 square miles to Scotland's nearly 30,000 – but since so much of Scotland is only useful for looking at, rather than exploiting in any real way, this brings the difference right down. Denmark is a bit like Holland, in that every patch of ground that can be profitably used is used, even if that use is for no more than a slightly sanitised recreation. Although there are lots of islands and coastline, as in Scotland, the concept of a Danish wilderness is unusual.

More to the point, Denmark, like Scotland, has an over-weeningly large neighbour to its immediate south (Germany) and, like Scotland, has had to face a turning-point in its modern destiny. *Modern* may be stretching it a little, but many Danes still treat 1864 as recent news bordering on current affairs. This was when Denmark, once the centre of a consid-erable little empire, lost its last extra-Danish possession, other than Greenland and the Faeroes, when Schleswig-Holstein fell into the hands of the Prussians. Humiliated by this rever-sal, Denmark experienced a collective nervous breakdown and was only able to face the rest of the world again thanks to a nationalist revival, driven forward by Pastor Nikolai Frederik Grundtvig. Even today, Grundtvig is spoken of with reverence, much as the great Kemal Atatürk is still revered by modern Turks.

Sometimes described as 'the spiritual architect of modern Denmark', his solution was a long-term drive towards better education at all levels of society, a new dispensation of learn-ing which would enable Denmark to overcome its losses and reinvent itself as the small, intelligent, independent economic unit it currently is. A Danish copywriter I once met pitched Grundtvig as a 'cross between John Wesley and Queen Victoria', which makes you wonder how many English copy-writers could name two Danish icons from the past couple of centuries. Grundtvig's legacy was then transformed into a practical reality by one Kristen Kold, the father of the modern Danish educational system. His endeavours now bear fruit in the eagerness of Danes both to see their schooling through and to come back and do endless night-school courses in later life.

Anyway, the thing is that Denmark faced this cardinal moment in its history and fabricated an inspiringly successful small country out of it. Of course, many other European countries have also recently reinvented themselves with great aplomb – Germany after the war, Spain after the death of Franco, France after the Fourth Republic. It's not a new idea. It's only new, in fact, in Great Britain, where modernisation and reinvention are regarded as something worse than an outbreak of cholera. But Scotland?

Admittedly, a measure of devolution from England and Wales isn't quite the same thing as a humiliating defeat at the hands of the Prussian army. It doesn't generate quite the same emotional heat or the same urgency for action. But given the way the Scottish quality press talks about little else other than 'What kind of Scotland do we want?', it would seem as good a time as any to go for that transformative moment, that point at which Scotland steps decisively into the twenty-first century and becomes something other than just another lump of Britain.

No obvious sign of a Nikolai Frederik Grundtvig coming forward, let alone Kristen Kold, though. Hard to think who could fit that spot, or have fitted it once. Walter Scott, I suppose. Ramsay MacDonald? Captain Kidd? Kenny Dalglish? James Clerk Maxwell? David Niven (yes, born in Kirriemuir)? The Earl of Balfour? Sean Connery? Robbie Coltrane? I'm getting desperate, here. Alex Salmond? Perhaps this is the wrong time to look and – more important – the wrong *order* in which to look, trying to shoehorn a leftover celebrity into the role of George Washington.

Still, if it did, if it managed to do a Denmark, the potential rewards would be huge, so far as I can see. Living standards would be almost universally good; the Scots would be one of the best-educated and most consensual societies in Europe; Scotland would enjoy the status of being the 12th equal richest country in the world on a per capita basis (place shared with Denmark, of course); the trains would run on schedule; spare time would be spent drinking, smoking and having heated arguments – as now, in fact, only in conditions of far greater comfort.

(On reflection, Scotland could do a lot worse than open up a cadet branch of the top Danish amusement park, BonBon-Land, which is near Copenhagen. We have Legoland in Windsor, why not BonBon-Land near Dundee? Replicating the Danish model exactly, this will offer rides such as the Water Rat, 'Which takes you through Karl Sludge's Underworld'; Seagull-Dropping Bicycles and Duckweed Boats, 'Which will keep your legs working hard'; the Flying Crock and the ineffable Horse Droppings; the world's highest rubbish tip; plus the 'Cheeky Dog Fart Switchback'. According to the promotional literature, 'Here there and everywhere, there's fun, pranks and high jinks and a great atmosphere that will make everyone in the family wildly happy.' But of course!)

The thing that seems to be missing, however, is a sense of communal ambition. Danes are a bit weird in that they are quietly proud of their homogeneity; they like to refer to themselves as a *tribe*. As the Germans would put it, *all their noses point in the same direction*, but this is with faint ethnic undertones and a strong compulsion to conform. I do not see this happening in quite the same way in Scotland. Nor, for that matter, do I see it happening in England, which could really do with a rethink and has, indeed, slightly embarked on one, but in a typically heel-dragging, muddled, reactionary sort of way. In fact, people like me sometimes look hungrily to Scotland, trusting that it'll give us a lead of some kind. After all, civil rights, drinking legislation, education and the law have all been handled differently up there. We either road-test new ideas on Scotland or borrow old ones from it. There's a sense that the smaller country could give the larger a lead, if only the smaller could pull itself sufficiently together. If only.

NINETEEN

Orkney, Shetland, the Outer Hebrides . . . these are all places which, I know, make many people's hearts leap, especially if they live in London and wouldn't know a crofter's cottage if it went and parked on their front lawn. Londoners yearn to go to these hopelessly distant and inaccessible spots – especially the Shetland Isles – because they are the last bits of the UK to be truly wild and free. Londoners nod their heads, recidivist hippies the lot of them, and murmur, 'Now that *would* be somewhere to visit. That's a *really* special place. *Celtic twilight*.'

What the hell are they thinking of? Why are these names so cripplingly evocative? What the Londoners are thinking of is that if you can struggle out as far as Lerwick, or, failing that, the Butt of Lewis, then somehow you will be presented with a landscape, a light, an atmosphere, a vision of being which is so different and so revealing that you will come back changed ineradicably for the better. That there is somehow an essential goodness up there, a goodness predicated not least on the distance between these outposts of Scotland and London.

What's more, legend has it that even the filthy Scottish weather will play benign tricks on you. A friend of mine was once up in the Orkneys around Easter. He came back deeply tanned and horribly at peace with himself. 'Like a Greek island,' he whispered, 'but without the tourists. And so *clean*.' Of the Outer Hebrides, another London tourist breathed that they were 'all water and rock and light. *Magical*. No trees, though, apart from one very small bent one. And it didn't rain, much.'

I am not persuaded. Here I am, car ready, Taymouth Castle slowly becoming a distant memory. All I have to do is hare off to Scrabster to pick up the hour-and-a-half ferry ride to Stromness and be there, part of it all. Or I can retrace my steps to Ullapool and catch the Caledonian MacBrayne (or CalMac, as we old hands refer to it) ro-ro ferry to Stornoway, two and a half hours across The Minch. It's easy. But I can't bring myself to do that either. Why not?

I can't face the Orkneys or Shetland because they are just too far north, too far from the world as I know it. If we take the Mediterranean as the centre of the universe and work our way out from there, then you see my point. There are those who thrive on the wilderness and relish the absence of the big city. I am the opposite. Wilderness scares me, especially if it is an island wilderness and there is the possibility that having got on to an island, I may find myself trapped there for ten days by a series of gales sweeping in from the north-west with nothing to do, nothing at all, but kick pebbles along some crappy track and drink myself into dismal oblivion in some lino-infested Shetland boozer and run out of books to read and end up gnawing lichens by the seashore. Then the weather will finally lift and I will run weeping and laughing back on to the ferry, white-haired and quite mad from my incarceration and have to live out the rest of my days locked in the attic.

The other snag with the isles of Orkney and Shetland is that I suspect them not to be Scottish at all, and therefore conveniently beyond the ambit of this book. Consider this: Orkney only passed into Scottish hands at the end of the fifteenth century, in compensation for the non-payment of the dowry of Margaret of Denmark. And before that, it was all Norsemen and Danes. I mean, look at the names: Stromness, Shapinsay, Papa Westray, Scapa Flow. They call the midsummer twilight, the one that allows you to read a book outdoors all night, the 'Grimlins', from the Norse word *grimla*, which means to glimmer. Stromness is described in my guidebook as 'reminiscent of a Norwegian fishing village'. The place is no more Scottish than Wimbledon.

As for Shetland? Same as the Orkneys, only more so. Ruled by Norsemen until the fifteenth century, and then absorbed into Scotland in the same dispensation as the Orkneys, the isles of Shetland are on the same latitude as Greenland and a minimal four hundred miles south of the Arctic Circle. They are as close to Bergen as they are to Aberdeen. The absolute most northerly tip of Britain is up here, in the form of a lighthouse on Muckle Flugga, and the wind blows even worse than down Leith Walk. Apart from oil, fish and a population of 20,000, there is nothing at all there apart from – I'm told – some amazingly well-equipped schools and other public buildings, built on oil money. This really is *ultima Thule*, the limit of the Roman world: the name being awarded by Tacitus, who invoked the mythical island of Thule, the island on the edge of everything, to indicate how dreadful and distant Shetland was.

Well, what about the Hebrides? Yes, okay, easier to get to – five hours more or less from Oban to Barra, or South Uist, courtesy of CalMac. I was around the area anyway, and yes, I could go and get the tang of peat smoke and listen to the cry of the curlew and put up with all the Gaelic (the road signs, I read, are in *nothing but* Gaelic, and you have to get a handbook from the Western Isles Tourist Board to translate). But then the

only town in the Outer Isles is Stornoway and it has a population of no more than *8,000* people. This is genuinely
frightening. There must be more than 8,000 people living in
my street, let alone my part of London. But Lewis has to make
do with that number for what is effectively its capital city. I'm
sure it's gorgeous and bleak, but gorgeous and bleak, when you
get to my age, are not enough. Necessary, but not sufficient.

If you want some kind of substantiation for this point of
view, then take a look at an excellent book entitled *Patterns of
the Hebrides* by a photographer called Gus Wylie. This is one
of those handsome volumes of black-and-white photos of life
out there, *up* there, each picture vying with the last for the
most windswept, bleak, treeless, bare, stony, cold, sheep-
ridden and comfortless imagery. The crofters smilingly
display their dentistry in tiny cold front rooms and next to
wire fences. Coaches rust away by stone walls. No one dares
remove their sweater. There is an awful lot of peat. The pictures are beautiful in that frozen, sepulchral way that
black-and-white photography and creative printing can
achieve. They also absolutely confirm everything I have sus-
pected about the Hebrides and in a very real sense remove the
need to go up there and cross-check for myself.

So call me deficient, but the more I thought about it all,
and the more I leafed through Gus Wylie's pictures, the less
enthusiasm I could muster, particularly as I would be going
not in spring or high summer, but on the fringes of winter
when, quite apart from anything, there wouldn't be any daylight for more than about ten minutes a week. And even if I'd
been able to go at the height of whatever passes for summer
up there, I have a first-hand report of someone else's summer
trip to the Hebrides which resulted in 'mist, drizzle, incredi-
ble midges, really flat, er, rain'.

Yes, the people are supposed to be very friendly, and I'm
sure we could have yarned about the death of nearby St Kilda

or the poisoning of Gruinard Isle by anthrax (by the British government in 1942). And we could also have laughed about the fact that Gruinard is in The Minch, but much, much closer to the mainland of Scotland than any of the other islands! That would have been fun.

But there was a clincher to all my indecision and sore-eyed map-scouring. The clincher was Skye.

I know I mentioned Skye before, but I didn't tell the whole story, such as it is, because I felt somehow embarrassed to. You see, Skye is one of those quintessential names, packed with romance and drama, a name brimming with longing. The 'Skye Boat Song' is one of those songs that, despite its full-on mawkishness and push-button hand-wringing, still gets under the skin and prickles the eyes of every suburban home-owner. *Even though* it commemorates that foppish waster, Bonnie Prince Charlie:

> Carry the lad that's born to be king
> Over the sea to Skye . . .

And so on. You only have to say 'Skye' and everyone pauses, as if touched by the memory of a long-lost and dear family relation. It is an island of myth. It is even a Sri Chinmoy Peace Island, and Sri Chinmoy, poet, peace campaigner and paranormal weightlifter, does not dispense these honours frivolously.

Which is why it was such a let-down to get there: the myth, like most myths, doesn't bear examination in the light of reality. It wasn't just that Skye is no longer an island, now joined to the mainland by a crummy cement bridge which has a leg stuck on the islet of Eilean Ban, where Gavin Maxwell (*Ring of Bright Water*, *A Reed Shaken by the Wind*) ended his days in a lighthouse cottage. Nor that this linkage now transforms it into a peninsula of rather less visual interest than the larger landmass to which it is attached. It was the whole experience. I was on Skye for the best part of a day, and an awful lot of my time seemed to go in negotiating an endless streamer of grey road, beneath overcast skies in a greasy drizzle, while boggy scenery skated past on one side, two-bit hills and rusty bracken on the other. Could have been anywhere in Scotland, could have been Wales. When I wasn't tailgating some knackered old van or a truck with a tarpaulin over the back and nameless island produce underneath, I occasionally had the leisure to gawp at some additions to the picture – watery inlets, heather, sparse roughcast houses with mould streaks. Call me jaded, but that's how it was.

So I was desperate, naturally, for Portree/Port Righ to give me a lift. This is where Flora Macdonald hid the Bonnie Prince, where he took leave of her (along with some shirts and the chicken), the place where all tourists tend, the capital of Skye. How did it pan out? I spent about an hour trying to park in a perfectly simple open-air car park with an enormous number of free spaces. Not Portree's fault, no, I own up to this one. When faced with limitless possibilities for parking, my mind tends to overload and leaves me unable to choose one space in preference to another. Then I had to go and get change for the ticket machine. Then I had to work out the best way on foot from the car park to where the action was. It was a concatenation of small, easily managed but irksome details which dragged me down before I'd even started.

That and the fact that when I worked out where the action was, there really wasn't much action to be sampled. There's a wee harbour girdled with cottagey houses and impregnated with that pleasant rank smell of seaweed and sludge. There is the Royal Hotel, which is where Macdonald is supposed to have said goodbye to Prince Charlie. Instead of the seventeenth- or eighteenth-century structure you might have hoped for, what's there looks to be mainly nineteenth-century with a cornflake-packet modern extension shoved on the end and the whole thing drenched in whitewash. I spent a good five minutes staring at it, wondering if there were maybe two Royal Hotels and I was outside the wrong one. There is also a cranky little fortified tower just off the harbour, inside which is a tiny metal spiral staircase. I lumbered up this thing, which was soaking wet from a recent downpour and consequently represented a significant physical danger, and stood at the top in a breeze looking down at the town. This is where it tells you that Skye is a Sri Chinmoy Peace Island, by the way. Nearby was a terrifying Free Church of Scotland chapel in which the good people of Portree could be scared out of their wits by the prospect of eternal hellfire, working on Sundays, Catholicism (look at the people of Barra and Eriskay! Damned in their worship of the Antichrist!). You can tell how Sabbatarian they are in the Protestant islands when you learn that CalMac were only recently allowed to run any ferry services at all on the Lord's Day. Before then, Sunday was a non-travelling day. The chapel hard by Portree had a notice of times of services: the word *Sunday* was not to be seen; only *Sabbath*.

And the rest, once I got away from the dainty, muddy harbour and the blustery pointless stone tower? Just stuff, just the things you find anywhere: newsagents, banks, a social centre, patches of common ground with springy green turf and dog crap, houses with machine-made Belgian-style lace curtains in the windows, parked Fords, schoolkids swinging their backpacks at each other, knee-faced blokes in quilted anoraks puffing up lanes. Portree, in other words, is just a place. But it is a long way to come from south-west London to find just a place.

Embittered, I drove a whole lot more across some other neither-here-nor-there parts of Skye before springing back across the expensive cement bridge and Gavin Maxwell's old

drum, skulking beneath lorries, and into the weary embrace
of Kyle of Lochalsh.

So the point is this: Skye is as close to the Outer Hebrides as
you can get without actually being in the Outer Hebrides.
From one to the other is between fifteen and twenty miles.
From London to Skye is about five hundred and fifty miles.
What more was I going to get in that trip across The Minch?
Other than seasickness? Skye had rendered the whole scheme
redundant. You know, you have to be flexible in your aims. You
mustn't let yourself be tethered by assumptions. You mustn't (I
chastised myself at the wheel of my soon-to-be-redundant car)
let yourself be forced into positions just because of some idiotic
cultural presupposition. No! I might have been ricocheting
around Scotland like the ball in a Bally pinball machine but my
super-erratic progress did not indicate a lack of purpose. Just
because Bill Bryson (in *Notes from a Small Island*) and Paul
Theroux (in *Kingdom by the Sea*) describe relatively conventional circuits looping clockwise around the country, there was
no reason for me not to describe a sequence of random squig-
gles and cross-hatchings, like an Etch-A-Sketch in the hands of
a two-year-old. My journey was propelled by a mixture of fear
(*I don't want to leave Edinburgh*) and obligation (*Oh God, I've got
to anyway*): a reactive way of doing things, a series of reflexes.
But it still had its own inner logic. Glasgow, with well over half
a million inhabitants and the third most visited city in Britain,
was calling me and I could no longer resist. It had to be done.
I hurled my Highlands & Islands guidebook back into my bag
and headed due south. I couldn't put off Glasgow any longer.
It would be like *Hamlet* without the Prince or *Coronation Street*
without Elsie Tanner. Or did she leave, anyway?

And, yes, for no reason I can adequately put my finger on,
I did feel a pang of guilt at not doing that extra twenty miles.

Twenty

So there I was, short-arsing around an HMV shop, looking for the CD with Alex Salmond singing on it and not finding it. But the hunger to buy was strong in me. Normally, I leave if I can't get what I think I want, preening myself on my self-control. But this time I wanted to leave with something purchased. It was a long moment of irrationality. After ten minutes of dithering over compilations of Scottish pipe band music, I walked into a pile of bad-taste-looking videos, including one called *Rikki Fulton: The Time of His Life*. Obviously a comic, from the mugging face-shots on the case. Never heard of him, but there you are, central to Caledonian culture judging by the ziggurat of boxes in the centre of HMV. So I bought it, assuaging the hunger and promising myself a rare treat at the same time – being able to pillory the Scots for their legendarily poor taste in comics.

After all, once you get past Sir Harry Lauder this terrible blank space opens up in which only a few freaks survive, like Andy Stewart, Jimmy Logan, that weirdo Stanley Baxter who was always doing elaborate Christmas TV parodies of movies you didn't know, the Godawful Krankies. This is a desert of comic talent which elides into the desert of Scottish pop music (Wet Wet Wet, Big Country, Simple Minds, the Proclaimers, Travis, all evidence that Scottish pop music only thrives when pop music as a whole is going through a low patch), the two together confirming that prejudice that Scotland is (a) not funny; (b) not funky.

The existence of Billy Connolly only serves to emphasise this cruel truth. His amazing success highlights the fact that nothing else the Scots find funny is funny, including *Oor Wullie*, by the way, and *Rab C. Nesbitt*, which is simply incomprehensible.

So when I got home, I jadedly shoved the tape into the video machine, willing Rikki Fulton to live down to my expectations. *Make me laugh, Scotsman*, I sneered at him, propped up imperially on the sofa, my teeth bared.

Picture my rage and confusion when he actually did. I mean, this is not laughter in the way Connolly can make you laugh – exorbitantly, shamingly – but you know, you could see the point. There was a lot of character-playing stuff, Dick Emery/Harry Enfield, that kind of thing, only done by this guy with a face like a horse and apparently a hundred years old. I suppose Russ Abbott would be a near comparison, south of the border: not everyone's scene, but the guy clearly keeps his constituency happy.

Except that if the tearful encomia from all the other celebs on *Rikki Fulton: The Time of His Life* were to be believed, Fulton is beyond Abbott, and is in the rare air which surrounds a true national comic institution. He is a Connolly who never sold out, a person adored by the generations, including Gregor Fisher, Bill Bryden and Donald Dewar. They queued up to shout his genius. They said that the Francie & Josie double-act he did with a guy called Jack Milroy was up there with Morecambe & Wise and Martin & Lewis. Well, okay, the bit they showed *was* good – two geezers who'd been doing it a lifetime and had the patter and the timing down to fine art. Certainly, I could find it in myself to complain about the 1950s sensibilities of Fulton's act – the buttoned verbal collar, the propriety of Fulton's stage drunk, the aroma of Dundee hanging over things, even though Fulton is from Glasgow. But then the guy's so old he's even retired, now, so I can scarcely blame him for acting his age.

No, I was obscurely cross, partly because by being entertaining he was denying me a platform from which to spout my superior conceits; and because if he was halfway decent, how come he hadn't tried harder to make it in England? This is an indispensable part of any Scottish success. In America they can get away with not having to export their media heroes: they don't need to. In France, they don't want to. But *that* list of Scots expats who needed England to get into the frame and then, even, conquer the world: where was Rikki Fulton, with his astonishingly camp '50s forename?

He'd been on the radio with Frank Sinatra, for God's sake, even done a bit of backchat with the greatest popular vocalist of the second half of the twentieth century. Why wasn't he fronting *Sunday Night at the London Palladium*? Or *Opportunity Knocks*? And becoming an international star in the sense that he would have been a star in both Scotland and England? I found this in particular a hard one to swallow. Even Jimmy Shand and Kenneth McKellar had to go down this road at one time. Why not him? Just because a load of Jocks happened to like him playing Supercop and the Rev. I. M. Jolly?

I am still brooding over this one. I know I shouldn't take it so personally, but I do. It's like Elvis never coming over.

TWENTY-ONE

God it was cold and wet. I'd walked from Union Street just outside Glasgow Central Station, along Gordon Street for a few yards, then up West Nile Street, right along Bath Street and into Cathedral Street, just to get to St Mungo's Cathedral and the Glasgow Necropolis past that; and the rain was beyond rain, beyond weather and into some other kind of medium altogether. If this was Glasgow rain, then it was telling me something. It was telling me that I might have considered Edinburgh rain or even Highland rain to be the real thing: whereas in fact, Glasgow rain was rainier, more pluvially torrential than anything I could previously have imagined. It wasn't just like standing under a cold shower, because the wind that rushed down the streets drove it capriciously at me from all available planes. It was more like standing under one of those body-pummelling showers that has outlets running up the sides of the shower stall as well as a head directly above you. One of those showers that tries to drown you. Or it was like standing under several showers at once. With all your clothes on.

But if you are standing under several showers with all your clothes on, at least you know that, *mutatis mutandis*, you can turn the shower off. So I suppose this wasn't even like standing under several showers, but more like having thousands of little demons or imps chucking buckets of water over me from several directions simultaneously, with no prospect of their ever stopping.

Down south, down in the fastness of London, even the worst downpours end at some time. Up here, it was long past what I would have regarded as the normal cut-off point for rainfall and it was simply raining itself into new dimensions of rain and time. My clothes had turned from their normal drab dry colours to a darker, soaked shade. They had then surprised me by turning even darker with inundation, an inky wetness that I'd never seen before, even when they came out of the washing machine.

As I crawled up Cathedral Street, the side roads were starting to flood. I had to squirm past a bit of scaffolding with a queen-sized footbath of brown water in the way. 'That puddle's too big tae cross,' an old bag said helpfully. 'Ye'll have tae go round.' So I did, getting sprayed by a happy-go-lucky passing car.

Not as badly as two guys further up the road, though. Fifty yards ahead, a puddle had formed by the roadside of such enormity that when a bus coincided with these two blokes marching east along the pavement, the plume of grey-brown spray that the bus threw up over them not only soaked them but soaked them completely from head to foot. This is no exaggeration: it was a wall of water some seven feet high. The two guys actually disappeared from view for a split-second before reappearing like a couple of gannets hit by a squall, furiously shaking the water from their anoraks.

What's more, there was nowhere to shelter, no easy door-ways or tolerant shop awnings, because this is the territory of the University of Strathclyde, and all the possible shelter was in lumpy grey institutional monoliths set back yards from the roadside, up tarmac drives and crouching behind green landscapes, among which grey armies of students moved, ducking the rain. I carried on due east, soaking up water.

Five minutes later, I reached the cathedral. 'A perfect example of pre-Reformation Gothic' it said in my book, which is the kind of thing I like on a weekday, except that by the time I got there, it was shut. At four in the afternoon, it was shut. This was 50 per cent of the justification for my trip, gone.

So I started to despair. I was wetter than if I had just sat in a bath of iced tea on a mountainside. I was cold. I was astonishingly furious at my own stupidity for getting so wet and was of course fretfully planning to retrieve things in some way not yet clear to me, some way that would redeem everything, however awful. Somewhere in the back of my mind I had assumed that the church would be open, as are most large churches at four in the afternoon. I had also assumed that it would have a few of those big, finned, circular, cathedral radiators, like things from a ship's boiler room, against which I could have pressed my body and steamed. Instead I stood in the shelterless archway of the locked cathedral entrance, staring at a fantastical Victorian Gothic wrought-iron gas lamp opposite, unlit and richly morbid. I might well have been crying by this point, only the rain trickling down my face hid my tears. *Oh fuck*, I thought. So I went to the boneyard.

To be candid, this was the main reason why I'd battled out to the east of central Glasgow in the first instance. Cathedrals are good, but it's not everywhere that has a city of the dead two hundred feet above sea level, accessed by a Bridge of Sighs (crossing what was once the Molendinar Glen, now Wishart Street), and which is also Scotland's first non-denominational 'hygienic' graveyard. Originally conceived in the 1820s and modelled on Père Lachaise in Paris, the Glasgow Necropolis is where respectable dead nineteenth-century

Glaswegians went to be placed in their family tombs or interred with some insane piece of statuary on top of them. It is a big draw, and yet (because Scottish, bare, windswept, rain-scoured) much less kinky or perverse in its character than, say, Highgate Cemetery or even Père Lachaise.

I staggered up the side of the cemetery hill, its paths made up of trip-the-fuckers unreliable mud and cinders and streaming little torrents of rainwater like the Highlands. I was gasping for breath as I laboured under the weight of my clothing (doubled by the amount of water it had taken in) and tried not to start weeping again. There was no shelter here either, only the downpour and acres and acres of soot-blackened stone.

But what a place! The forty-five-degree pathway up is lined with mausolea bearing what struck me as over-zealous and redundant DANGER KEEP OUT notices from the council. I don't know what kind of freak would in this or any other lifetime try to climb into a ruined mausoleum in Glasgow, but then sensation-seekers resist taxonomy. Indeed, the council did close the cemetery for a while, on account of its being unsafe underfoot for all the drunks and ghouls who liked to plunder it after dark.

Now it's open again to all-comers and when I got there, I found that, as sooty, wet, Edgar Allan Poe/Bram Stoker cemeteries went, it was perfect. Ferns were growing abundantly through the shattered masonry and the oxidising ironwork. Streaks of moss and bleak mildew ran down ashlared faces. There were endless temple doorways to temples that didn't exist – I'd walk into a row of columns propping up a whiskery green pediment with awful bronze doors beneath, tilting in their frames, and find nothing beyond. They were drunken guards of a missing place. Stones, rust, not a single other living person. It could hardly have been more dead if it tried, unless I too keeled over and died, which was not beyond all bounds.

Then I reached the summit and stood in the lee of John Knox's fifty-foot memorial statue. All around were more chunks of Roman and Greek architectural references, fluted columns, sepulchral urns, swags, pediments, Ionic lumps. There was a kind of Islamic kiosk in one spot, gazing down on the Addams Family Royal Infirmary to the north. Glasgow lay below me in a lake of mist and rain, its spires, chimneys and high-rises poking out; the Drowned City. To my left was the Tennent's brewery steaming and billowing, the inside of a valve radio blown up in steel. It was faultless, but as the only non-corpse for a quarter of a mile in any direction, I simply had to get out of the rain and get a drink before I lay down like something off *The Raft of the Medusa* and turned blue. I made my way back down the Necropolis hill, over the Bridge of Sighs, and south towards Gallowgate to look for the Saracen Head, or *Sarry Heid*. This used to be the most notorious boozer in Glasgow, which must have taken some doing. Allegedly the modern world has intervened and it isn't any more, but I wanted to say I'd been there. Only I couldn't find it, and besides, my legs were dragging me back to the modest slum where I was staying in the middle of town and before I knew it, I'd got to the St Enoch Centre – which is the largest glassed-in area in Europe and looks like an Albert Speer-inspired collision between a railway terminus, an airship hangar and a shower cubicle. On the edge of this Crystal Palace is a pub called Fat Boab's, named after, I guess, the character in *Oor Wullie* who wears a boiler suit, is fat and is called Boab, i.e., Bob. A woman looked at me as I entered and said, simply, 'Oh dear, oh dear, oh dear.' I got this Glaswegian confection at the bar called a *hauf'n'hauf*, which is a measure of whisky plus a half of beer of some sort, which you drink as a chaser. I have to say I felt a lot better once I'd drunk it, and not even slightly inebriated. A man was standing at the fruit machine, drinking a cocktail of lager and Irn-Bru. Then I spotted the pool of rainwater which was forming under my seat as my clothes drip-dried. So I had to leave in case anyone saw me and presumed that I'd actually wet myself.

You will not be surprised to learn that I spent a high percentage of my time between Union Street and the Necropolis internally debating whether to get an umbrella, but failing to do so. Then wishing that I *had* got an umbrella and cursing my vanity and stupidity. I mean, I had several close shaves: first at a branch of Boots, where their collapsibles cost a stiff £13; then at a baggage'n'brollies store, where they were a much more reasonable £6, but done in an embarrassingly happy floral pattern.

Soon after that I entered what appeared to be a likely looking umbrella shop, which turned out to be a hardware store of appalling complexity. Blundering around the ground floor, I spotted a sign announcing CLOTHING UPSTAIRS, next to an escalator. So I went up the escalator only to find tremendous quantities of horseman's waxed topcoats, riding gear and tack room accessories, none of which looked like an umbrella. For half a second I toyed with the idea of trying to make a curry-comb or snaffle-polisher into something that would keep the rain off, then thought better of it and went to look for something that really was an umbrella. Ten minutes later and all I'd found were light-bulbs, vacuum cleaners, binliners, extension cables, groundsheets and toasters, so I looked for the way down to the ground floor and the weather again. But I couldn't find it. There was an escalator up but no escalator down and no sign of any exit of any kind. This made me quite apprehensive. Another five minutes went by as I made a further circuit of the waxed topcoats, saddle-soaps, ironing-boards and plug adaptors, before coming back to where I'd started, still no sign of a way out. I then genuinely panicked, spontaneously inventing the notion that all Glasgow shops are set as puzzles and cannot be left unless you are in possession of certain occult knowledge. My eyeballs swivelling, I began to revolve slowly on the spot as this idea took hold, until I revolved myself to the top of a staircase which turned out to have been there all along, offering freedom and the rain outside.

Then, shaken, I found some brollies at a key-cutters and shoe-menders, where they had an assortment on a rack for about £3, which were ideal and were so cheap I could have bought one and then thrown it into the River Clyde after use. But I still didn't buy one. Why not?

The reason became clear to me before I'd even made it as far as Cathedral Street, while I sat in the Lido café (in West Nile Street, used to be a real 2i's sort of rockers' joint – the reason I'd picked it out, in fact, although now just an amiable mainstream caff, another excursion without a point), nursing a cup of tea and a bacon roll, waiting for the rain to ease. The reason why I didn't buy a brolly was that there were *no* men with umbrellas in Glasgow. There were loads of sensible women with brollies, skittling down the pavements and keeping themselves dry. There were even one or two kids with umbrellas. But the men, the real men, were just determinedly getting saturated. One or two had the hoods of their anoraks up, but the rest were walking around with the rain coursing in rivulets down their faces and getting under their collars, their hair hanging like seaweed. The only logical inference? That brollies were for poofs.

Well, I didn't want to look effeminate at all, because this is Glasgow, where these things matter, and I am averse to standing out from the crowd in tough cities anywhere in the world. So after a few minutes' reflection, I knew that anything I felt about umbrellas would be useless and irrelevant because I was culturally debarred from using one, almost as much as I was debarred from wearing a kilt. The only way I could have explained away my being male and using an umbrella if challenged by a Glaswegian – bound to happen in the circumstances – would have been to play the Foreigner Card and act Dutch. As it turned out, I didn't feel confident enough to be foreign since the rain had already sapped my strength, so I contented myself with getting soaked and staying soaked and I think with hindsight it was worth the suffering.

This is the thing with Glasgow. No other city in Britain carries the same resonances, the same baggage of expectations and preconceptions. No other city would have stopped me using an umbrella if I'd had one. Name me anywhere else which conjures up images as big and gritty and threatening and pervasive as Glasgow: Manchester? Newcastle? Bristol? *Birmingham*? Uniquely, Glasgow comes fully formed with an armoury of perceived attributes. It makes you feel that you need to act in a particular way before you even arrive there. The word *Glasgow* opens up an entire lumber room of received ideas, including: ships/dead shipyards; *No Mean City* and the underworld of the Glasgow razor kings; the Gorbals; the Glasgow Empire, toughest entertainment venue in the country ('If they liked your act, they let you live'); the Red Clyde; *See you*; a punch in the mouth; colossal drinking, on a scale only equalled in Ireland, plus historically unequalled drunks; Billy Connolly; streets that look a bit like cities in the States a hundred years ago; that weird rebranding in the '80s in which Glasgow became Smiles Better, followed by its completely unanticipated re-emergence as City of Culture and Architecture; the Glasgow Smile; Sauchiehall Street; all those steam trains it used to make; happening/clubbing/young and red-blooded capital of the New Caledonia; belligerent *yang* to Edinburgh's snotty *yin*; Charles Rennie Mackintosh, who called Glasgow 'philistine'; the tenement city; Celtic and Rangers; Tennent's Super, the dreaded Purple Tin ('Obliterate them with the old purple tin!'); junk capital, where people think *Trainspotting* is; unhealthiest place in the nation; attracts some 2 million visitors a year.

One could go on. The accretions, the layers of material are more or less indefinitely complex, depending on where you start. For a Londoner, Glasgow's image lurches uncontrollably between the extremities of a place that smart people refer to as funky, lively, crunchy and full of that most nebulous quality, *vitality*, and a Caledonian Rome in the Dark Ages. It is a beast or a kind of rough-hewn angel. It is where you can club till dawn, buy slacks from D & G and watch modern ballet; and also get your faced filled in without even trying. It is boiling with new money and keeling over with generations of dismal neglect. It is the most outgoing, cosmopolitan of Scotland's cities, and putrid with sectarianism. It is where Scotland's tough modern economy is happening (the call centre capital of the UK, with over 130 centres in Scotland, nearly half located in the Glasgow area; IBM's complex up Clydeside; Livingston just down the road with Motorola; NEC; heart of Silicon Glen; 7 per cent of all computers in the world made here, etc.); and the place where the Second City of the Empire went spectacularly bankrupt.

Actually, the history of Glasgow, unlike the history of Scotland, is pretty easy to follow. Nothing at all happened for centuries, because the Dear Green Place (Celtic *glas*, green, and *cu*, dear) beside the Clyde could not be reached by boats of any size so far inland. Then St Mungo arrived, having resurrected the pet robin of St Serf after yobs killed it at some time between AD 500 and 1000. Mary, Queen of Scots was also there, followed by the plague, Oliver Cromwell, the building of Port Glasgow twenty miles downriver and the wretched Bonnie Prince Charlie, who found almost no support among the Glaswegian population, to the city's eternal credit.

Glasgow as we know it, or think we know it, only starts to happen in the eighteenth century, when it worked out a way to bring ships up the Clyde, from where it could begin a lavish trade in tobacco. Being that bit further west than Bristol or Liverpool meant that Glasgow-based vessels could make the Atlantic crossing to Virginia and other North American colonies that bit quicker. Thus arose the Tobacco Lords of Glasgow, who gave way in turn to the Cotton Lords of the late eighteenth/early nineteenth centuries, who in turn gave way to the monstrous heavy industrialists of the nineteenth and early twentieth centuries: the point at which the Glasgow of legend is born – overpoweringly rich, furiously constructive, inexpressibly poor and either way relieving its distemper with spirituous liquor. This is the insistent contrariness of Glasgow: precisely at the same time as the hugely profitable shipbuilding and engineering were getting into full swing, so were the poverty and appalling ill-health. As the shipyards grew, so there were Bread Riots on Glasgow Green in 1848; and in 1850 it was found that every other child born in Glasgow would be dead before its fifth birthday.

Nevertheless, at their peak just before the First World War, the Clyde's shipbuilders were producing half the world's tonnage of shipping. Around two ships out of every three launched anywhere in the world were launched on the River Clyde. The entire globe moved on steam trains and trams built in Glasgow workshops, and ships assembled in Glasgow docks. We wore textiles from Glasgow while drinking locally distilled whisky out of Glasgow glassware. We stuck Glasgow pottery around our houses and wrote on Glasgow paper. This was when Glasgow really was the Second City of the Empire. The nineteenth century brought with it abysmal poverty in the Gorbals and the East End of Glasgow, the benign virtues of the new middle classes in Hillhead, and the super-rich industrialist sponsors of all those churches, hotels, railways and hospitals you can see littered all over the city today.

Then it caves in. A guy called George Blake – no, not the spy – wrote a book called *The Shipbuilders*, marking the fall. This came out in 1935, and already Blake was able to describe 'the high, tragic pageant of the Clyde', whose shipyards were slumped in idleness, whose berths were empty, where there were only 'gaunt, dumb poles and groups of men, workless, watching in silence'. After the First World War, economic history saw to it that the Depression and a slump in the ship-building business – artificially kept booming during the war – nailed Glasgow's industries and gave us not only *The Shipbuilders* but also *No Mean City* ('Johnnie lay very still, his face a mask of blood, and Lizzie was stretched unconscious by the door').

Which is where we come in. For anyone born in the twentieth century, Glasgow is some kind of depraved apotheosis of the capitalist dream – a place where unbelievable wealth gushed in like water from a burst dam, and then gushed out again at about the same rate, leaving only dereliction, squalor, vice and drunkenness behind. And this is the legacy which all we British partake of. For instance: the only other time I can recall being in Glasgow was so long ago that I spent one afternoon watching one of the *Rocky* movies in the Odeon in Renfield Street and came out to confront the worst, most spectacular drunk I had ever seen, waiting for me on the pavement. Obviously I was younger then (I mean, *Rocky*), less experienced as to what drunks should or could look like, but even so, he was museum quality: hair sticking out like a toilet brush, puce eyeballs, jaw sagging to his chest, a tabard of puke down his front (spectacular puke, even, buttercup yellow with a thick aggregate of mobile food-stuffs swirled in), shirt tails flapping, one shoe missing and, as a show-stopping touch, the trousers dropped to knee height so as to let the piss run free down the noble incline of Renfield Street.

My first reaction was to be appalled. My second was to adopt an instant posture of callow touristical detachment: *Of course*, I remember thinking to myself, *this is Glasgow! How appropriate!* I found I could appreciate this abject human as a piece of *épater les bourgeois* street theatre, because this was indeed Glasgow, and Glasgow's reputation as a city depends on such gracenotes as the constant threat of violence and consummately degraded drunks. It was like rounding a street corner in Paris and catching your first glimpse of the Eiffel Tower, or getting to Seville and smelling *paella*: it was all of a piece with one's presumptions about the place.

Conversely, when I was back there this time, like all tourists I went to the Museum of Transport, opposite the Kelvingrove Museum and Art Gallery and, like all tourists, I ploughed my way through the mob of schoolchildren that lives there and made my way into the big upstairs room where they keep the scale models of ships built on the Clyde. These are very beautiful – everything from a gentleman's sailing yacht, to various warships we flogged to the Russians early last century, to the famous *Queens* – the *Mary* and the two *Elizabeth*s. These last were used in the John Brown shipyard's testing tanks to check the stability of the designs before they went ahead and built the full-scale liners. Some Scottish knacker with his wife and kids bent down and peered at the model of the *QE2* before straightening up and announcing in that thickwit know-all dad way, 'You see? The model of the *QE2*'s no as nice as the models of the earlier ships. Even the models weren't as well made by then.'

What he'd failed to take into account, of course, was the fact that the *QE2* is a less elaborate design than the *QE1* or *Queen Mary*. More modern in intention, therefore less fussy in execution, the endless lines and pipes and attachments of the earlier boats are streamlined away. The absence of detailing on the later boat indicated that it was never there in the first place, not that the modellers couldn't be arsed to include it. It was evidently as lovingly constructed as its delightful fore-bears and it was with some difficulty that I restrained myself from clearing my throat in a marked manner just to set Mr Know-Nothing straight.

The important thing, though, the determining quality of one's visit to the room of lovely old boats, isn't the perfection or otherwise of the models; it's the spirit of condolence in which you undertake it, as if paying your respects to the memory of a relative. Everyone knows that the Clyde was once the home of mighty shipbuilding enterprises, even if that's all they know. And despite the protestations of odd residual teakheaded Thatcherites that all businesses that go to the wall go because of the ineluctable rightness of the mar-ketplace at work, you can't look at these damn models (or the silent and sleeping Clyde itself) without feeling a weird sen-timentality crawl over you, a feeling of loss and regret, very nearly something personal.

Maybe this is because the transition from boom to bust was so catastrophic and absolute that you can't help but be awed by it. Maybe it's because the ships and the sea are romantic things and it's hard to say goodbye to that stuff without a pang. Maybe it's because Glasgow is obscurely lovable in some dodgy Celtic miasmal way. All I know is you don't get the same feeling in Manchester, which resembles Glasgow in many ways: histori-cally, economically and physically. Manchester's just full of stroppy Mancs. Glasgow's doom is more personally affecting, so much so that I went and bought an *In Memoriam* video called *Seawards the Great Ships* (written by John Grierson) after I'd looked at the models. *Seawards the Great Ships* is a thirty-minute film made in 1960 as kind of promo for what was then left of the Clyde shipbuilding industry. It failed, in that it didn't bring much extra shipbuilding work in, but succeeded in that it won an Oscar for Best Live-Action Short Film in 1961. And so stirring, so melancholy in hindsight – with its armies of shirtsleeved draughtsmen, its terrifying welders, its vast sheets of steel, its engines, its Vulcan poundings and thrashings, the great chains that stop the new-born ship from rushing down into the Clyde and then uncontrollably out to sea or into the opposite bank . . .

And another thing. So penetrating is Glasgow's mystique, I even dressed up to go there. Rather, I dressed down, dressing as I conceived a guy at large in Glasgow ought to dress in order not to get lamped for being English or soft or at all poofy. To this end, I put on jeans, a sort of horrible donkey jacket and some clumpy shoes.

As it turned out, what I should have worn was either trainers, a tracksuit/anorak top with Adidas written on it, jeans and a baseball hat (backwards or not; it was an option), plus the facial appearance of someone aged indeterminately between twenty-five and fifty-five, scored with lines and cicatrices and pock marks; or the middle-aged *homme d'affaires* look, which means (in Glasgow) a dark suit, dark shirt, tie (dark or contrastingly light; it was an option) plus a Terry Venables overcoat, now and again draped over the shoulders to indicate mobster savvy. What I actually looked like, I realised after half an hour there, was a very old student. Instead of looking so inconspicuous that I could pass anywhere in the city unremarked-upon, I was actually inviting a smack in the mouth. Still. The symbolism is everything, the compulsion to *dress up for a city*.

I wove my way back to my hotel pit, passing a man in the street who canvassed me at a glance and offered the word '*Aye*', along with a little gratified nod at my amazing wetness. When I got in, the hotel towel crisis had developed a little

further. The towel crisis started when I first got into my fabulously cheap B&B in the centre of town and found there
were no towels in my room. I went down to the reception
desk and asked for some towels. The proprietor (wearing a
grey sharkskin suit and deluxe matching hair, like something
out of *Tutti Frutti*) said, 'Oh. I'll get you some.' I went back
upstairs to my room. The phone rang.

'They're all at the laundry,' said the voice of the proprietor
down the line, 'but they'll be back in twenty minutes.'

So I decided to go out to get inundated and came back,
hours later, dripping. Towels arrive okay?

'They're not back yet,' the proprietor said from behind the
safety of the reception desk. Then he heaved a bin-liner on to
the counter and pulled out a brand-new towel, still with the
maker's labels stuck all over it. 'Have a new one,' he said.

I thanked him and went back upstairs to change, clutching
my single, small new towel.

As I was on the brink of peeling off my revolting wet
clothes before drying myself with my one towel, there was a
knock at the door.

'I've brought you another towel,' said the proprietor, handing me another towel. I thanked him warmly, took the towel,
closed the door and started to grapple with my clothing again.

Five minutes went by. I was pretty well advanced in the
matter of clothing removal by this stage when there was
another knock at the door. I looked down at my bare pink
legs and my flapping shirt tails and decided I couldn't answer
the knock in this condition. I dragged my wet jeans off the
radiator and started to force my legs back into them. It was
like trying to shove a Swiss Roll into an unlined chamois glove.
Bounding and leaping one-footed as I jammed the other foot
down the steaming tube of my jeans, I made it to the door. It
was the proprietor again.

'Oh. I forgot. Here's another towel,' he said.

Maybe the towels on their own would have been enough to make me leave. As it was, I had a whole portfolio of reasons to go. Among them:

– Another non-working bedside light, just as in Edinburgh. Unlike in Edinburgh, I could easily swap bulbs over from the dim ceiling light to the bedside lamp, as the ceiling was only just over six feet above the floor. Turned out, though, that it was the light itself that was broken, not the bulb. Or could it have been the socket it was plugged into? I was going to conduct some experiments in pursuit of this theory, only to find that the electric flex of the bedside lamp had been nailed to the wall, making it impossible to move. So I ended up in the sad yellow gloom of the overhead lamp all night. What is it with lights and hoteliers in Scotland?

– Perforated walls. I was convinced that I could smell cigarette smoke coming *through* the wall from the room next door. Yes, everyone enjoys a gasper now and then, but only by exercising a positive preference to do so and not in one's sleep at 1.30 a.m.

– Not that there was a fantastic lot of sleep, owing to the thinness of the cardboard-and-mastic mix from which those walls were fabricated. I knew things were going to be bad when I found myself listening to the regional news coming from the telly next door, while fighting with my wet gear after the last appearance of the hotel boss and his towels. Later that same day, I enjoyed the sounds of the late-night news coming through the plaster, followed by the toiling thuds and grunts of live sex in a cheap hotel room before the TV went back on and played a late-night movie which I, for some reason, was unable to get on my own in-room TV. Finally, some time after two, the room next door fell silent. But as I lay in the swirling darkness, I realised that I could make out another TV on a floor below, playing an insomniacs' motorsport programme, very distantly . . .

This is what happens when you pick a hotel on the basis that it is (a) the very first hotel you come to; (b) possessed of enough shelter to allow you to get out of the rain; (c) dirt cheap. Next day I packed up and fled, moving into the rather fine station hotel at Glasgow Central. I can think of no higher praise than to say that *every single* light worked in my new bedroom, and stayed working all the time I was there.

Then I lit out for the Clyde, looking for its high tragic pageant. Is this really fair? I mean, after all the labours Glasgow has expended turning itself from The Graveyard of Hope to European City of Culture, what kind of wantonly perverse, mean-minded homunculus would actually go grubbing around for the marks of failure and defeat?

Let me say in my defence that only by looking for crap can you give a place the chance to refute the allegation of crappiness. I didn't know what I was going to find once I stepped down on to Clyde Street and Broomielaw, running alongside the river, and it could have been a dazzling inversion of all my expectations, a slap in the face to my London presumptions. If I'd just swallowed the tourist props and headed off to the new monster John Lewis up Buchanan Street, or hung around the smartypants Princes Square development (it has its own Foucault's Pendulum) nodding and muttering how true it was that Glasgow is the second biggest retail centre in the UK outside London, how could I have known what was really happening? How could I have known whether Glasgow was reborn or whether someone had simply dressed up the corpse in a surprisingly lifelike way?

On top of which, we in London have a nicely ruined once-working river of our own, along which industry and trade used to thrive on an unparalleled scale before collapsing into utter economic barrenness. It is called the Thames, anywhere from Tower Bridge down to Gravesend. So don't get on your high horse and tell *me* about terminal decline.

I rehearsed these arguments in my head until, stiff with feistiness, I hit the Clyde, the stilled heartbeat of a great city and – and what? And it is, yes, a bit like the lower reaches of the Thames, Deptford way. You look at it, silently pay your respects to the lives it consumed one way or another and shrug and acknowledge the ruthlessness of the world, but it's not an unfamiliar feeling.

Items of interest on the way, schlepping between the Suspension Bridge on Clyde Street and the Clydeside Expressway, opposite Govan?

– Bits of collapsed walkway, one of which was being photographed artistically by a couple of awestruck Japanese students.

– An immense blue crane standing preserved at the water's edge, a thing of such monumentality that it's hard to believe that humans built it. It is called the Finnieston Crane and, when it was put up in 1932, was the biggest crane in Europe. They used it to load complete railway locomotives on to ships which then set sail for the rest of the world bearing Glasgow's finest engineering to the end of the line. Next to it, and hopelessly trivialised in comparison, is a newbuild City Inn, a line of morose-looking cabbies standing under its tinny porch.

– The North Rotunda of the Harbour Tunnel, now turned into a casino, while the tunnel itself (for pedestrians, like the Greenwich foot tunnel) has been filled in with sand by the council.

– Bollards the size of tree-trunks, still with their faded working numbers painted on them, waiting for ghost ships.

– The beautiful Clyde, beautiful like all rivers, chocolate brown and swollen by the rains.

– The complete absence of other people on this public utility, with the exception of the giggling Japanese retrophiles and one indescribably sad-looking guy sitting on a wooden bench. He was thin, inadequately dressed for Scotland and the colour of feta cheese. He had a tin of Tennent's Super, the old Purple Tin on the go. One and three-quarter miles I walked, there and back. He was the only other recreating person I saw (apart from the Japanese) and it wasn't even raining.

– The London Docklands-style condos and new-retro flat-blocks going up on the south side, punctuated, Greenwich Dome-esque, by a massive silvery metal slug lying inertly at the west end on Pacific Quay. This turns out to be Glasgow's new IMAX cinema. Next to it is a great tall metal tower being fussed over by mobile cranes. This is apparently The Tower and next to it will be the Science Mall; the whole enterprise coming under the heading of the £75 million Glasgow Science Centre.

– The odd seagull.

Was there tragedy on the Clyde? Not really. Tragedy needs bigger players, even though Glasgow as a whole sometimes seems like a character out of a film. Is Glasgow slightly like London? Without a doubt. And about a hundred times more like London than Edinburgh could ever be, with its grandeurs and its modulations and its pretensions. Glasgow is much more like London in its mish-mash of rich, squalid, shambolic and noble. Down by the water's edge, that Docklands feeling of waiting for the rest of the world to turn up is as pronounced in Yorkhill as it is in SE8. You have to understand that this is high praise, so far as I am concerned. Even the weather had that sullen London overcast look to it.

The snag was that I hadn't come all this way just to find something that reminded me of the Thames down past Wapping.

So having effortfully made my way out west along the Clyde and then back again towards the centre, I decided that I had to launch myself on a senseless cross-town slog to get something more Scottish down me. Aiming erratically at the

Kelvingrove Museum and Art Gallery (which I'd been within spitting, or at least walking, distance of forty-five minutes earlier) I jumped on the Glasgow Underground, bound for the Kelvin Hall stop.

It should come as no surprise that Jack Milroy and Rikki Fulton – as Francie & Josie – used to sing a number called 'The Glasgow Underground', nor that I have a copy of it. According to them, 'the Dolce Vita' can be found buried in the city's clay and you haven't lived until you've been down there. Live performance on my CD, greeted with standard-issue Caledonian rapture by the groggy audience. And of course, how like London – the only other city in the UK with a subterranean mass-transit public railway system. Apart from Newcastle.

But *look*: the point is not that it's actually like the London Underground. For a start, Glasgow's system comprises a circular route about six and a half miles long, with fifteen stations; the London Underground has two hundred and seventy-five stations and two hundred and fifty-plus miles of track.

But even leaving that to one side, there is a more important distinction. In the carriages of the London Underground, there is room for a fully grown man to stand up, move around, sit down, as there is on the Paris Metro and the New York Subway. In the Glasgow Underground, there is just room for a fully grown man to crouch down on the floor with his head between his knees. The whole system is physically absolutely tiny, being built in 1896 for malnourished Glaswegians and has never seen the need to get any larger. Also, the rolling stock is painted a dazzling shade of satsuma, hence its local sobriquet, the Clockwork Orange. On top of this, most stations only have a single, central platform set between the two tracks, and this platform is built on the same Mighty Atom scale as the trains. The result is that at times of peak use, you will stand there with a baby-buggy shoved up your nose and someone's *Evening Times* slapping your arse while you do your best not to let yourself be pushed on to the electrified rail. The last time I used the system I forgot to squat down on my haunches in order to clear the carriage doorway and nearly knocked myself out on the edge of the train roof.

If you can find a seat, then it's like being Alice in Wonderland, when 'she found her head pressing against the ceiling, and had to stoop to save her neck from being broken' after drinking psychotropic drugs from a bottle. And it's no better for the locals, because what with the Welfare State and a hundred years of nutritional progress, they're all the same size as me (apart from the children, of course) and they too end up squatting on their seats.

But anyway. I made it out to the Kelvin Hall stop, marched out the wrong way and found myself in a tiny, reeking back alley. I looked down at my feet and realised that I was staring at a recumbent jobbie, so huge, bulky and fully rounded it could only have been human. With a scream, I bolted back the other way, toughed it past the ruined newsagents and teashops of the Dumbarton Road, found the Kelvingrove Museum and Art Gallery and, recovered from the jobbie scare, tried to live it large. This was easy, as I was among the Kelvingrove's terrifying Jacobean fantasy stonework, busy admiring the green slime/red stone combination of the outside and the grey, sad interior, like a dead man's suit with curlicues and a huge church organ in the Centre Hall. Plus the usual provincial assortment of gravy-brown paintings, suits of armour and plaster ichthyosaurs. Plus numerous white-haired Scots ladies and their white-haired husbands, chomping on sandwiches in the cafeteria. Oh, plus (let's be honest) some Rembrandts, some Millets, Monets, Van Goghs, terrific stuff, but, in the end, not what I was there to see. Any more than I was there to see the famous Burrell Collection on the other side of town, with its Chinese ceramics and very old bits of furniture. I mean, these things I can get at home.

The Kelvingrove building itself is, nevertheless, splendid – authentically scary, vast, encrusted with flanges, brackets and copings, and topped off with an entire Family Assortment of domes and spirelets. Even better, it points the wrong way. This means that as a rule, you go in through the back door on the Dumbarton Road, rather than the front door, which tries to outface the crazed wickerwork Gothic steeple of Glasgow University across the River Kelvin. The front entrance is at the back and vice versa, because the city authorities changed the course of the main road while the building was being put up, having failed to tip off the architects beforehand. Evil-minded people like to claim that it wasn't the fault of the local highways people at all, but that the architects simply got it wrong (held the plans upside-down, or something); as a result of which, one of them committed suicide by jumping off the top floor. But this is no more than malicious conjecture.

Even better was the Museum of Transport across the way. As well as containing the Valhalla of hand-crafted effigies of ships, it has a real shambles of a collection of wheeled vehicles, chucked more or less wherever space will allow. Thus, we have some trams, railway engines, a Mini on top of a curved metal pole, a crashed car (don't do drugs and drive, kids!), a leery cut'n'shut, some old motorbikes, an awful number of ancient motor vehicles with Scottish connections (the Argyll and the Arrol-Johnston being two that cleverly pre-empted the rest of the British motor industry by imploding in the 1930s), some trolleybuses and a bewildering caravan from the Faslane Peace Camp down the road.

It is, in other words, one of those authentic British bughouse collections (like the Pitt Rivers in Oxford, or, better still, the Sidmouth Motor Museum, which is remarkable for not containing any cars) and gets a lot of its appeal from its what-the-hell-have-we-got-here lack of pretension. A couple of dazed Canadian tourists (doubtless in search of their roots and painfully stuck for diversion, having found them) stood irresolute and shrugging amid a pile of old Scottish sports cars.

'Let's go down the end there,' said one.

'Yeah!' said his friend, brightly.

They didn't move.

And yet, it still wasn't *quite* what I was after.

What I was after was a Glasgow tenement building, because the Glasgow tenement is one of those little synecdoches that summons up the whole city in the mind of the southern dilettante. The very word *tenement* conjures up a strange admixture of Glasgow characteristics.

On the one hand you have the historical Glasgow tenement of bestial deprivations: one toilet between four families, the Gorbals, a dozen bodies in one room, small children sleeping in a chest of drawers, infestations, violence, chronic illness and death. On the other, you have the fact that modernity swept through Glasgow about fifty years ago and most of the tenement slums were knocked down after the war, their populations shunted off to East Kilbride or Easterhouses or up psychotic new flatblocks dumped where the slums used to stand.

Which leaves the remaining tenements to be prized as works of architectural distinction – fine, spacious buildings containing handsome apartments much esteemed by the local professionals. Thus they mirror the way in which Glasgow has taken its heritage, turned it inside out and presented it refreshed and rehabilitated to the new century.

Symbols of changing Glasgow, I thought, sounding like a tourist board flyer in my own head. *That's what I want.*

TWENTY-TWO

I'm going to have to let you down here. All I can do is apologise. I know that you, like me, wanted to know more about the deep-fried Mars bar. I know that, like me, you probably didn't believe in its existence. You had it down as one of those silly, gassily implausible myths that Londoners like to trot out in front of one another when stuck for something to say about Scotland. You didn't really believe that anyone could eat a Mars bar, frozen, dipped in batter and then deep-fried at a chip-shop counter. Neither did I.

Unfortunately, I still don't, because I never managed to find one. Nor did I find the legendary deep-fried pizza, the deep-fried multiple hamburger (a burger in a bun, the whole coated in batter, fried, then served inside another bun), nor the deep-fried Snickers bar.

This was not for want of trying. I've lost count of the number of chippies I went into while I was up there, conning the food selections anxiously for filth. KEBABPIZZABURGER-CURRYSPUD was just one sign over just one fast-food joint that I keenly inspected. I lived on chips and beer, beer and chips and blew up like an advertising dirigible, but I could never quite find the stuff that makes Glaswegians drop like flies. Coronary heart disease is the single biggest cause of death in Scotland, which in turn has one of the highest rates of CHD in the world, on account of all the awful crap they eat, but could I find one of its principal causes? No.

I do know that food writers like to talk up the restaurants in Glasgow and Edinburgh, because, after all, they have columns to fill and it makes a change from boosting some twinkling gastroshrine in Shoreditch or the Thames Valley. Paul Richardson for instance, in his book *Cornucopia: A Gastronomic Tour of Britain*, does a quick job on Scotland and ends up at Ullapool having an orgasm over a 'hauntingly flavoured piece of roasted kohl rabi'. Fair enough, and without a doubt the centre of Glasgow (as opposed to the moonscape of the Highlands) is bursting with new restaurants long on halogen spots and lightly tanned wood finishes. And the hake I ate in Plockton was okay. But this is not nearly characterful or appalling enough for a Londoner who can get swank food all day every day if he's mad or rich or hungry enough.

The best/worst I could do was in Nairn, where I got a deep-fried haggis in batter. This I consumed in the car park next to the sea, where the front should have been. You can actually get deep-fried haggis all over the place, and they call it a Haggis Pudding. No, I'm not going to make puerile fun of the haggis, because it can be a delicious thing, what with all the minced spicy gizzards and entrails that go into it, plus its mordant air of threat as it lies on the plate like a bomb about to go off. You have your neaps and tatties and you drink an entire year's-worth of whisky on Burns Night, and this is a real treat. But the central component of a chip-shop Haggis Pudding is not one of these Fat Boy-shaped haggises. It is a sausage thing with a definite haggis interior but a torpedo exterior. Not too bad a haggis filling, but a bit dry, especially when accompanied by some parched, overwarmed chips.

The real problem set in with the batter coating. On this outing, with this Nairn Haggis Pudding coming in at £1.95, the batter was like leather or fabulously tough fatty cardboard. Maybe it had been sitting in the hot cabinet a week too long, or been bitumenised for a prolonged life, but either way, once my teeth were into it, it was hard to get them out again. It was as if I'd bitten into a hot road. Oh, and the look of the thing: it was like a pallid sea cucumber or a big white crusty turd. And when I broke it in half, it looked like a drug-crazed nightmare confusion of the two, a pallid sea cucumber filled with shit, something out of William Burroughs.

In Aberdeen, by way of contrast, there was the thing called a Mock Chop, which the girl who sold it to me couldn't account for. It was some kind of processed meat product, the scrapings from Europe's worst abattoirs, no doubt, rendered down, compressed, sliced, and seasoned along the lines of Spam. Then it was battered, fried and served up to me, an anonymous flap of meat with the inevitable muddle of chips alongside. It was faintly peppery and chewy, like I suppose a shoe insole must be after a day in August. I've eaten worse.

It was the ambiguous nature of what I was eating that really bothered me – or, rather, the frankness of the ambiguity of it. I will complacently pig out on any amount of awful de-natured, factory-processed filth – like commercial ice-cream, chainstore burgers, industrial margarine – because I can (if I want to) read the ingredients off the packet and assure myself of what it is I'm shoving into my face, no matter how gross and unnatural these ingredients are. But eating something entirely unidentifiable I only do (with misgivings, naturally) in the Far East or France. And for the record, I absolutely draw the line at dodgy *tisanes* and those sea-squirt things for which we English have no name but which the French call *violets*. Scotland is neither France nor Vietnam. So that was a problem with the Mock Chop; the taste was no worse than a McDonald's.

The upshot of this? I never got near the Promised Land of deep-fried confectionery bars. I was always stuck somewhere on the wrong side of the mountains, packing my mouth with chipfat and gargling on beer, but never getting that full barbarous influx of sugars, carbohydrates, fats and syrups, topped off with a ghostly benison of fag smoke. Maybe if I'd liked Irn-Bru even slightly, I might have got that full, degenerate fat/sugar bodily sensation – and yes, they drink Irn-Bru in Glasgow more than they drink the tapwater. But I didn't. And I would mention in passing that the tapwater in Glasgow, straight from lovely Loch Katrine, tastes horrible, too.

News just in for smokers: Glasgow Council is to lift its ban on smoking in Glasgow's public buildings. More specifically, the smoking ban, introduced in June 2000, is being relaxed for private functions held in the council's public spaces. Why? Because it was costing the council thousands of pounds in lost bookings – for example, in the case of the university researcher who cancelled his wedding reception at the Winter Gardens upon being told that his guests wouldn't be allowed to smoke. Astonishing that they even considered instituting a ban in the first place. Walk around Glasgow, you see gaspers everywhere. Cigs keep you warm. An ASH Scotland spokesperson said: 'This is a backward step for Glasgow City Council.'

TWENTY-THREE

Having exhausted the Transport Museum and dodged safely round a party of enormous suede-headed Glaswegian teenage vandals squabbling over cigs on the steps outside, I set off up towards Hillhead and beyond. I was hunting down that tenement thrill with the avidity of an urban fox after someone's discarded chicken wrappings.

Bourgeois Hillhead is so swamped with students I can hardly get through them, but, my upper lip glistening with a fine dew of perspiration (no rain! nearly a whole day goes by without rain!), I break out on the north side and lurch through the Botanic Gardens. I stare weepily at beautiful Victorian Gothic ironwork, rusting and richly mossed, the greenhouse glasswork fogged with algae from the last century, stumble past children in buggies and some pretentious student types taking photographs of leaves with a tripod.

Soon after that I am aware that we are leaving the polite museum/university/parkland nexus and lurching towards a scuzzy end of town. The buildings around me start to fray at the edges, the shops give up trying to flog books or bank accounts or amusing knick-knacks and just get down to the basics of Snickers and Irn-Bru. In fact I have a Snickers on the go myself, by this stage, nicely deliquescing in my hand.

This means that when a group of fairly brutal-looking schoolgirls standing in a shop doorway hail me as I trudge past, my mouth is too full of Snickers to make a meaningful reply. The roughest one shouts to me, 'Hey, mister! Could you get me on the Net?'

Something like that. But what with all the corn syrup, peanuts, partially hydrogenated soybean oil, lactose, milkfat and sugar in my mouth, I can't even say, 'What?'

Still, it does get me to speed up a bit, in case the schoolgirls decide to rumble me for any more confectionery I might be carrying about my person. Putting some space between me and them, I am now up on the crest of a ridge, with lowish newbuild social housing lying below, a main road blocking my way, and, to the left, a couple of ranks of redstone nineteenth-century terraces, four or five storeys high, stretching away down the far side of the ridge. This is Maryhill and these look like tenements to me.

I pound across the road, straight into the arms of a chip shop. It occurs to me that the Snickers has only gone so far and that I really need a concentrated blast of fat and starch to keep up the pace. Inside the chippy, a derelict is propping himself against the melamine counter. Serious dereliction, I mean: four-day beard, exploded trousers roughcast with dirt, anorak limp on the shoulders and looking as if just used to wipe down all the platforms on the Glasgow Underground, eyes like punched lychees, aroma of paint thinner.

'Gie's a pie,' he croaks across the counter.

'How much have ye got?' says the chip guy to him.

'This.'

'Ye cannae get a pie for that.'

'Well what can you get for that then?'

'You could have a wee bottle of lemonade.'

The poor old fucker snorts a bit, trembles where he stands and allows a few hisses of gas to escape. I start to feel so sorry for him that my hand begins to reach involuntarily into my pocket to buy him a packet of chips, when he forestalls me by muttering, 'Ah, forget it,' and wanders out into the street.

'He was jist tryin' it oan,' the chip guy says brightly to me. So I take him at his word and ruthlessly buy the packet of chips the wretched derelict couldn't afford.

And then I spot my tenement. It is a defining moment. On the other side of the road stands a solid line of architecture, a continuous wall, a bit like a section of the Kelvingrove Museum, peeled off, ironed out and set up as a cadet branch in a rougher neighbourhood. There are shops along the ground floor, but the upper storeys bear the kind of machine regularity I guess is part of the tenement look; and there is a little doorway in the centre, leading through to the space which separates one tenement from another.

Robotically packing chips into my face, I cross over the main road and stalk the tenement from closer to.

What do we make of this, given the fact that we are from the London suburbs and that our delight in the successful application of the Golden Section in architecture may not be equalled by that of the people who have to live in that architecture, especially if it is getting on a bit and covered in mould? How do we pass judgement on a grouping of nice old redstone buildings in two parallel rows with an alley running between, some little yards abutting the back doors, weeds here and there, a parked car, shreds of litter? When we look at the waterfall of algae running down one end where a leaky pipe has clearly been leaky for years, do we take a snap of it, offbeat photorealist style, or do we mutely and Englishly sympathise with whoever has to live there with the damp? When we observe that it is so quiet in the tenement close that you can hear birds sing, where does that leave us? Up here in Maryhill, we have the nineteenth-century solution to the problem of mass housing. Down in the old Gorbals, across the Carlton Suspension Bridge, we have your post-war New Brutalist flatblocks. Just below the Maryhill tenements, we have the late-twentieth-century compromise of lowbuild pan-British vernacular social housing. So where would you go? Which of these options do you praise, which do you blame?

It's the usual snag of buildings and their contexts. Any of these would be okay, provided you match them up with their environments. This means you have to relocate the New Brutalist somewhere in mid-Manhattan and give it a doorman and a makeover; roll the classic tenement down into Glasgow centre (on account of the fact that up here on the Maryhill Road it just looks old and forlorn, a friendless geriatric); and leave the consumer-friendly, featureless lowbuild exactly where it is. Would I live in a Maryhill tenement? For sure, on account of its dignified shape, its solid proportions, its patina of age. Just as long as it wasn't in Maryhill.

These laboured ratiocinations were making me thirsty, so I went to the pub. The nearest was a mere block away, back across the road, so I went there. It was also the toughest, meanest, shittiest-looking boozer I think I have ever been into, and it was only weakness and a Saharan thirst that got me through the front door.

I wasn't even sure it was open for business, at first. It had every single window boarded up and the kind of paintwork you get on very old trawlers that are about to be broken up for scrap. Even the terrible boozer in Aberdeen had windows. I only guessed that this one was open because of the chalk-board notice outside offering cheap beer and a happy hour that started in the morning and ended at midnight. Breathing deeply, I shoved my way in.

It was very dark inside, not surprisingly, given the lack of windows. In fact, it was like the inside of a tyre factory, apart from a bit of playful electricity around the bar itself, and up the far end, where a statutory giant TV screen was showing cable programmes with the sound gone. In fact, there were no fewer than four tellies in there. There was this giant one, two more bolted to the walls and one atop a battered plywood box that looked like a coffin made of driftwood. Hard to tell what the furnishings were like – banquettes down the walls, mangled pixie stools elsewhere, tables like battlefields, I think – on account of the darkness. There was a pea-souper cigarette fog. And the joint was completely full of men who looked like tramps plus their tramp-like lady friends. So full, in fact, that there was only one free place to sit (and this well before peak time of 7 p.m., I would add), right up against the Cinemascope TV screen. But neither this nor any of the tellies was being watched by the mob. They were too busy yelling their heads off at each other.

Key ingredient of the afternoon's colloquy? *Fuck*. Never have I heard the word *fuck* used so often, so liberally, so persistently. It wasn't there for emphasis. It wasn't even there for punctuation. It was just there. It had a life of its own, necessary because it was necessary, as fundamental as air: 'It's no the fucking problem, I said. It's the way you fucking dae it. If I was tae fucking put the fucking thing over there, I'd be fucking wasting my fucking time. I'd be fucked before I even fucking started. It's no a fucking question of fucking time. That's no the fucking issue . . .'

All this delivered in the aggrieved-yet-reasonable tone of Glasgow intercourse: permanently disputatious without *quite* picking a fight. I listened, transfixed, to a huge bloke next to me in a beard and a leather jacket, furiously debating some arcane point with a small bespectacled tramp, before getting up in a welter of *fucks* and stumping out of the pub. At which point, the small speccy tramp got up with his half-finished pint and wandered over to another table, where an even more furious man was talking to a third tramp. The specs guy was plainly one of Nature's listeners, while the really furious man elaborated some point about modern technology to his audience.

'Ye shouldnae get a fucking black line across the screen, right?' he complained. 'It's not meant tae fucking dae that. There is no fucking way it should fucking *dae* that.'

Someone said something back to him, which launched him on another outbreak of language.

'Oh, aye, you get the fucking menu up, *I* got the fucking menu up! I pressed seven and I got fucking twenty-seven and there's no fucking way I wanted fucking *twenty-seven.*'

But here's the weird thing. I sat there, nursing my pint of heavy and fiddling with a beer mat, and had I been in a boozer in London with this sort of racket going on around me, I would have been finishing up quick and slipping out of a side door before things got too unsavoury. But up here, here in (let's face it) run-down, dosser-filled, beat-up Maryhill, it was a hoot – and largely because of the Glasgow Voice.

Everyone knows of course that there's an easy way to impersonate demotic urban Scots: you simply exchange a short U for the short I, chuck out half the alveolar stops D and T and stare a lot. Thus, a *bun liner* is a large plastic sack which fits inside the domestic trash bin, a *fush tea* is battered cod with chips, the *Mussussuppy* flows south from Minnesota down to New Orleans and out into the Gulf of Mexico, a *to'al stoa'er* is a good thing.

But Glaswegian has this mad rhythm to it, a need to place stress according to a sense of vocal aesthetics rather than to emphasise elements of meaning. It's more like Italian, with its reiteration of emphatic sound shapes and patterns.

Compare Londoners, even animated ones, who tend to bunch lumps of words together in more or less featureless estuarial groupings, only breaking out into accentuation when a point arrives that *has to be made*, i.e., *So you and Bri and Dee are all coming along in DAVE'S MOTOR? I mean I'm only asking cos I don't SEE how you're gonna FIT IN. D'you know what I mean?*

Glasgow English, on the other hand, likes to keep a certain dance-band swing, the front half of the sentence getting a little beat going before the second half closes (ideally) with a stress followed by an unstressed syllable, to lead the speaker back out into space. You could see this in a gag made by Glasgow Council leader Charles Gordon, when posing for the smudgers with Scotland Office Minister Brian Wilson and a female Cuban dancer called Maite, in order to promote a festival of Cuban arts: 'Two chancers and a dancer,' he observed. Or rather, two CHANcers and a DANcer. When the furious man said, 'I pressed seven and I got fucking twenty-seven and there's no fucking way I wanted fucking *twenty-seven*,' he actually said, 'I PRESSed SEven and I GOT fucking TWENty-SEven and there's NO fucking WAY I wanted FUCKing *TWENty-SEven*.' Hence all the fucks: rhythmic elements to keep the beat sweet, and also to emphasise that you do feel quite STRONGly about your SUBject. And this, like Italian, or New York English, is a real boost for the unwary tourist. Does Glasgow buzz? Well, yes, partly because the Glaswegians are all shouting away at each other in this vivacious demotic.

Anyway. There I was, swilling placidly away and instead of feeling deeply depressed and unnerved, I was very nearly relaxing into my heavy like an old friend.

The crazed bearded guy having moved on, I was at liberty to get the occasional blast from a table of oldsters a couple of feet away, all well bevvied up, the prune-like women so small and crushed by life and misfortune that they were taller when seated on their pixie stools then when standing up. Did this stop them laughing their decrepit arses off? No. Some he-tramp rounded off a story whose beginning I had long missed with the line, 'So the dog fell in the fucking canal and I said, "It's not ma dog, what dae ye want me tae do about it? I canna fucking swim!"'

They all erupted, laughing so much they had to take their fags out of their mouths and cough, the sound of loosening phlegm rattling like gunshot around the table. Then the furious guy next door cranked up the volume again, 'But you get the fucking black line, which is fucking ridiculous.'

'It's fucking absurd,' agreed his interlocutor.

'Aye. Right enough it fucking is,' shouted Mr Furious, and he too exploded in a howl of laughter.

Meanwhile, people were staggering back and forth to the bar, accumulating pints of lager and heavy and the odd chaser if they were in funds. You have never seen so many torn sweaters and deep-crust trousers in one room.

'He said it was mine!' screamed an oldster, setting the table rocking again.

It was almost *fun*. What a notion! I must have been delirious with exhaustion and the fat/sugar high from my street meal. Up here? In Maryhill? What was I thinking of?

Then the thought occurred to me that if, for some unimaginable reason, I ever lived here, within a week I would be straight on the Scooby Doo, smoking sixty a day and I would never draw a sober breath. It was one of those moments of conscious disengagement, one of those fleeting perceptions of oneself in a wholly other state, a parallel self. I could have been *Chazza* and had that permanently sparring, affronted way of speaking and walked down the street the way your Glasgow man is apt to do, with that slight roll, nearly a swagger, and even, sometimes, *whistling*, which is

something so little done in London these days that it counts
as street theatre.

I got up to stagger to the Gents. A few minutes later, I found
myself stumbling back out towards the pitch-black bar, the
call of Nature attended to. And I realised that Mr Furious
was on the far side of the bog door, waiting to come in. My
head cleared with blinding immediacy. At once I saw that all
this drunken hilarity was just a fantasy of my own making, a
delirium. Glaswegians are not happy, laughing inebriates.
They are the most bellicose and violence-prone citizens in the
whole of the UK and I was Target Number One. Mr Furious
was going to whack me there and then, thus asserting the
inalienable moral right of all Glaswegians to connect fist with
nose, when faced with a middle-aged sissy from the south.

I held open the bog door for him, tensing myself for the
blow.

'Chirz,' he said politely, walking through. 'Right, pal.'

One of the oldsters slipped off her pixie stool and buckled
on to the floor. Laughter broke like a wave over her. I propelled myself out on to the street, my head spinning.

Then it was as if I'd never been to Maryhill. When I fell out of
the Underground at Buchanan Street, I had one of those tran-
sitory moments of epiphany: I got that Big City mood for just
a second, that sensation of having been miles away somewhere barren and terminal, then having returned with a rush
to the warm, busy life of great town. I'm *back*, I thought; back
to the real world.

And Glasgow did look like a *bona fide* city, the let's-get-on-
with-it street intersections, the monumentality of the
buildings, the enormous numbers of people marching at dazzling speed from shop to office, the lights, the smell of diesel,
pavement dust, perfume, fag smoke, a hint of chunder. Bad

lads were wandering off into the darkness with pool cues in cases under their arms. Nearly all the girls were pretty, while the men (and the women who weren't pretty) had faces like drowned rats or used teabags. There was a lot of Irn-Bru going down.

In my delirium at getting back to society, I immediately, helplessly and compulsively twinned Glasgow in my mind with New York City, even though Glasgow is actually twinned (I think) with Dalian, in China, Nuremberg, Rostov-on-Don and possibly Turin. New York, as we know, is the city to end all cities, the citymost city in the world, or at least Manhattan is, and Glasgow has just a savour of the Big Apple about it. As in New York, you have to walk quicker in Glasgow. Like New York, you have the thrilling, restless architecture. Like New York, you have the compelling vitalities of the way the people speak. Dammit, they just used it *as* New York in the film version of Edith Wharton's *The House of Mirth*, the one with Gillian Anderson in, with Glasgow doubling as turn-of-the-century NY before they'd worked out how to put up skyscrapers. This is no small achievement. If I lived in a city that looked a bit like Manhattan, I would bore people to tears with the intelligence.

The only drawback is that people don't live much in the centre of Glasgow. They do in Manhattan and they do in the middle of London; this is partly because London has no middle so there's no pronounced cultural reason not to live anywhere except the City. And some people even live there. But Glasgow (a bit like Manchester, again, that other instantaneous Victorian city) is offices and shops and bars and restaurants, the virtues of hard work and self-gratification, but no homes. It is a pleasure centre with photocopying facilities.

Even if you go out west in the direction of Kelvingrove, the west end of Sauchiehall Street past the sordid M8, as I did one dazzlingly bright morning, out to the lovely early-nineteenth-century terraces and the handsome ashlared villas, it's still all offices. All the lawyers and the accountants and quantity surveyors hang out there, in buildings which would once have been the homes of the professional and mercantile classes. So consciously under-resourced is this part of town, with no shops or tradesmen to unsettle the paradigmatic urban calm, that the lawyers and accountants have to rely on mobile snackwagons which you can see parked up on every other street corner, handing out styrofoam coffees and greasy buns.

But if people don't live here, does it matter if all you want is that cosmopolitan the-world-comes-to-Glasgow street vibe and the lights? With a spring in my step I headed for the Horseshoe Bar, the longest continuous bar in Europe at 104 feet long, in a boozer very little changed from its last major remodelling in 1884, spattered with horseshoe motifs. Full of geezers, naturally, the evening paper stuffed under their arms, chucking the drink back like clockwork, shouting their heads off. In my pomp, I went up to the bar and commanded a pint of eighty shilling. The barman (no sorrowing Edinburgh barmaids here, no brooding melancholy) doubtless spotted my Englishness and my relative unfamiliarity with the concept of drinking recklessly in Glasgow pubs. So he came back at me: 'Tennent's, or the Cally?' he asked.

But I was hot, too hot for him.

'Pint of the Cally, please,' I rejoined, since I knew that the Cally was the Caledonian brew, as opposed to the Tennent's. Didn't miss a beat. Just stood there, cool as you like and ordered it. *Cally*. And he poured it for me, as well.

A bit later on, I wondered about trying to find the fighting Glasgow, or, rather, observe it for the purposes of tourism. Of course, I hadn't a clue where to look and no desire at all to start a fight or get caught up in one. So I made do with some tousled yobs being moved on by the Polis from the entrance to Glasgow Central Station. *Cally*, I sniggered to myself. It felt like home.

On the last day, to top it all off, I went to the theatre for a laugh. Damn, I was feeling good about Glasgow by now. I could have stayed for weeks. The place was one huge good-looking bar with museums. I had even – and this really shows how at ease I felt, what a sense of blithe compromise I'd reached with this part of Scotland – given up worrying about kilts. There are several places to buy a kilt in Glasgow (MacDonald MacKay in Hope Street; Hector Russell in Buchanan Street, to name but two) but I was now so relaxed I couldn't even work up the energy to get angry about tartan. Like a reformed drinker, I didn't even stick my head round the door of a kilt shop, let alone finger the plaid.

Anyway, *Braveheart* had put me off. I mean, how could anyone seriously buy into all that crap? (Although, thanks for the title, Mel.) Glasgow was too big for that. Glasgow, like all great international cities, was bigger than the country it inhabited.

So I had to do one last thing and then go. There were two choices open to me, apart from *The Nutty Professor II: The Klumps* or banging house and trance at the Shag Tag. I could go to the legendary Citizens' Theatre to see Eric Bogosian's 1983 monologue *Funhouse*, a conspectus of transgressive male sexuality from insurance salesman to full-body rubber fetishist, performed by a man in high heels and a leather thong. Or I could go to the Pavilion Theatre up Renfield Street, to catch the family variety show *Not Another Very Special Hogmanay*, a piece of old-fashioned music-hall with a twist about a Hogmanay celebration that goes wrong, months from Hogmanay. Indeed, now that the dreaded Glasgow Empire has been flattened, the Pavilion is deemed the Home of Variety in Glasgow, or a 'somewhat old-fashioned commercial theatre favoured by comedians', as it says in my guide.

At the Pavilion Theatre box office, I found I was lucky to get a seat, and this was only the first night. 'Oh, it's very popular,' said the woman at the desk, redundantly, as there were already hundreds of very old men and women being bundled out of coaches, or fighting their way up the hill on foot, some stopping every twenty yards or so for a smoke. The average age was easily eighty-eight, but they were all rich with Glaswegian pawkiness and had paid special OAP prices anyway, so they were going to see this thing or die in the attempt. I handed over my tenner and joined a slow-moving crowd of geriatrics stumbling up a savagely steep and apparently endless flight of stone steps leading up to the Top Circle. 'You go ahead, dear,' they kept saying to me, motioning me forward, so I had to surge on up the stairs in order not to lose face. To be honest, I would much rather have leant against the wall and coughed and gasped like them, but when you're fifty years younger, you don't get the choice.

Inside, the Pavilion turned out to have a nice semi-ruined Edwardian interior (it opened in 1904) with plenty of filthy old plaster mouldings and baroque-derivation curlicued embellishments. It was also very small, like the Underground, built for tiny but brutal people from another era. Up (breathless and grey-faced) in the Top Circle, I was jammed into a seat the size of a coffee-cup and pitched forward at an angle of forty-five degrees. A very fat woman nearby looked as if she was never going to get out of her seat, once in. In order to leave the building, she would have to unbolt the chair from its neighbours and walk around Glasgow with it stuck over her arse like a bustle.

Occupying the rest of the seats were normal-sized Glaswegians with carrier bags full of crisps, chocolates and non-alcoholic beverages. And, to my surprise, they were not all pensioners. This was partly because some of the old bags almost certainly never made it up the hundreds of steps, anyway, and were lying like fish on the stone slabs downstairs. But also because among the oldsters were people evidently in their forties, thirties and even teens – as in the case of the family party in front of me: two girls, a pustular boy and a mum. What were *they* doing there? Especially the boy, who had the statutory shellsuit/trainers/limp hair/crinkle-cut sneer of early teenage and looked as if he would have been a thousand times happier on a PlayStation or looking at porn.

Was I wrong. The lights went down, the curtains parted, the stage filled with four men, four women and a five-piece band, who promptly performed a succession of Scottish Country Dancing jigs and reels.

I rocked back in my seat. It had only taken seconds, but this was Andy Stewart and his Highland Fling all over again. This was Kenneth McKellar territory, the terrible mummified hand of Scottish light entertainment, biscuit-tin Scotland, the stuff I thought I'd put behind me the moment I worked out how to keep dry in Glasgow (don't go out in the rain). It was retrogressive and dreadful and the family in front were loving it, *even the teenage boy*. He was bouncing around in his chair. He was funnelling sweets into his gob. He was clapping along with the beat, for God's sake.

After a bit, the dancers fluffed their way through the last number and the stage cleared for the meat and potatoes of the evening. The meat and potatoes, the main course, was, in essence, a crude way to get some superannuated variety turns onstage one after another and let them do five minutes of their acts, within the overarching structure of a half-hour TV sitcom. A corner of the stage had been turned into the sitting room of a Glasgow flat, where a couple of dismal middle-aged losers were watching Hogmanay on an imaginary telly. There was a lot of stuff about losing the savings for the

Christmas turkey and taking a dram too much refreshment at the local boozer. But the main thing was to keep the OAPs and misguided youngsters in the audience happy by creating a freakish demi-world, a confusion of media and realities, in which the two losers in the onstage flat watched an invisible TV on which conceptually appeared, live, the acts actually appearing on the same stage as the two losers.

This meant that the stage lights blinked on and off, the couple pretended to settle down to watch one of their favourite acts on the telly and we (and they) discovered a cabaret couple like Sonny and Cher but in their fifties meandering onstage to sing country-tinged songs of loss and yearning. They could have been doing it in the back room of a pub, but were in fact doing it on the other two-thirds of the stage. Who were they? What were their names? The thick broth of the performers' accents meant I could only understand half of what they were saying and there wasn't a programme. So I sat and stared, my mouth hanging open with horror and amazement.

Whoever they were, they were followed by two incredibly old women wearing mini-skirts, joke-shop hats and ill-advised tights, like an acid-trip Elsie and Doris Waters or two-thirds of the Beverley Sisters. Then there was a sort of Scottish Gerry Marsden, with a big false-teeth grin, rock'n'roll footwear and a banjo, who sang a song about the 'Barras' market at the east end of town. And there was even a stand-up comic called Lex (that much I did catch) who was as old as his audience and did a drunken roué act, wearing a silk top hat, white scarf and overcoat.

I was especially transfixed by him, partly because I could understand his Glaswegian (he kept shouting and repeating himself as part of the turn), and partly because his act was so astonishingly antediluvian. I mean, it was not just pre-war but essentially nineteenth-century in its origins, the sort of thing

Charlie Chaplin did with Fred Karno, or James Finlayson, or, for that matter, Dan Leno or Flanagan & Allen. He told risqué music-hall jokes. He did the stage drunk stagger. He even had a painted cloth backdrop, which he hit with his cane from time to time.

Between them, these terrible old derelicts (plus a snappy compère like a Caledonian Bruce Forsyth) crashed their way through precisely those tunes which make me want to stick my head in a sack and which I vowed I would never listen to again. Those 'Good Old Scottish Songs', as they oxymoronically dubbed them: 'Roamin' in the Gloamin'', 'A Wee Deoch an' Doris', 'Donald Where's Yer Troosers?'.

It was a drug-hell nightmare, not least because absolutely everyone else in the packed 1,400-seat auditorium was enraptured. Everyone other than me laughed, shouted back at the performers, clapped along. They smacked each other's forearms with excitement. They bundled crisps into their mouths as if they were posting their Christmas mail. I had left, not just England, but the United Kingdom and indeed the planet as a whole. This was family entertainment lifted straight from the deep freeze of the 1950s, hastily microwaved and served up, patchily scalding, in front of the twenty-first century for people still reading *Oor Wullie* and *The Broons*. It was family entertainment such as does not exist in the rational world.

Oh, but did I mind? Did I care? Well, I was so eager to be a Glaswegian for at least half of the show that instead of running screaming for the exit, or at least to the politely named Refreshment Bar, I sat sweatily with the others, if not clapping along with the rotten dancers or the senile Sonny and Cher, then at least showing my approval for the very old stand-up called Lex and the MC who wasn't Brucie.

The great Jack Milroy was a different matter. I didn't even know he was on the bill until just before he made his appearance. But having thoroughly digested the Rikki Fulton story and got wise to Scotland's greatest double-act, Francie & Josie, I was now only too aware of what a name Milroy is. (Milroy is even on the cover of my *Rikki Fulton: The Time of His Life* vid, done up in his F&J outfit). No matter that the same woman who had compared Inverness unfavourably with Chiswick also groaned noisily at the mention of F&J, saying, 'God! All those Christmases ruined, having to go see Francie & Josie in panto . . .' This was class entertainment, Scotland-style. I was going to give Jack Milroy my full attention and appreciation.

So when the MC asked us to put our hands together for 'international showbiz legend, Jack Milroy', however many eyebrows this appellation might have raised in LA or Berlin, I was in there with the rest of the mob, whistling, applauding, hooting. And they really did go nuts for him. I almost felt a spasm of pity for the other superannuated toilers who'd been working away for the thick end of two hours before he came on. Nothing they'd done had produced anything like the racket that greeted Milroy. The man is clearly adored, a legend of the variety stage.

He sprang onstage in the Francie sub-Ted red suit and daftie wig, beaming furiously as the house erupted. I wondered if maybe Fulton was going to come on too, in the blue Josie suit. But no. Fulton is retired. So how was Milroy going to do the Francie & Josie act without Fulton? Easy. He dealt with the problem of Fulton/Josie's absence by re-creating him in reported speech. Thus, he fed himself lines from an abstract Fulton and then went off into whatever gag he felt like telling.

Pretty elderly material, it has to be said – the joke about the expensive parrot, or the one about the duck in the trousers, well, you know, not so fresh that you'd want to eat them – but it's always a pleasure to watch a real pro in action. After all, the guy has his patter so finely crafted you could forgive the maturity of the actual jokes. He works his audience with the ease of a man unwrapping a Twix, and they were his to do with as he liked. When he finished after about twelve minutes, I thought they were going to break the theatre up. He almost made up for those Good Old Scottish Songs.

So is that it? A ripping night out with one and a half thousand clapping Glaswegians? That warm glow of losing yourself in the mass? Well, it was, up to a point. The point at which it wasn't came with the first anti-English joke of the evening. It came when the old slapper who was marooned on the sitcom side of the stage reflected on the larger meaning of Hogmanay, and how one's thoughts sentimentally tended towards those far away, and who could not be present.

'At a time like this,' she said, 'I feel sorry for all the Scots who can't be in Scotland. All the ones in Canada, Australia, New Zealand . . .' She bowed her fat head. 'Of course, the ones I feel sorriest for are *the ones in England*!'

This was met with a cheer like a howitzer going off and a good forty seconds of applause, yelling and stamping. It was the biggest reaction they'd had up to then. It wasn't just a joke, in fact, it was also a yelp of rage, *Braveheart* on fart powder. And me? The rictus of hilarity I stuck on my face was a front, obviously. I thought, *Shit. Now they're going to beat me up*, and, like a plain-clothes Special Branch officer at a meeting of Republican terrorists, or an undisclosed leper, very self-consciously did nothing at all to appear conspicuous.

So I sycophantically giggled, clapped and even tapped my toes along to the jigs and reels, until the interval. At which point I had to tousle my accent as well as look happy, since I was perched at the end of a row and everyone had to push past me in two directions to get to the Refreshment Bar or to the she-wrestler handing out ice-cream tubs. 'Thank you,' they all said civilly, or 'Chirz,' as they stepped on my English toes. 'Ur,' I said back, neutral, uninflected, from no country, trying not to fart with terror.

Second half started, my heart rate began to slow down. It was tame stuff and the English were not mentioned. I began to relax.

Then the Brucie MC started to lament the passing of the good old ways. The good old ways in this context included being able to make jokes that were sexist, homophobic and, yes, racist. And – well I never – *racist* in this context meant jokes against the English. And to remind us all of the heritage which had been lost, he went right ahead and told an anti-English joke.

'The ship is sinking, right? All the crew has to get into a life-raft to get away. The captain says, "There are too many of us in this life-raft. I shall have to ask three of you brave lads to make the final sacrifice so that the life-raft doesn't sink and the rest of us may survive." So the Irishman says, "I do this for the glory of Ireland," and throws himself overboard. Then the Welshman says, "I do this for the glory of Wales," and throws himself overboard. Then the Scotsman says, "I do this for the glory of Scotland," and throws an Englishman over-board . . .'

Well, they went ape for that one. We had a tempest of applause, zoo-level howls of savagery and mirth, the building shaking with the release of psychic energies. I thought, if they find out now, I'm dead, I'm lynched. I'm going to end up as paste. A dead Englishman! It doesn't get any better than that! Even in a joke! *For fuck's sake, you petty bigots*, I wanted to say, *have you no self-respect? Are you so low that your best idea of fun is to cling to centuries-old hatreds?*

So much for cosmopolitan, open-armed Glasgow. So much for the tolerance of the big city. *You have a great city to cele-brate*, I rambled on in my head, *and rapid growth in the call centre and telecommunications industries, but what you really*

*enjoy is lurching back through the generations and tiny-mindedly
pissing on your next-door neighbour! You tossers!*

The fact that I said none of these things was due in part to
the noise, above which even Iron Maiden would have found
it hard to make themselves heard; and in part due to simple
fear.

My buttocks clenched with stress, I waited for the rabble to
settle down and prayed that Brucie-in-a-kilt would either fall
off the edge of the stage or suddenly recall having taken a
delayed-action laxative a couple of hours earlier. He didn't,
but at least he stopped telling English jokes. And let's be
honest, part of my yelling and cheering for Jack Milroy was
because Jack, God bless him, gave no sign of wanting to start
the trend up again.

Burdened with lugubriousness, I trudged back towards my
hotel where all the light-bulbs worked. *Betrayal* was a word
drifting around my consciousness in a melodramatic fashion. *Betrayal*, I said to myself, and *Typical bloody Scotland*.

With hindsight, I also wanted to say that the single most
alluded-to piece of writing that I came across in the Scottish
media all the time I was up there was the speech delivered by
Renton about a fifth of the way through Irvine Welsh's
Trainspotting, in the chapter entitled 'The Glass'. This diatribe, in which Rents explicates the Anglo-Scottish problem,
is a kind of manifesto for national psychosis: 'Ah don't hate
the English. They're just wankers. We are colonised by
wankers. We can't even pick a decent, vibrant, healthy culture
to be colonised by. No. We're ruled by effete arseholes.' Which
mixture of spinelessness and poor taste therefore leaves the
Scots as 'the most wretched, servile, miserable, pathetic trash
that was ever shat intae creation'.

The fact is that *Trainspotting* first came out in 1993, but
was still being liberally alluded to seven years later, even with

the new Parliament in place and everything to play for. So what does that say to you about Scottish self-belief? What a fool I was to think that Glasgow was above history, that anyone could go there and enjoy it simply as a big, interesting, handsome, internationally minded city. Suddenly, it looked provincial. Suddenly, all the IRA and UVF and Rangers and Celtic sectarian graffiti seemed much more prominent on the street walls. Suddenly, it seemed small-time and every bit as wedged in the broom-cupboard of history as *Not Another Very Special Hogmanay*.

I got back to my room, made a cup of tea with the horrible Glasgow tapwater and bitterly transcribed the jokes before I forgot them.

TWENTY-FOUR

I sat on the train south. A couple of gnarled Scots were at the table opposite. They spent an unusual amount of the five-hour trip complaining about the price of two cups of coffee from the buffet. 'Two pounds forty!' they kept saying. 'That's never two pounds forty! It was only ninety-five pee last time!' The rest of the trip went on demolishing a sack of sweeties they'd bought with them.

I stared out of the window for a few hours, as you do, and then composed my Plan For Scotland. With St Andrew's Day approaching (30 November, all the expats determinedly getting stotious on a bottle of Johnnie Walker) even as I write, this seems as good a time as any to wheel the Plan out.

It is very simple. You keep Edinburgh and Glasgow, chuck Aberdeen, let Dundee and Inverness fight it out for third place. You get rid of 85 per cent of the Highlands, as they're not worth anything and get in the way of communications. Thus scaled down, Scotland can then be detached from England at the join, to cheers and wild oaths from the

Scottish side and a sigh of relief from the English, and floated down to the latitude of the Mediterranean Sea.

Still too big to go through the Straits of Gibraltar, it will have to be anchored off the coast of north-west Africa, a bit like a much larger Madeira. And there you have it. It is the Darien Scheme reborn. You get all the restless energies, abilities and style of the Scots, but with weather that doesn't kill on impact. It is foolproof, and there is only one condition: that the English get to keep the oil.

What do you think?

Now you can order superb titles directly from Abacus

☐	Father's Race	Charles Jennings	£6.99
☐	Greenwich	Charles Jennings	£7.99
☐	People Like Us	Charles Jennings	£6.99
☐	Up North	Charles Jennings	£6.99

The prices shown above are correct at time of going to press. However, the publishers reserve the right to increase prices on covers from those previously advertised, without further notice.

──────────────── ⬭ABACUS ────────────────

Please allow for postage and packing: **Free UK delivery.**
Europe: add 25% of retail price; Rest of World: 45% of retail price.

To order any of the above or any other Abacus titles, please call our credit card orderline or fill in this coupon and send/fax it to:

Abacus, PO Box 121, Kettering, Northants NN14 4ZQ
Fax: 01832 733076   Tel: 01832 737527
Email: aspenhouse@FSBDial.co.uk

☐ I enclose a UK bank cheque made payable to Abacus for £ . . . .
☐ Please charge £ . . . . . . to my Visa/Access/Mastercard/Eurocard

Expiry Date ☐☐☐☐   Switch Issue No.   ☐☐

NAME (BLOCK LETTERS please) . . . .

ADDRESS . . . .

. . . .

. . . .

Postcode . . . . Telephone . . . .

Signature . . . .

Please allow 28 days for delivery within the UK. Offer subject to price and availability.